"Attention, MOVE! This is America!"

"Attention, MOVE! This is America!"

Margot Harry

Banner Press • Chicago

Published 1987
Printed in U.S.A.

Banner Press, P.O. Box 6469, Chicago, IL 60680

LC 87-1384

Contents

Introduction

The Cobbs Creek Park neighborhood of West Philadelphia was born at the turn of the century. Formerly a tough, down-at-the-heels blue-collar mill community, the area was transformed once the Frankford El was completed in 1906, affording workers access to inner-city jobs. Hundreds of rowhouses soon sprung up, designed by "the rowhouse king of Philadelphia," E.A. Wilson, the architect for more than twenty-five thousand of the structures throughout the city.[1]

For nearly half a century the neighborhood was predominantly Jewish, with people either commuting to their jobs or establishing small neighborhood businesses. But starting in the mid-1950s—reflecting a "white flight" pattern occurring on a massive scale in many of the older eastern cities—the Cobbs Creek residents pulled up stakes and piled into the nearby, newly created suburbs.

As the whites left, Blacks began moving in to replace them. Today the neighborhood is 95 percent Black, comprised of people who viewed moving to the Cobbs Creek area as a major step up and away from Philadelphia's vast and festering ghettos. A stable, quiet, and proud neighborhood, its residents include teachers, postal workers, keypunch operators, civil servants, small businessmen, and retirees. Most of the houses are owned rather than rented, and it's the kind of neighborhood where people work two or even three jobs to pay off the mortgage and send their kids to college.[2]

Philadelphia historians refer to the style of these rowhomes as "colonial revival"—three-bedroom, two-story houses of brick with colonnaded front porches, second-floor bay windows, gabled flat roofs, and tiny back yards in which neighbors can plant small gardens and gather for outdoor barbecues. Many of the Cobbs Creek residents have added aluminum siding, carpeted their porches, or remodeled their homes' interiors. As one resident describes the neighborhood:

"I grew up in South Philadelphia. And you know how when you grow up you think about how things should be? Well, I always wanted to live in a place with a few trees and a yard. And when we moved in here, it was like everything I had always dreamed of. It was so beautiful and everybody worked on their houses. We worked to make the whole neighborhood better—and we did. It was a wonderful place to live. You couldn't ask for more."[3]

The 6200 block of Osage Avenue is part of this neighborhood. It runs east to west, and immediately to its north and south are the carbon copy streets of Pine and Addison. Running perpendicular to 6200 Osage on its eastern end is Sixty-second Street; on its western end runs Cobbs Creek Parkway, and immediately beyond that stands Cobbs Creek Park. It is a small, pleasantly shaded park with a quiet creek running through it, a place where adults can relax or jog and take their kids to play (see map on opposite page).

But one house on the 6200 block of Osage was different. Not at first, not in the early 1960s when Louise James and her young son Frank moved into 6221 Osage, nor for two decades after that. Louise worked for the telephone company and kept pretty much to herself, and the neighbors liked Frank, whom they found shy but smart and friendly. But by 1981 some things were going on that made the neighbors curious and a little concerned. For one, Louise James started referring to herself as Louise Africa, and her now-adult son called himself Frank Africa. For another, Louise Africa started to care for about a dozen children. Who and where are the parents, neighbors wondered. Then in 1982-83 several other adults, all dressed simply in t-shirts and blue jeans and wearing long dreadlocks, began to live at 6221. They were members of MOVE.

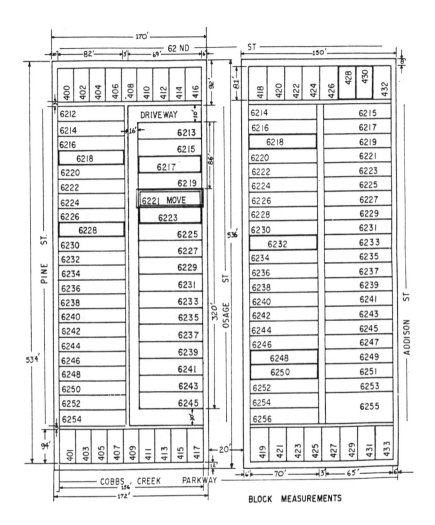

BLOCK MEASUREMENTS

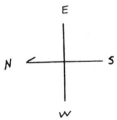

MOVE is an organization of predominantly Black radical utopians. Formed in 1972, their numbers have been estimated to be between 50 and 150, and most of them and their supporters are believed to live in or near Philadelphia. Practically since its inception, MOVE has been attacked by various authorities and the mass media. Members have been described as filthy, their homes as vermin-infested, and they have been consistently portrayed as a violent back-to-nature cult led by a supposedly messianic madman known as John Africa. In more recent times they have also been described, among others by Philadelphia's first Black mayor W. Wilson Goode, as "urban terrorists."

But such terms fail to explain why MOVE so vexes and appalls the authorities. MOVE refuses to respect present-day America and its prevailing values. Its members openly defy official power and tirelessly preach against a system they consider utterly corrupt and destructive of life on this planet, particularly through the use of modern technology. And when threatened and confronted by the authorities, as they have been throughout their short and stormy history, they do not back down. MOVE members have explained the purpose of their organization this way:

> MOVE's work, John Africa's revolution, is to stop man's system from imposing on life, MOVE's work is to stop industry from poisoning the air, the water, the soil and to put an end to the enslavement of life—people, animals, *any* form of life. The purpose of *John Africa's* revolution, MOVE's work is to show people how corrupt, rotten, criminally enslaving this system *is,* show people thru *John Africa's* teaching the truth, that this system is the *cause* of all their problems (alcoholism, drug addiction, unemployment, wife abuse, child abuse, child pornography, every problem in the world) and to set the example of revolution for people to follow when they realize how they've been oppressed, repressed, duped, tricked by this system, this government and see the need to rid themself of this cancerous system as MOVE does. MOVE is revolutionaries, we are the vanguard, the spearhead of *John Africa's* revolution. Our work is to confront this system up front to show people not only that they *can* fight this system and win, but to show them the urgent *need* to fight.[4]

When asked how MOVE sees this revolution coming about, Gerald Africa, a MOVE spokesperson, explained:

> Through information. See, we've always stated that our purpose is to inform people. People are only led through information.

And they're led through misinformation. What you have in civilization today is the misinforming of people by governments and major media only for the purpose of exploiting and oppressing people. This is why the government takes such a strong attitude in handling MOVE, because they know that we have the power and the expertise given to us by John Africa to lead people away from the government. And they can't stand it. The government is like a vampire that feeds on the blood of the innocent. And every citizen that is denied it, it starves. You don't have to drive a silver bullet through the government. You just deny its blood. And people are its blood.[5]

A major confrontation between MOVE and the authorities occurred in 1977-78, when Philadelphia police blockaded the group's Powelton Village compound for nearly a year. This included a fifty-day siege in which no one was allowed in or out of the house and food and water were cut off in an effort to starve them out. This confrontation eventually climaxed in August 1978 with a massive police assault that included high pressure water hoses, a battering ram, bulldozers, and automatic weapons. In the subsequent trial, nine MOVE members were each sentenced to thirty to one hundred years in prison, charged with murdering a policeman who almost certainly died in his fellow officers' crossfire.[6]

Because of the siege at Powelton Village as well as numerous other incidents with the authorities and police over the years, the MOVE members who came to live at 6221 Osage Avenue in 1982-83 soon began to fortify the house in preparation for other expected confrontations. Neighbors watched uneasily as MOVE hauled tree trunks from Cobbs Creek Park into the house, and listened as they hammered, sometimes late into the night. They also observed MOVE members carrying out large baskets of dirt, leading some to speculate that the group might be digging underground tunnels. The neighbors also took note as wooden boards were nailed across the second-story bay windows, and then as two wooden bunkers, reinforced with railroad ties and metal sheeting, were constructed on the flat roof, the larger one in the front covering over the distinctive cornices and pediments.

In addition to these major and, in their eyes, rather unusual and seemingly unnecessary house alterations, some of MOVE's more conservative neighbors also found the group's lifestyle difficult to tolerate. They complained about MOVE's practice of taking in stray dogs and cats, and of leaving raw food on the ground which they said created obnoxious odors and drew hordes of flies – some claimed even rats. They also were angry about a pen constructed to house animals at the back of MOVE's house, which they said blocked access to a common driveway and created a fire hazard.

Some of the neighbors also disapproved of how the MOVE adults were taking care of the children, whose parents were imprisoned MOVE members, including those who had been found guilty of killing a police officer during the Powelton Village confrontation in 1978. According to some of the neighbors, the children were ill-clothed and poorly fed. They said they sometimes saw the children eating out of garbage cans and would call them into their own homes to feed them. MOVE countered that the children had sufficient clothing, were well-fed through a diet consisting of nourishing natural foods, and were sick much less frequently than most other neighborhood kids. There also were reports of residents and MOVE members getting into a couple of physical scuffles, and that one of MOVE's next-door neighbors moved out shortly after one such incident.

But what some of the residents seemed to find most intolerable was the frequent use of a bullhorn and loudspeaker system that MOVE had rigged up. According to some of the neighbors, MOVE members would get on the sound system for hours on end, sometimes late into the night – castigating the U.S. government and local officials, demanding the release of their nine comrades jailed for the 1978 Powelton Village incident, and frequently criticizing the neighbors themselves for trying to buy into the American mainstream rather than helping MOVE to get their railroaded, imprisoned members out. For instance, when neighbors held a Fourth of July barbecue in 1984, MOVE got on the sound system to denounce "all those motherfuckers out there celebrating a white man's holiday."[7]

The liberal use of profanity on the loudspeaker system also upset some of the neighbors. Said one person, a strongly religious woman living directly across the street from MOVE: "It attacked me in a way, just to hear it. I prayed about it. I talked to the Lord and asked for some change. I asked him, 'How could these people become like this?'"[8]

On Mother's Day 1984, a contingent of neighbors met with several MOVE members, at MOVE's behest, in front of 6221 Osage to discuss and attempt to deal with some of the problems. MOVE was particularly interested, it appeared, in trying to explain why the neighbors should assist in the battle to get imprisoned MOVE members released. But the meeting, some of the neighbors felt, achieved nothing. According to one neighbor, "They told us that John Africa taught this and John Africa taught that, and that we were living all wrong. We came away believing that they didn't care what we thought, one way or the other."[9] MOVE, however, saw things in a different light. They felt the meeting ended badly because of a small group of neighbors within the larger contingent who seemed more intent on attacking MOVE and disrupting the discussion than trying to talk things out.

Some of the residents were also upset with the response of city and state officials to whom they had been going for more than two years with their grievances. This included meetings over the summer of 1984 with Mayor Wilson Goode, someone the respectable and law-abiding Black citizens of Osage Avenue felt would surely help them. Said one of the residents who met with him, "He told us to have patience and everything would be taken care of."[10]

On May 1, 1985, a group of the residents, spearheaded by the conservative Osage Avenue block association and its captain, Clifford Bond, conducted a well-attended and subsequently well-publicized press conference at which they announced their intention of taking matters into their own hands if Goode and other officials didn't take some kind of immediate action against MOVE. Because of MOVE, they claimed, their stable, prized neighborhood – a neighborhood in which they had invested so much of their lives – was going to pieces. Less than two weeks later, they would watch it go up literally in smoke.

On Monday, May 13, 1985, at approximately 5:25 p.m., a Pennsylvania state police helicopter hovers sixty feet over 6221 Osage Avenue. Harnessed securely to the inside of the chopper's cabin, Lieutenant Frank Powell, commander of the Philadelphia Bomb Disposal Unit, the "bomb squad," leans outside and hurls a green canvas bag toward the roof below. Extending from the bag is a lit 45-second fuse attached to a bomb. As the bag hurtles downward the helicopter rears quickly up.

Inside the house are thirteen MOVE people – seven adults, six children. On impact the bomb throws off a fierce wave of heat of 7200 degrees Farenheit, melting tar roof materials into flammable liquid and turning wooden debris into flying kindle. The whole of MOVE's roof convulses, the entire area shakes. Glass windows half a block away completely shatter.

White puffs of smoke rise from MOVE's roof, followed a few minutes later by black plumes of smoke and flames. In a while the flaming front bunker on the roof collapses into the second floor of the house, and the fire soon begins its race down the evacuated sixteen other rowhomes on the same side of Osage as 6221. So intense is the radiant heat that houses on the other side of Osage, about thirty feet away, and the ones on the south side of Pine Street, about twenty feet away, also burst into flames. The fire, initially allowed to burn, is not declared under control until midnight.

Of the thirteen people who were inside 6221 Osage, eleven are dead – six adults, five children. Mangled, burned, carried away in zippered nylon bags – mostly in pieces. Only 30-year-old Ramona Africa and 13-year-old Birdie Africa manage to survive. As for the once attractive and stable neighborhood, both sides of Osage Avenue, the south side of Pine Street, and a section of Sixty-second Street are destroyed. The only things left are the smoldering brick walls, standing in rows like giant grave markers. Altogether, sixty-one rowhomes have been totally destroyed or gutted, 250 people are without homes.

The bombing and fire were the culmination of a massive assault by the Philadelphia Police Department that began many hours earlier, before dawn on May 13. MOVE obviously had been correct, following the 1978 Powelton Village assault, to expect and prepare for another such violent confrontation. But they probably couldn't foresee to what lengths the authorities this time would go, as MOVE's laboriously constructed fortifications proved ultimately unable to withstand the ferocious onslaught which included the use of a powerful bomb and a deadly arsenal of weapons far surpassing what had been employed some seven years earlier.

The May 13 assault and its horrifying results immediately became known across the U.S. and around the world, as banner headlines and page one news stories described the death and destruction. Many people were shocked. Yes, they said, perhaps such a thing can and does occur in other places, but in the U.S., in Philadelphia, the city of the Liberty Bell, and with its first Black mayor in charge? Uncomfortably stuck in this glaring and ugly light, and with the U.S. facing an internationally embarrassing situation of grave proportions, local and national officials and others attempted to justify what had happened.

Philadelphia was depicted as a beleaguered city confronted by a cult of zealots who had terrorized a conservative Black community for years, and who had stockpiled explosives and automatic weapons for a violent confrontation with the authorities they intended to provoke. The fire itself was blamed on MOVE, as officials claimed that shortly before the assault, MOVE members poured gasoline on their own and adjoining roofs. Officials also insisted that since some of the neighborhood residents had been asking for help for years, the city administration, reluctant but out of other options, finally had to go in with heavy firepower and a bomb. In this manner, an "in your own backyard" version of a policy carried out many times in Vietnam was developed: "We had to destroy the village in order to save it."

Edward Rendell, Philadelphia district attorney at the time of the police operation and subsequently a candidate for governor of Pennsylvania, remarked: "These are people who essentially committed suicide and murdered their own children."[11]

Mayor Wilson Goode stood at City Hall on Tuesday, May 14 and said the prior day's assault, bomb and all, was a political necessity. "If I had to make the decision all over again, knowing what I know now, I would make the same decision because I think we cannot permit any terrorist group, any revolutionary group in this city, to hold a whole neighborhood or a whole city hostage. And we have to send that message out loud and clear, over and over again..."[12] On May 14 alone he delivered this message several times.

He described MOVE as "a group dedicated to the destruction of our way of life. We have listened to their rhetoric, we have seen them kill a police officer and we have listened to them threaten the life of the President, the governor, the mayor, judges and police officers. We watched them for three years turn a neighborhood of peaceful homeowners into chaos and frustration." Goode also stated that "the MOVE group wanted a violent confrontation" and thus could hardly complain now that they got one.[13]

Other mayors rushed to defend Goode's decision. The mayor of Milwaukee sent "hats off praise to Goode," and Miami's mayor described Goode as "a very considerate and thoughtful man."[14]

Los Angeles Police Chief Daryl Gates called Goode "an inspiration to the nation. I think he has provided some of the finest leadership that I've ever seen from any politician. And I hope he runs for national office. He's jumped onto my heroes list, and by golly, that's not a long list."[15]

National officials also moved quickly to praise the operation. U.S. Attorney General Edwin Meese III stated before a police convention in California: "I think that Mayor Goode...in the very rational and reasonable way that he's handled a very difficult situation...is a good example for us all to take note of."[16]

Approval also came from groups like the Black Clergy of Philadelphia and Vicinity, who assembled before the rubble on Osage Avenue to state their "universal support for Mayor W. Wilson Goode and his handling of the MOVE confrontation."[17] The organization of Black policemen of Philadelphia commended the police commissioner for "the planning that went into that operation, the manner in which he carried out the operation without the unnecessary loss of lives..."[18] Clearly to them, the deaths of eleven MOVE members were necessary.

Many national Black leaders, such as the Reverend Jesse Jackson, remained silent in the immediate aftermath of the May 13 events. Black congressman John Conyers of Michigan did say, "In our community among Black leadership, we are totally outraged," and he called the assault "the most violent eviction notice that's ever been given in history."[19] But the actual content of his criticism merely expressed tactical differences with what occurred on May 13. According to Conyers, "The whole point of the matter is that there were any number of reasonably forceful alternatives that we could have employed that weren't." He then suggested the possible use of SWAT teams, armored vehicles, or, as was attempted in 1978, starvation under siege.[20]

Support also came from some of MOVE's neighbors, even as their homes lay in ruins. Milton Williams, one of the outspoken critics of MOVE whose home was destroyed in the fire, said: "Now everyone knows how dangerous they [MOVE] are. This is the lesson for everyone – not to let them breed anywhere...It was well worth it, because they're out. We'll be back and we'll be a community again, *without* MOVE."[21]

Clifford Bond, head of the Osage Avenue block association and another of MOVE's major adversaries, said of the deaths of the MOVE children: "If you study biblical times there were children killed at the drop of a hat. In Beirut they're killing children by the boatloads. Who cries for them? The Lord's given those [MOVE] children peace. He'll bring them back with a different mind and a different body . . . It might sound morbid, but I'm kind of glad God took those children."[22]

But in sharp counterpoint to these various declarations of support and efforts to justify the assault, there was widespread and deep-seated rage. Exclaimed one man moments after he watched the bomb drop, "Do you know what they've just done? They've dropped a bomb on babies! You think we can sit down and let them drop bombs on houses? Do you know what they've started here?"[23]

And as the flames lit up the sky, the cry of "Murderers! Murderers!" rang out from among many of the hundreds who had gathered at the barricaded corners close to the MOVE house. Rocks and bottles were thrown at the police. Plainclothes detectives and staff members of the Crisis Intervention Network trained in crowd control worked to pacify the milling throng.

But despite their efforts, heated debates and arguments broke out as individuals outraged by what they were witnessing moved from corner to corner. A large number of those gathered, especially among the Black youth, were on the verge of battling the police toe to toe, as cops moved in with riot clubs. Within a few minutes of receiving the first reports of anger in the streets, Mayor Goode telephoned the city solicitor to find out what emergency powers he had should it prove impossible to contain the bitterness and outrage.

In street corner conversations over the next several days, comparisons tumbled out. A Black student from South Africa compared the actions of the police to what happens to Black people in his country. Others compared the bombing to Hiroshima, Dresden, Grenada, El Salvador, Vietnam. "They think they're in Vietnam dropping bombs," commented one Black youth. "It makes me feel like I'm living in one of those countries where they just go and bomb you out," one woman told reporters. Mayor Goode came under heavy criticism, as people debated the value of electing Blacks to political office. Exclaimed one Black youth, "We were all excited when we got a Black mayor, and now look what he's doing to us!"

Nor did many of the residents of Osage Avenue and Pine Street agree with the comments of neighbors like Milton Williams and Clifford Bond. As they surveyed their destroyed homes and neighborhood, many expressed shock and anger. "I wanted action but I wanted it done in a peaceful way," said one resident. "I didn't want it done with this kind of violence." Said another neighbor, "We never expected them to burn the whole block down." On the day after the assault, in the shade of the trees of Cobbs Creek Park, a Black man gazed at the ruins and spoke of the neighbors who had complained about MOVE: "The people on that block were ignorant to the facts of what the American government is capable of doing, what they will do. They didn't think these people were gonna drop a bomb on all their houses. They didn't know what they were dealing with, and I don't feel sorry for them."[24]

Controversy and people's anger continued to swell as more facts tumbled out in the days immediately after the May 13 assault. Explanations offered by Mayor Goode and other city officials were openly and defiantly questioned. Officials speaking together at the same press conferences offered different accounts of what occurred on Osage Avenue. Signs of a falling out among some of these top officials began to emerge, *not* on whether it was right to eliminate MOVE—on that no disagreement was expressed—but on the correctness of some of the tactics employed and who was responsible for them. In addition, information fed to local reporters by police involved in the operation frequently contradicted what was being reported from the top.

Confronted with a rapidly deteriorating situation and also growing criticism of his own role, Mayor Goode issued an executive order within days of the May 13 operation for the formation of an "impartial commission" to investigate the events leading up to May 13 and what happened on the day itself. After months of closed interviews with more than nine hundred people, and after several weeks of televised testimony from ninety witnesses in the fall of 1985, the Philadelphia Special Investigation Commission (PSIC) issued its final report on March 6, 1986.

The commission found that the operation against MOVE suffered from poor planning, inadequate intelligence, lack of proper training of police personnel, and poor supervision. Mayor Goode was singled out and criticized for "abdication of leadership." Specifically in regard to the aerial bombing of the MOVE house, the commission concluded that it was "reckless, ill-conceived and hastily approved. Dropping a bomb on an occupied row house was unconscionable and should have been rejected out-of-hand by the mayor, the managing director, the police commissioner and the fire commissioner."[25] The commission also concluded that the deaths of the five MOVE children were "unjustifiable homicides," although it left open the possibility that the MOVE adults, who were roundly criticized and attacked throughout the public hearings and in the commission's report, were themselves perhaps partially to blame.[26]

To many people who expected nothing more from the commission than a crudely thrown-together whitewash, these seemingly frank and hard-hitting conclusions came as something of a surprise. Perhaps here at last was a fact-finding commission that really did call things out for what they were, and no matter who got hurt. But as will be shown in the following chapters, there is more than one way to conduct a whitewash, and while Mayor Goode's commission was forced by the very severity of what occurred on May 13, 1985 to give the strong appearance of impartiality and letting the chips fall where they may, at bottom its final report and findings are nothing but a cover-up for the horrible crime committed that day. For what happened on Osage Avenue was not the result of bureaucratic bungling, inadequate intelligence, improper training of police, or poor planning. Simply and truthfully put, it was a carefully planned, premeditated massacre. In fact, a full-scale plan to assault the MOVE house had been developed and was ready to be implemented in August of 1984, and major elements of this plan were carried out nine months later, on May 13, 1985, including use of a bomb on the roof. Also, intelligence reports from Philadelphia's Civil Affairs Unit, the city's political police or "red squad," as well as other critical information collected from city agencies by the Philadelphia Police Department's Major Investigations Division, were instrumental in formulating this plan.

Further, just a couple of months after he had become mayor in January 1984, Wilson Goode started to consult federal and state authorities about what to do about the "MOVE problem," and federal agencies including the FBI were specifically consulted by the Philadelphia Police Department to help plan the attack and help acquire high-powered military weapons, including the powerful contents of the bomb itself. At the same time, neighborhood spies and snitches were recruited and tensions that existed between MOVE and some of the neighbors on Osage Avenue were taken advantage of and deliberately exacerbated in order to justify the forthcoming attack as something the authorities were forced to do despite their peaceful, conciliatory intentions.

Then on May 13 itself, what amounted to an occupying army surrounded the MOVE house in a search-and-destroy mission reminiscent of Vietnam and other counterinsurgency campaigns against foreign "enemies of the U.S."—right down to the camouflage paint on the cops' faces. The house was hit with hundreds of smoke and tear gas grenades, then ripped by ten thousand rounds of ammunition and high-powered explosives. Mission still not accomplished, a powerful bomb was dropped which turned the house into a roaring furnace. Positioned in the back alley, waiting to see if any MOVE members would attempt to escape the blaze by emerging from the back of the house, were sharpshooters from the police department's stakeout unit. And when MOVE members did try to escape the suffocating and unendurable inferno, they were met with a deadly hail of bullets.

The commission's concentration on such "criticisms" as inept planning, inadequate intelligence, and improper police training and supervision serves not only to cover over the well-planned and premeditated nature of the events of May 13, 1985, but also to justify its major recommendations at the end of its report, which consist of a blatant call for a major strengthening of the city's police and intelligence apparatus so that future such assaults can be carried out even more professionally and effectively. In this respect, it must be said that the commission existed not only to whitewash a massacre but also to condone it, and in so doing the commission, as well as the massacre itself, reflected and concentrated the reactionary ideological and political tenor of today's America.

This tenor was ably captured by Philadelphia City Representative Dianne L. Semingson, who, shortly after the May 13 assault, explained why eleven Black people were murdered: "There's going to be an effort to make the city's actions known as being absolutely necessary. I hope people will see it as the *New York Times* did yesterday, as the police going against a home of radicals, showing that we won't tolerate deviant behavior that affects others."[27]

Intolerance of "deviant behavior" is a hallmark of the "Resurgent America" of the 1980s, and a large-scale offensive has been unleashed against all those who fail or refuse to conform to the vision that this is a white, Christian, male-dominated, and English-speaking country that is well on its way to overcoming its "problems" of the 1960s and '70s and reestablishing itself as undisputed heavyweight champion of the world.

Much of this offensive is disguised as sincere and desirable efforts to deal with various social problems. Children are fingerprinted, supposedly so they can be more readily found if kidnapped; police roadblocks are set up, supposedly to catch drunk drivers; censorship laws are passed, supposedly to deal with pornography. But the Black people of South Africa can readily explain what lies behind fingerprints, roadblocks, and censorship laws.

Nor is it any coincidence that at the same time these things are going on, the White House applauds attacks on women's right to abortion; there is serious talk of setting up concentration camps to deal with homosexuals and others who have contracted AIDS, or who don't even have the disease but are simply carrying the virus; courts hand down decisions giving the police even greater power and freedom to conduct searches, kick down people's doors and arrest them without having to show cause – and a known racist and fanatical opponent of civil rights, women's rights, immigrants' rights, and radical and revolutionary groups is appointed Chief Justice of the Supreme Court, pointing to even greater repression to come.

Yet another major component of this fascistic offensive, also masquerading as benign and in "the public good," is the nationwide campaign to prevent the use of all languages except English. In November 1986, for example, an initiative was passed in California declaring English the official language of the state. The initiative's proponents claimed they were only trying to help immigrants assimilate, but the actual essence of this initiative is not only to suppress the use of all languages other than English but also to suppress the people who speak these other languages, especially the millions from Mexico and Central America as well as the hundreds of thousands from different parts of Asia, and to enforce "national unity" and blind obedience to the American way.

This goes hand in hand with the recently passed Immigration Reform and Control Act of 1986, whose major "amnesty" provision is designed, as numerous congressmen have not been shy about pointing out, to induce immigrants to "come out of the shadows," thereby enabling the authorities to update computerized lists of the names, addresses, recent histories, family members, etc., of millions of immigrants, and thus enhancing, among other things, the possibility of mass deportations at some future time, perhaps during a declared "national emergency."

There is also the so-called "war on drugs," which includes sending five hundred federal police agents for duty on the U.S.-Mexico border, yet another way to go after immigrants. This "war" has also involved new ways for the U.S. to intervene in its explosive "backyard," such as the sending of troops and military equipment to Bolivia and the possibility of doing the same in Peru, where a major revolutionary struggle is under way.

The nationwide "war on drugs" has also meant Congressional passage of hundreds of new laws, including expanded use of the death penalty, search and seizure without warrant, and the use of illegally obtained evidence—all of which can later be used more broadly and openly against political opponents. This "war" has also legitimized indiscriminate raids and the introduction of new "drug task forces" and networks of informants inside the ghettos and schools. The children of the '80s are now even being told that it is their patriotic duty to turn in their parents of the '60s, and New York's mayor has called for the building of two concentration camps on the edge of the city to detain ten thousand people, many of them young Blacks and youth from other minorities, who are awaiting trials involving drug charges.

At the same time that all of this is going on, America "on the rise again" supports the apartheid regime in South Africa, bombs Libya, invades Grenada, prepares to invade Nicaragua, and creates many other incidents in Central America and all over the world—all of which are the arrogant acts of a reactionary bully in their own right, and any one of which could also serve as the catalyst for a global nuclear confrontation as the U.S. frantically steps up its militarization in preparation for a showdown with its Soviet rivals. In fact, the entire fascist crackdown on the home front represents a major effort to secure a quiescent and loyal citizenry in order to conduct such a world war. These are anything but normal times, and political conformity and allegiance to this Resurgent America are demanded. People either must do what they are told or get the punishment they deserve.

Such is the social and political context for the statement by Philadelphia City Representative Dianne L. Semingson that what happened on May 13, 1985 was to demonstrate that "we won't tolerate deviant behavior that affects others." Nothing could make it clearer that the silencing of eleven Black radicals was not the result of bureaucratic bungling, "improper" police training and supervision, etc., but instead was the conscious political execution of determined and unapologetic rebels. This is not the story that Mayor Goode's special commission has told, nor is it the story being told by the major executives of American power in Washington, D.C. and elsewhere who stood behind this massacre, who sanctioned and applauded it. But it is the real story, and it will be told here.

1 | The Plan

On May 14, 1985, as the remains of the eleven MOVE members were still being removed from the smoldering ruins, Mayor Wilson Goode held a press conference. Staring stonily, almost defiantly, into the television cameras, he said: "I would do it over and over again, because it was the right decision. I do not like the result, but based upon my information, it could have been much worse."[1] Interviewed later that day by ABC-TV's Peter Jennings, Goode defended his decision to drop an "explosive device" on MOVE's house. He said the device had been "determined to be absolutely safe by those professionals on the scene, and I believe that the only thing that went wrong was that a fire took place after that."[2] The device, he said, "did in fact work. It achieved what it was supposed to achieve."[3] In a televised address to the citizens of Philadelphia that evening, Goode took full responsibility for the events of May 13: "I stand behind the decisions made and I stand behind my managing director, police commissioner and fire commissioner. They did outstanding jobs under extremely difficult circumstances."[4]

These words are obviously not those of an apologetic blunderer. The fire was not intended, he says. Everything else was. This flies directly in the face of the special commission's finding that the whole operation was marked by poor planning and inadequate intelligence, and of those officials who have tried to cover up the events of May 13 by characterizing them as a "tragic mistake." As Ramona Africa, the sole adult MOVE member to survive the massacre, said one year after the May 13 events:

"A number of officials are *still* tryin to convince people that May 13th was just *'a bad day'*. That's like *Hitler* tellin people not to judge him by *'one mistake', the holocaust!* May 13th was *not* merely *'one day'*. The events of May 13th represent the results of *deliberate planning, surveilling, photographing, interviewing,* and tryin to pass the *horror* of May 13th off as 'a bad day' is like tryin to pass slavery off as a *bad investment."*[5]

Indeed, testimony at the commission hearings themselves by various city officials and others corroborates Ramona Africa's contention that the events of May 13 were the result of extensive surveillance and planning.

For two years prior to May 13, 1985, the Philadelphia Police Department's (PPD) Civil Affairs Unit and Major Investigations Division (MID), the department's major intelligence-gathering unit, had the MOVE house on 6221 Osage Avenue under constant surveillance.[6] Other MOVE houses in Philadelphia and elsewhere were also regularly surveilled. For example, when the police in Chester, Pa. raided a MOVE house there on May 13, 1985, at the same time that the assault had started on Osage Avenue, Vice-Captain Richard Conway revealed, "We had been waiting to do this for well over a year so it would not become a safe house in the event anybody fled from Philadelphia."[7] Officers George Draper and John Cresci of the Civil Affairs Unit testified before the commission that they carefully monitored MOVE's activities on Osage Avenue. This included meetings between Draper and some of MOVE's neighbors, at which they would inform him of MOVE members' daily movements and habits.[8]

In the course of presenting their comprehensive report to the commission, Draper and Cresci revealed their intimate knowledge of how many meetings MOVE had in every year since 1973 (in other words, essentially since MOVE's inception); how many and where MOVE held demonstrations and what took place at them; and how active the police considered MOVE to be at any given time.[9]

The commission also called a host of officials from various city and state agencies to testify, including the Department of Licenses and Inspections (L&I) and the Department of Water. The

commission's major line of questioning of these officials was why
certain things weren't done about MOVE earlier, such as shutting
off the water to 6221 Osage if bills were unpaid, or why no action
was taken when MOVE began construction of a bunker on their
roof without the proper building permits. But, probably uninten-
tionally, this line of questioning also revealed just what these
agencies *were* doing—activities hardly in their normal line of
work.

In the fall of 1983, for example, the Department of Licenses
and Inspection and detectives of the PPD's Major Investigations
Division began to carry on a discreet affair. MID Detective Nate
Benner met with Rudolf Paliaga, chief of the district operations
for L&I, and shared with Paliaga files on six MOVE properties in
Philadelphia which the PPD had under surveillance, surveillance
photos of 6221 Osage Avenue, and police-drawn sketches of
possible escape routes from Osage Avenue. At MID's request, L&I
provided police with information about the MOVE house, for
example the thickness of the walls of 6221 Osage. L&I inspectors
also started a regular practice of conducting drive-by inspections
of Osage Avenue. These inspections were never recorded and
clearly were not to check for housing code violations. They *were*
an integral part of the extensive covert surveillance operation
that was going on in preparation to "solve the MOVE problem"—
even down to the point of making sure that the people inside 6221
Osage would not be able to escape what the authorities had in
mind for them.[10]

The newly elected Mayor Wilson Goode also began paying
immediate attention to this problem and its ultimate solution. In
March 1984, Managing Director Leo A. Brooks and head of Civil
Affairs James Shanahan were given a detailed briefing on MOVE
and what had been happening on Osage Avenue.[11] This briefing
included field reports from the officers who had been surveilling
MOVE and who also were gathering information from Osage
Avenue residents.

Goode then asked Brooks to give the same briefing to other
elected Black officials who represented the area which included
the Cobbs Creek neighborhood. Brooks—who had given up a
thirty-year career in the army, where he had attained the rank of
major general, to become Philadelphia's managing
director—characterized this meeting as strictly informational in
character, with no action yet being contemplated. But this was
not true. As Brooks himself remarked, the briefing of the politi-

cians was designed "to make sure that they were familiar with the circumstances as they existed at that time so that if things did become more volatile, or if the behavior did become more disruptive, that they would have the background from which we would be moving."[12]

That "moving" is what Goode and his associates had in mind can readily be seen from key developments in May of 1984. In late May, Police Commissioner Sambor summoned to his office Sergeant Herbert Kirk. At the time of his meeting with Sambor, Kirk was a 27-year veteran of the Philadelphia Police Department. His expertise included training and certification by the FBI and the state of Pennsylvania in special weapons use for "non-normal" tactical situations. The FBI, other federal agencies, and the military also trained him in SWAT tactics, and he spent four years in the Navy as a weapons specialist.[13] Sambor asked Kirk to formulate a plan, the object of which was to remove MOVE people from their Osage Avenue home. According to Kirk's testimony before the commission, the plan was supposed to be designed to extricate MOVE "with the least amount of force possible."[14] Kirk poured over aerial surveillance photos of MOVE's house. According to Kirk, the photos showed a three-foot-by-three-foot trap door cut into the roof, with three-foot-high wooden pallets around it in a barricade fashion.

Kirk also asked the Fire Department to bring one of their trucks, armed with a high-pressure line known as a "Squrt" gun, to the Fire Academy. There a mock-up of the MOVE house was constructed to see if the Squrt gun would move and drive the pallets off the roof. It did.[15]

The idea, said Kirk, was to drive the pallets away from the trap door in order to send an assault team onto the roof to throw tear gas into the house and force the MOVE members out. Kirk contacted the Department of Water and asked them to check if the water pressure of hydrants on Pine Street, where the Squrt guns would be located, would be sufficient for the assault. The pressure was fine.[16]

Kirk's next visit was with Lt. Frank Powell, commanding officer of the PPD's bomb squad, or Bomb Disposal Unit (BDU). For more than six months, Powell had already been studying photographic blow-ups of the MOVE roof supplied by aerial reconnaissance. In a bit of wit, and as one more example of how absurd and misleading is the commission's claim that the May 13 massacre was based on poor planning and inadequate intelligence, Powell said, "I probably know that roof better than my own neighborhood."[17]

Powell and his experts then went to work on designing an "entry device" that would blow a hole in the roof to enable the assault team to deliver the tear gas. According to Kirk, the experts blew up seven or eight charges on a facsimile of the MOVE roof until they found one "that would work every time, and then we tried that three or four times to make sure that it did work and that the size of the hole that it made was constant."[18] No poor planning here.

Kirk then provided an outline of the entire plan, the contents of which certainly throw into question what he meant by saying the idea was to get MOVE members out of the house "with the least amount of force possible":

> The plan was for one assault team to scale to the rooftop after the Squrt guns had done the job of knocking the barricades away from the trap door.
>
> When the rooftop team secured the roof, the water would then be turned off, the entrance device placed on the roof, detonated, and the tear-gas generator would start to deliver tear gas into the property. The tear-gas generator delivers a high volume of gas in a very short time. It would have filled the house in a matter of minutes. Thus, driving anyone inside, outside unless they had breathing equipment. And the longer the gas generator ran, the more the oxygen would be displaced. So even if they had gas masks, sooner or later they would have failed.
>
> [Police would have] two outer and inner perimeters. These were manned by stakeout personnel. The containment teams' responsibility was to place under arrest anyone in the property driven out. The second team *to give them fire cover should a fire-fight develop once these people were driven outside the property.* That is the basic plan.[19]

In other words, if MOVE members were to be forced out of their house, they stood an excellent chance of being shot. As a backup, Kirk had in place plans for a lateral entry into the MOVE house by using explosive charges on the adjoining walls of the houses on either side of MOVE's. In this case, too, the object was to drive the MOVE members into the open.[20]

Kirk also testified before the commission that the only written copy of the plan was contained in a three-inch-thick folder, complete with surveillance photographs and the results of the testing of various explosives. But the folder was never produced by the

PPD in the aftermath of May 13. In fact, Sambor and others such as Lt. Powell denied having any knowledge of such a written plan. Yet Kirk testified at the hearings that the last time he saw the folder, in August 1984, it was in his file cabinet and that he had shown all of the plan to Sambor and parts of it to Civil Affairs Captain Shanahan.[21]

In the same two-month period during which Kirk was working on a military plan, authorities also attempted to establish the legal and political basis for an assault on MOVE members on Osage Avenue. On Memorial Day, May 28, 1984, Mayor Goode met with a delegation of Osage Avenue neighbors who complained bitterly about MOVE and demanded that something be done. Over the July 4 holiday, neighbors were back at City Hall to meet with the mayor. This time they brought Goode a tape recording they had made of MOVE's speeches. They told him MOVE was threatening over the loudspeakers to provoke some kind of confrontation with the police on August 8, the sixth anniversary of the siege at Powelton Village.

These reports, coupled with the claim that MOVE members were bringing explosives into their house, were critical components in establishing the political basis for a police assault. MOVE was portrayed as armed and dangerous. Managing Director Brooks told the special commission that "during the months of June and July, there was a growing feeling, and it was reported to me several times by the police commissioner, that he had received it through his intelligence sources, that they [MOVE] were going to make a public excitement that day . . . There were implications that there might be hostage-taking, that there might be all sorts of things, fire, whatnot, explosives and whatnot."[22] At his meetings with the neighbors, Goode expressed sympathy and determination to do something, but also his concern that he did not yet have a strong enough legal case against MOVE. He wanted felonies rather than misdemeanors. According to one of the residents at the meeting, he told them "he wouldn't make a move until he could do a *complete* job because it was more harmful to us if he locked them up on minor charges."[23]

In an eighteen-page analysis of all the possible criminal charges that could be brought against MOVE members, the District Attorney's office expressed the same concern: ". . . there is probably cause to support arrests, searches, and prosecutions against MOVE. Unfortunately the most sustainable charges are misdemeanors. MOVE members arrested for misdemeanors will likely remain free on bail pending trials...and thus be given a public forum for venting their doctrine at length.... If convicted of misdemeanors most MOVE members would not be given substantial jail sentences."[24]

Significantly, during this same period city authorities actually went out of their way *not* to make certain arrests of MOVE members that could have been made. For example, on May 3, 1984, while a MOVE member was being interviewed in front of 6221 Osage by a TV news crew, another MOVE member with a hood over his head appeared briefly on the roof with a shotgun. Over twenty-five cops in riot gear soon appeared and took up positions around MOVE's house. But surprisingly, no arrests were made.[25]

Similarly, when Yvonne Haskins of the Philadelphia Parole Board issued a warrant in June 1984 to have Frank Africa picked up for failing to meet with his parole officer, she was visited by none other than "red squad" leader Capt. Shanahan, who told her not to pursue the warrant and that the PPD would not assist the board if it attempted to arrest Frank Africa.[26]

It is also highly revealing that when August 8 did roll around, the authorities still did not have in hand the felony charges against MOVE they wanted. This indicates that as they began to deploy their forces on August 8, and despite Kirk's contention that the whole purpose of his plan was to flush out MOVE members only to arrest them, arrests were not what the authorities had in mind.

At 6 a.m. on August 8, 1984, hundreds of police and firemen assembled a few blocks from the MOVE house. Two other MOVE houses in Philadelphia were also put under surveillance. The police had assembled an arsenal that included fifteen police wagons, two armored cars, a bomb-disposal unit, a K-9 dog team, mounted police officers, and fire trucks with mounted Squrt guns. Residents on Osage Avenue were told to evacuate their homes and mail delivery to the block was suspended for the day because authorities said it was too dangerous.[27]

MOVE's response to all this was to get on the loudspeaker to declare they were not intimidated and would not come out of their house. They also continued to demand the release of the nine members arrested for the death of the police officer during the 1978 Powelton Village siege.

What followed was a very tense twenty-four hours, but the police at the end of that time did not storm the house. Why they didn't is not altogether clear. Sgt. Kirk testified at the commission hearings that he had no idea why the plan was not implemented.[28] Mayor Goode and other city officials insisted that the police were there solely in a reactive posture, and that when MOVE took no offensive action, police action was not needed. However, Ramona Africa felt the police had counted on provoking MOVE into some kind of violent confrontation by setting off a cherry bomb, but that MOVE had seen through the provocation and didn't respond.[29] Or perhaps because the authorities had not yet obtained felony warrants, they felt they still lacked a sufficient legal cover for an all-out assault.

In any event, what is indisputable is that August 8, 1984 ended up being a foretaste of and dress rehearsal for May 13, 1985. MOVE was given a strong-arm message of what might happen if it persisted in its rebellious activities; the complaining residents were now more fully aware of what the city might be prepared to do, ostensibly in their behalf; and officials got a reading both on how MOVE was likely to respond to a major show of police force, and also how the public itself would react to such a confrontation. Significantly, many of the people who gathered in the neighborhood on August 8, most of them Black, were furious with the heavy hand of the cops. City Councilman Lucien Blackwell testified at the commission hearings that because there was so much anger, August 8 turned out to be an embarrassing moment for the Goode administration.[30] This public outrage is perhaps another reason why there was no assault on August 8, and pointed to the need for the authorities to attempt to further isolate MOVE.

Over the next six months or so, Goode and his administration proceeded with some care in regard to "the MOVE problem." In the aftermath of the May 13 massacre, the mayor's commission would assail this careful approach as a policy of "appeasement" toward MOVE, of continuing MOVE's "right to exist above the law."[31] The commission complained that nothing had been done in October 1984 when MOVE began to construct a bunker on the roof of 6221 Osage, apparently to replace the flimsier structure made of pallets and in obvious response to what MOVE had learned on August 8 of police intentions. The commission also railed at various city agencies for failure to do anything about unpaid MOVE water, gas, and electric bills; about MOVE children remaining out of school in flagrant violation of truancy laws; and about non-enforcement of various health code regulations.[32]

By raising a hue and cry about "appeasement," the commission adroitly conjured up a picture of the days leading up to World War 2. MOVE is thus equated with Hitler and the Nazis, and Mayor Goode is equated with the British Prime Minister who was criticized for attempting to appease them. If only something had been done about MOVE/Hitler earlier, the commission argued, perhaps a violent confrontation could have been avoided. But the commission's cry of "appeasement," in addition to putting the onus for the May 13 assault on MOVE (after all, while Prime Minister Chamberlain was seen as wrongly attempting to appease Hitler, it is Hitler who is blamed for starting World War 2), is not at all supported by the facts and represents a rather flimsy and transparent effort to divert people from what was actually going on in those months leading up to the massacre.

Precisely because MOVE refused to be intimidated on August 8 by "the Kirk plan," and also because so many people expressed outrage over the heavy show of police force on that day, it was essential for the authorities to have firmly in place the legal, political and military components before another confrontation with MOVE. As opposed to any notion of "appeasement," the authorities were summing up the lessons of August 8 and were carefully preparing for a showdown.

Mayor Goode himself *told* the commission that a violent confrontation with MOVE was unavoidable:

> I don't think...that there is anything that anyone could have done that could have prevented a violent armed confrontation with the MOVE organization. *I believe that an armed confrontation was inevitable from day one.* That any time any group which is a terrorist group decides that it wants to go into a neighborhood, to in essence, hold that whole neighborhood hostage, and ask in return for releasing that neighborhood, the release of persons from prisons who have been sentenced by a judge over which the mayor has no control. There is very little anyone can do with that.[33]

The commission also seems to conveniently ignore Goode's comments immediately after the events of May 13, 1985:

> Every indication I've received for the past several months, over the past year, was of the nature that if, in fact, the police came in to arrest anyone there would be an armed, violent confrontation. Therefore, I moved with the full knowledge – with the full knowl-

edge – that, in fact, there would be an armed, violent confrontation.

And I want to say to all the people that as mayor of this city I stand fully accountable for having made that decision. I stand behind that decision, and I just hope that the casualties will be very few.[!][34]

It must be said again that these are not the words of an inept blunderer and certainly not those of an appeaser. Further, in their testimony before the commission, Managing Director Brooks and Police Commissioner Sambor made the same point. They also offered the same obligatory disclaimer that the inevitable armed confrontation would obviously be not their fault but MOVE's.[35]

By the spring of 1985, there were many signs that the showdown was not far off. Surveillance of the MOVE house and MOVE members' activities had of course continued throughout the period. Lt. Frank Powell continued to study his aerial reconnaissance photos of the MOVE roof. Civil Affairs officers continued to meet with some of MOVE's neighbors who, by continuing to complain and demand that something be done about MOVE, were unknowingly contributing to the destruction of their own neighborhood.

MOVE actually hadn't been on their loudspeaker much over the last seven or eight months, perhaps reflecting how they too were feeling out the situation after August 8. But on April 29 they did get on the sound system, in response to several police officers lurking in the back of their property and setting their dogs to barking. Some of the neighbors then immediately phoned in a complaint about the noise MOVE was making, and shortly thereafter a contingent of cops arrived on the scene.[36] No arrests were attempted, even though Civil Affairs officers said that MOVE members threatened their lives and that of the mayor. Instead, officers tape-recorded and took notes of MOVE's loudspeaker speeches, thus collecting information that would later turn up in the warrants used as the legal justification for the assault on May 13. In fact, the events of April 29 strongly suggest a deliberate police provocation, for on the very next day Police Commissioner Sambor alerted key subordinates to begin developing plans for an assault on MOVE.[37]

The pace now really picked up. On May 3, just two days after some of the Cobbs Creek residents held their well-covered press conference at which they repeated their demand that strong action be taken against MOVE, Goode called a meeting that included Brooks, Sambor, District Attorney Edward Rendell, and City Councilman Lucien Blackwell. At this meeting Goode and his associates began to lay the legal and military basis for the forthcoming assault. According to Brooks, the outcome of the meeting was that "Ed Rendell was to go back . . . and reinterview the citizens, take depositions, reinterview the police officers who had been in constant, recent constant surveillance, and decide whether he had sufficient information to go for a warrant, and that he would report that back the following week."[38] And unlike the August 8 confrontation, Goode and the other authorities this time wanted heavy legal charges definitely in hand. As a legal pretext for the coming violent assault on MOVE, charges about health code violations simply would not do. One cannot storm a house claiming it was to rid a neighborhood of raw food lying on the ground.

Brooks also reports that on May 7, Rendell "came back and showed some of the depositions, some of the statements. And it was the conclusion of the mayor at the end of that meeting . . . that Rendell was to go back and obtain the warrants . . ."[39] It was also at this meeting, Brooks adds, that he told Sambor to start putting together an operational and tactical plan.[40]

This of course came as no surprise to the police commissioner, who had already instructed his subordinates right after the April 29 incident to ready an assault on MOVE. Nor was it necessary for them to start from scratch, since they could and did borrow major elements from the plan designed by Sgt. Kirk and company in preparation for August 8, 1984.

As was true of Kirk's plan, Sambor's called for the initial use of smoke, gas, and water. But unlike the earlier plan where a lateral entry was the backup to a rooftop assault, now a major element of the new plan called for the use of "insertion teams" that would employ explosives to blow small holes into the walls on both sides of 6221 Osage Avenue in order to get the tear gas inside the house. This was necessary, said Sambor, because trying to insert the gas via the roof had been made much more difficult by the large front bunker MOVE had built after August 8. As a major contingency, however, and similar to the Kirk plan, there also were to be water cannons or Squrt guns on hand to try to eliminate the front bunker. And if the insertion teams failed, the plan called for the use of explosives on the roof.

Sambor adamantly denied that the use of explosives on the

roof was contemplated at any time prior to the afternoon of May 13, but Sergeant Albert Revel, one of the key planners for the May 13 assault, revealed at the commission hearings that placement of explosives on the roof was planned as a backup days before May 13.[41] Mayor Goode also denied at the commission hearings that he knew anything in advance of May 13 about the insertion teams' use of explosives. But Sambor informed the commission that the mayor wasn't telling the truth and that he had gone over the plan with the mayor, including the insertion teams' use of explosives, prior to May 13.[42]

Sambor testified that his plan was essentially in place by the evening of May 10 and that on May 11 he told Goode the operational details: "I told him about the evacuation. I told him the time would commence somewhere around 10 a.m. Sunday [May 12]; that we hoped to have the majority of, if not everybody, out by 10 o'clock that night; . . . that we had set up the entire operation; that we anticipated at no later than 0300 [3 a.m., May 13] to have everybody out and to begin the final preparations for the confrontation."[43]

It was also on May 11 that the city authorities got the arrest and search warrants they wanted as a legal basis for the forthcoming assault. On that day, Judge Lynne M. Abraham, sitting in her Society Hill home, signed warrants for the arrests of four MOVE members known to be inside 6221 Osage. Frank James Africa, Conrad Hampton Africa, Ramona Johnson Africa, and Theresa Brooks Africa were charged with seven specific crimes, including four felony charges – criminal conspiracy, possession of explosives, riot, and improper influence in official matters.[44]

Judge Abraham also wrote out a search warrant at the request of the Civil Affairs Unit, which claimed that MOVE had an illegal cache of weapons and explosives inside 6221 Osage. This was not only an important legal but also political justification for what was to come, and went hand in hand with rumors flying in the press and elsewhere that MOVE not only had a large cache of weapons and explosives but was threatening to shoot police and Mayor Goode and blow up the whole block.[45]

Those familiar with U.S. history, as well as many based on their own life experience, will not be the least surprised that the authorities and police, with the help of the mass media, pulled out all the stops in trying to convince the public that the hail of bullets and weapons they were about to unleash was nothing more than the droppings of an offended dove. But the authorities did have two major public image problems to contend with as they prepared for what they called the "inevitable" armed confrontation. One was the MOVE children inside 6221 Osage. They could not be charged with anything, and while the adults could be portrayed as armed and dangerous, what could be said about the children?

Goode testified before the commission that at the May 7 meeting with Brooks, Sambor, etc., he told Brooks to work through the Police Department, the Department of Human Services, and the Law Department to make sure the children were removed from the house before the assault.[46] But Brooks took no action in regard to this, and in fact left town the next day without even saying anything to his staff about how to proceed.[47]

Irene F. Pernsley, the city's human services commissioner, says she didn't learn of the problem with the children until May 9, when she got a call from Sambor saying they were supposed to be picked up and held until after the confrontation. This, of course, should have been no problem, since through their surveillance the authorities knew that the MOVE adults took the children every day and always at the same time to Cobbs Creek Park for them to exercise and play, and always returned with them at the same time.

But there was a problem. Pernsley told Sambor "that we do not have the authority to just pick up children while they are at play or while they are in the park . . ." and then asked him "on what basis it was being proposed that the children be picked up, inasmuch as we only operate on the basis of reports and allegations of neglect and abuse of children."[48] She then told the commission, perhaps in another unintended moment of revelation that the hearings were replete with, that in her entire tenure as human services commissioner she had never received a report about abuse or neglect of children at 6221 Osage and therefore let Sambor know that she "would be unable to honor that request."[49]

The commission also reports in its findings that on the evening of May 9, "the City Solicitor's office gave the Police Commissioner specific instructions to take the children from 6221 Osage Ave. into protective custody at the first opportunity. Nevertheless, the City Solicitor's office did not attempt to secure the legal authority to remove and detain the children until the morning of the confrontation, when it was too late."[50]

Indeed it was. And when Goode met with Sambor on May 11 and 12 to go over details of the plan, he knew that the children were still inside the house but did nothing to delay or stop commencement of the operation. As Ramona Africa said: "MOVE children walked the streets daily, rite up til May 11, 1985 and were never with more than *two women*; police officials knew this and so did Wilson Goode. If Wilson Goode had any interest in the safety of MOVE kids, he had every opportunity in the world to have them picked up, *especially* during the week before May 13, 1985 when Wilson Goode, no doubt, knew the date of his murderous attack."[51] In fact, on May 11 a car driven by a MOVE supporter approached a checkpoint placed across Osage Avenue and manned by the police. (The checkpoint was part of the first deployment for the confrontation to come two days later.) In the car were at least two MOVE children. But the police simply permitted the car to go to 6221 Osage, children and all.[52]

The commission concluded from all this that Goode, Brooks, and Sambor had been "grossly negligent" and risked the children's lives. This is grossly ridiculous. All the evidence points to a much different conclusion: the authorities had ample opportunity and time to pick up the children and simply decided not to do it, leaving them to share the same fate as the adults. Perhaps their attitude is best captured in the words of one of the neighborhood residents who wanted MOVE out and didn't care how. On May 12, as the operation started going into full gear, he said: "What I'd do is call them out. Tell them they got so many minutes. And if they don't come out, I'd level the place kids and all. . . . You don't want to leave any kids growing up wanting vengeance."[53]

A second major public image problem the authorities had to contend with involved negotiations. People would want to know what kind of efforts the city had made to talk MOVE members out of the house before deciding they had no alternative but to attack them. Accordingly, an article appeared on the front page of the *Philadelphia Inquirer* one day after the confrontation.[54] The article states that three private citizens delegated by Mayor Goode to negotiate with MOVE told him on May 9 that they were somewhat optimistic because "MOVE wants out" and would be willing to leave their house under certain conditions.

Supposedly MOVE wanted "an ironclad guarantee from Goode himself that they would not be arrested" upon leaving 6221 Osage. Goode then was said to have sent word back the following day that there would be no immediate arrests, but that the mayor couldn't promise there would be no arrests at any time in the future. Then, the article continues, the negotiators lost their former optimism because MOVE refused the mayor's terms and "reverted to their original, non-negotiable demand" for the release of the nine MOVE members imprisoned for the death of the police officer during the 1978 Powelton Village siege.[55]

The article then quotes Goode as saying he received word from one of the negotiators on Saturday, May 10, that MOVE had sent him a message "not to bother anymore talking to them. They would not talk to me anymore about this matter.... At that point, we decided we could not negotiate them out and had to go in and serve the warrants."[56]

However, Gerald Africa, a spokesperson for MOVE and the individual involved in these negotiations, maintains he never said any such thing. Nor was it the position of those in the house, he stresses, that they would come out if Goode promised not to arrest them. But, Gerald Africa says, there most certainly was an agreement reached by the negotiators and himself, one that Goode flatly rejected. MOVE members agreed to come out of the house and thus prevent a confrontation if either Goode or Pennsylvania Chief Justice Robert Nix would give them a verbal agreement that the courts would review the cases of the nine jailed members. MOVE also wanted the nine released on bail pending the results of the review. This was hardly an unreasonable demand, and in fact there already was a precedent for it. As part of settling the confrontation at Powelton Village in 1978, the authorities had agreed to release several other imprisoned MOVE members on the same review basis. But Goode and the other authorities now refused to consider such a compromise.[57]

All it would have taken, said Gerald Africa, even right through May 13, was a phone call to him giving nothing more than verbal assurance that the cases of the nine members would be reviewed. But the call never came. Said Gerald Africa: Goode "never was about negotiations. And I stayed by this phone and watched my brothers and sisters die, even up until the last, even until it was over, waiting on the mayor or anybody from government to call me so that I could go up to Osage Avenue and tell them to give up."[58]

As the early morning hours of May 13 approached, MOVE broadcast to police over the loudspeaker that in order to proceed with negotiations, they should contact radio talk show host Irv Homer, news director at WDAS Barbara Grant, and channel 10 news reporter Harvey Clark. But the police did nothing about this offer. Homer didn't even learn of MOVE's request until he read about it in the newspapers several months after the massacre.[59]

Chauncey Campbell, a member of the Philadelphia chapter of the NAACP, was one of the last people to talk with MOVE. On the afternoon of May 12 he spoke with Theresa Africa. He asked her if the people inside the house were aware of what was going on outside, how the police were bringing in lots of weapons and how it appeared as though a violent confrontation was about to start. She said: "I know – they're here to kill us." She then asked him to go back to tell the ministers, to tell the journalists, particularly the Black journalists, to tell everyone that MOVE had no intention of initiating anything with the police, that anyone familiar with MOVE's philosophy knows MOVE doesn't believe in killing anyone or anything, not even a fly. She said MOVE reveres life, including their own, that they therefore had no intention of committing suicide. "Tell them," she said, "that we want justice. And tell them that we want to live."[60]

2 | The Assault

At 5:35 a.m., May 13, Police Commissioner Sambor lay on his stomach in the doorway of 6218 Osage Avenue, directly across and only about ten yards from the MOVE house. Extending forward a bullhorn, Sambor shouted: "Attention, MOVE! This is America! You have to abide by the laws of the United States."[1] People in Philadelphia, throughout the country, and around the world were soon to get a vivid demonstration of just what Sambor was talking about.

Tactical and operational deployment for the coming confrontation with MOVE started in earnest about twenty hours before Sambor issued his command. It was Mother's Day, a warm and sunny morning on which many people in the neighborhood were anticipating a relaxing day of family outings. The selection of Mother's Day to begin the operation was no coincidence, and serves as yet another example of how carefully planned and premeditated was the forthcoming assault.

Sambor chose the date and Mayor Goode concurred. Goode says he asked Sambor if "he thought, since May 12 was Mother's Day, he wanted to wait a few days beyond that. He said no, that he felt that May 12 was a good day, that he would hope the people could leave, go to church, go visit their relatives and not return home, that would be from a point of view of secrecy and security the best way to work it."[2]

"The best way to work it" meant that, by order of the Philadelphia Police Department, the neighborhood was to be evacuated. Residents were ordered to leave home by 10 p.m. and be prepared to stay away for 24 hours. Refusal to comply with the order, it was stressed, would lead to arrest. Some of the residents were angered by the order. One elderly couple refused to leave their home until the police banged on their front door with a crowbar and threatened to break it down.[3] Another infuriated resident questioned, "Why should I leave? This wasn't declared a disaster area. I don't see any reason to leave, unless they're planning to blow up everything around here."[4]

But faced with the prospect of arrest, people angered by the police order started to leave along with those who were already leaving uncomplainingly. The Black neighborhood began to resemble a scene common in South Africa. The streets bristled with barricades. Prior to the 10 p.m. deadline, residents had to show identification before they were permitted to go to their homes. Detectives with clipboards manned checkpoints at street corners, writing down the names and addresses of anyone attempting to get behind the barriers. Police helicopters buzzed overhead. Reporters and TV crews flocked to the scene and large crowds began to gather at the barricades.

During this period several community activists tried desperately to work out a peaceful resolution, apparently unaware that Mayor Goode and the authorities had already concluded that negotiations were useless and a violent confrontation was inevitable. Long-time West Philadelphia activist Novella Williams contacted Goode by telephone and pleaded with him to call off the operation and not kill the MOVE people. Goode replied that there was nothing to worry about and that if he backed out now he would appear to be "irresponsible."[5]

As the hours passed and tension increased, a group of Black women from North Philadelphia who had arrived on the scene called on mothers and grandmothers to prevent the police from storming the MOVE house. One person at a barricaded street corner recalled a woman hollering to people, "Do the same thing we did in Powelton Village"—a reference to people breaking through the police blockade in 1978 to deliver food to MOVE. She said, "I was there at Powelton Village. We knocked down them barricades. We went through there. They weren't stopping us from saying what we wanted to say."[6]

But this was not 1978. The police would allow no one onto Osage Avenue and the barricades were not breached. There was a heavy air of intimidation. When one person in the crowd started loudly to condemn the police, yelling at them, "Y'all out here to kill MOVE!" he was arrested and taken away in handcuffs.[7]

After the 10 p.m. evacuation deadline the police conducted house-to-house searches, threatening and roughly removing stragglers. With the neighborhood finally stripped of its dwellers – about 500 people living in some 125 houses – the police made their move. A deserted neighborhood was transformed into a battlefield.

In the early morning hours of May 13, utility crews cut off the gas and electricity to the 6200 block of Osage Avenue. At approximately the same time, Squrt guns on remote control booms were positioned on Pine Street, behind the MOVE house. Members of the Bomb Disposal Unit and sharpshooters from the stakeout unit also arrived on the scene, carrying sandbags and duffle bags stuffed with weapons. An eyewitness to the arrival of the stakeout unit describes the scene:

> About 3 a.m. SWAT cops were coming with helmets, bulletproof vests, shotguns. . . . They had rifles and guns. One guy was in the back of the paddy wagon, putting his works, his thing, together. He's putting it all together in the paddy wagon. He had one of those black things you carry in your hand. And this one man said, "Oh, that's explosives in there." You know, like they threw those things in Vietnam, grenades.
>
> There was maybe three paddy wagons full up with a lot of them cops coming in. . . . Each paddy wagon had four or five plainclothes men with suits on [who would] go to the paddy wagon, give them their orders with a sheet of paper, tell them where to go at. . . you know, you give your orders. In front of everybody they was doing it. . . . I mean, it was just like Vietnam all over again. That's how it was. . .[8]

Police reports after May 13 indicated that, all told, there were seventy-seven police involved in the assault.[9] This figure doesn't include the hundreds of other cops who were involved in various other operational aspects of the assault, such as crowd control. They were organized into ten teams, including several rooftop teams, and they surrounded the MOVE house in a roughly diamond-shaped configuration.

Mayor Goode told the commission that he ordered Sambor to

hand-pick all the police officers who would be on the assault teams. The reason, Goode said, is that he wanted to make sure there would be no one involved who had "a hot temper," or who "may have been emotionally attached" to the 1978 confrontation at Powelton Village.[10] What Goode was referring to in particular was an incident at the end of the Powelton Village siege in which one of the surrendering MOVE members, Delbert Africa, was attacked and severely beaten by four cops as he emerged from the house with his hands in the air. The incident, captured on film by a TV crew on the spot, created a public furor and led to a trial of three of the officers. They were acquitted, adding fuel to the fire over the beating. And the whole matter was a serious embarrassment for the police department, which was then (although certainly not for the first time) under pressure because of widespread allegations of corruption and brutality.

Goode had to explain this question of hand-picking police personnel because despite what he claims were his orders, several of the seventy-seven cops surrounding the MOVE house on May 13 in fact *had* been involved in the Powelton Village siege, including at least one who participated in Delbert Africa's beating. Goode could not explain how these cops ended up being part of the May 13 assault. He told the commission he only learned of the situation subsequently, from a newspaper account. When asked what he then did, Goode replied: "I basically have indicated to the managing director my displeasure with the fact that I felt that my instructions were not followed in that regard."[11]

But Leo Brooks wasn't about to take the rap. In reply to a commission question about whether any instructions were given specifying that cops involved in the 1978 beating of Delbert Africa should not be involved this time, Brooks responded: "I did not give that instruction, nor did I hear that instruction given."[12] Gregore Sambor also denied having heard such specific instructions. So did District Attorney Edward Rendell. What did Goode have to say to this? Did he or didn't he give these specific instructions? Goode could only reply lamely: "I don't recall those words, but I'm sure that in my instructions that that was definitely implied."[13]

Exactly who and what was deployed against MOVE on May 13 caused some other memory problems as well. There was the important question, for example, of what kinds of weapons the police officers were carrying. A police report issued after the assault indicates that the cops were equipped with a powerful arsenal. Sixteen cops were assigned M-16s.[14] The M-16 is a potent weapon developed for use in Vietnam. High-velocity bullets from an M-16 usually kill rather than injure their target.

Thirteen cops had 12-gauge shotguns with deadly 00 buckshot; two others were armed with .22-caliber rifles equipped with silencers; and there were also Browning automatic rifles, 30.06 rifles with scopes, and .357 magnums on hand. But that was just the beginning. Seven others were equipped with Uzi submachine guns; there were two M-60 machine guns and one .45-caliber Thompson machine gun. There were also two .50-caliber machine guns with armor-piercing ammunition ordinarily used to take out jeeps or trucks. To top it off, there was a 20mm. antitank gun.[15] Significantly, many of these are war-fighting weapons and are not normally found in city police department arsenals.

Who decided that such weapons would be used? Police Commissioner Sambor, the logical choice since he was the person responsible for overseeing development of the assault plan, told the commission he had no idea. He could not recall anything being said about this at a May 9 planning session attended by FBI representatives, two dozen top police officials, etc. Nor could he recall anything being said about this at any other time leading up to May 13.[16]

But Sergeant Albert Revel, one of the three police officers Sambor designated to develop the details of the plan, had much better recall. He testified before the commission that at the May 9 meeting, "the commissioner wanted to know what we had in our armory as to the availability of automatic weapons. And [Sambor] was told we have. . .all the 16s, and the Uzi's, and the .50s."[17] At that same meeting, Lt. Powell told Sambor there were other heavy automatic weapons available, and asked if the police commissioner thought they were necessary. Sambor said, "If you can get them and they can be transferred legally, . . .get them."[18]

One of the reasons why the city's top officials were having great difficulty remembering such important matters is that none of these principal decision makers wanted to admit that through their own conscious design, in the early morning hours of May 13 the MOVE house was surrounded by large numbers of well-trained, lavishly armed police, and that a carefully developed plan existed to turn them loose. Over the years and through a series of probes, investigations by various commissions, etc., the Philadelphia Police Department had earned a well-deserved reputation for being one of the most brutal in the country, particularly in encounters with Blacks and other minorities. And the cops who surrounded the MOVE house on May 13, including the "veterans" of the 1978 confrontation, had a long-standing hatred of MOVE, both because of the embarrassing 1978 trial of three of their fellow officers and also because of numerous other confrontations with MOVE where the radical Black group had refused to back down. They were itching to go, and they wouldn't have long to wait.

Fifteen minutes after Sambor informed MOVE that this is America and announced that four people inside 6221 Osage were under arrest, the only thing to come from the MOVE house was the defiant reply: "We ain't got a motherfucking thing to lose. So come on down and get us."[19] The authorities knew that the MOVE members wouldn't come out. Sambor expressly told the commission that,[20] and so did Goode when he confessed he knew from day one that a violent confrontation was inevitable. For one thing, the authorities understood that as a matter of principle, MOVE always refused to back down in the face of intimidation and force. In the negotiations several days earlier, Gerald Africa had offered Goode a way out, but he wouldn't take it. He knew the MOVE members wouldn't surrender without some kind of compromise, and now were left only with the option of defending themselves.

Another reason the MOVE members could not and would not come out is that such a deadly ring of firepower had been established around their house that it was only logical – given the whole history of police attacks on their organization, to say nothing of the long history of police murders of other Black revolutionaries, such as Black Panther leader Fred Hampton – for those inside to assume that if they did attempt to emerge, they stood an excellent chance of being cut down.

Thus when the fifteen-minute deadline passed and MOVE had not surrendered, the police and authorities hoped it would appear that they now had exhausted all legal and other remedies and had to attack – which is what they proceeded to do. It began with police firing tear gas and smoke projectiles at the front and rear of the MOVE house. Osage Avenue and several blocks around were plunged under a choking, blinding blanket. Moving under this cover into two homes on either side of the MOVE house were the two insertion teams whose task was to blow three-inch holes into MOVE's walls in order to flood the interior with tear gas. At the same time, the Squrt guns on Pine Street opened up, pouring a thousand gallons of water a minute onto MOVE's roof with the object of destroying the front bunker.[21]

A minute later came the first shots. Sambor claimed that MOVE fired first. When asked by the commission how he knew, Sambor replied with admirable simplicity, "Because I was there."[22] But others who also were there saw it differently. Said one Black youth, for example: "The police fired first. I know that for a fact 'cause I saw it. I had my binoculars and everything."[23]

But it isn't necessary to try to sort out conflicting eyewitness accounts. Sambor himself, after claiming MOVE fired first, went on to give important evidence to the contrary. The commission asked Sambor about the nature of the initial gunfire:

Q. Did it sound like automatic fire to you?
A. It did, yes, sir.
Q. And I take it you are familiar with the sound of automatic weapons?
A. I have heard automatic, yes, sir.
Q. As you know, Commissioner, there were no automatic weapons found in the MOVE house, and I suppose an obvious question is: Do you have any theory as to why you believe you heard automatic weapons fired [by MOVE], when there were no automatic weapons found in the house afterwards?
A. I can't explain that, sir, and – I can't explain that, sir.[24]

Indeed, after the massacre the only weapons found in the ruins of the MOVE house were the burned and twisted remains of two pistols, a shotgun, and a .22-caliber rifle. No automatic weapons.[25]

Besides initiating the firing with their automatic weapons, the police also didn't spare the ammunition. The commission reports that in a period of ninety minutes, from 6 to 7:30 a.m., the police fired at least ten thousand rounds at MOVE. Thirty-two cops "admitted to firing their weapons. One shooter acknowledged that, from his post, within 50 feet of the house, he fired 1,000 rounds from his M-16 semiautomatic rifle."[26]

According to a list of weapons that was subsequently obtained from the police by the *Philadelphia Inquirer*, the fired ammunition included 4,500 rounds from M-16s; 1,500 from the Uzis; and 2,240 from the M-60 machine guns.[27] The *Inquirer* article further points out that "A note to the inventory list suggests that the two officers with M-60 machine guns in 6218 Osage Ave. exhausted their original supply of 400 rounds of M-60 ammunition. It states: '1,840 rounds brought later from the Police Academy.'"[28] One day after the massacre and before all this information was made public, city officials were claiming that on the morning of May 13, 75 percent of the gunfire came from MOVE.[29]

So many police bullets were whizzing through the air that the crowds at the barricades had to hit the ground and hide behind the tires of parked cars. While the police had their main weaponry trained overwhelmingly on MOVE, it appears that all this firepower and the tear gas were also used to try to prevent any civilians from witnessing the assault, and to discourage any notion of interfering.

One person at the barricades at Sixty-second and Pine recalled people saying:

> "They're shooting at *us*. They're trying to kill us. They don't want us to see." I mean, the media got on the ground their ownselves during that whole time. Every time a gun would shoot the media was all on the ground. They were scared to death.... Me and this girl were going down through this little street, just walking...before we know it, cops is shooting at us, at our feet. Me and the girl got down on our knees like this, crawling, trying to get back from where they were shooting at us.... It was a constant bumbumbum, bumbumbum, don't shoot her, just scare her good enough. It was that kind of thing. It was to make me know that you can't get up there but so far.... If I had gotten through that block I could have seen everything that was going on.[30]

The police during this period also pushed back the barricades, shoving TV camera crews covering the scene live further and further away. When cops discovered reporters holed up in houses behind the barricades and fairly close to 6221 Osage, they confiscated their notebooks and tape recorders; rolls of film were deliberately exposed.[31]

The smoke and tear gas, the tons of water, the ten thousand rounds of ammunition were not the only elements brought into play in the early stages of the attack. There were also the two insertion teams, Team A and Team B. Each team apparently was composed of seven police, all members of the city's stakeout and bomb disposal units. Team A was headed by Lt. Powell, chief of the BDU, the person who had been studying surveillance photos of the MOVE roof since well before the August 1984 confrontation, and the one who would be designated later in the day to drop the bomb. Another member of Team A was William Klein, who made the bomb. Also assigned to the A-Team was Terrence Mulvihill, a veteran of the 1978 Powelton Village confrontation and one of the officers who had been charged with beating and kicking Delbert Africa.[32] Heading up Team B was Sergeant Edward Connor, Powell's predecessor as chief of the BDU.

At the very beginning of the attack, under cover of the smoke and tear gas, Team A entered 6223 Osage, the house next to MOVE's on the west, and Team B entered 6217, two houses to the east. It soon was abundantly clear that these teams' mission was more ambitious than just blowing three-inch holes in the walls for the insertion of tear gas. In fact, the word "insertion" is not at all appropriate to describe their real purpose. "Demolition" is much more to the point.[33]

In a period of roughly four hours, from approximately 6:15 a.m. to 10:45 a.m., the two teams set off a total of nine major explosions. Team B used a charge to open a three-by-four-foot hole in the porch wall between 6217 and 6219 Osage Avenue and followed up by hurling increasingly more powerful charges of HDP boosters through the hole at MOVE. HDP boosters have a substantial blast wave and detonate at the very rapid rate of twenty-six thousand feet per second. By comparison, "slow" dynamite detonates at a rate of eight thousand feet per second.[34]

Team A used preshaped hatch charges on the common wall between 6223 and 6221. They also used detaprime boosters as stun grenades. A stun grenade generates lots of light and noise but is not designed to cause serious physical injury. But detaprime boosters are not standard issue stun grenades. Because of the tremendous detonation wave and pressure produced by these boosters, they are more commonly used to detonate or boost other explosives, and when used in close confines they are capable of turning ordinary objects into flying missiles. In effect, by employing these boosters Team A had fashioned their own fragmentation grenades which were capable of causing serious bodily harm and possibly death.[35]

When the two teams had finished their work that morning, the fronts of four houses on Osage had been blown out or damaged. In 6223, where Team A had been located, the basement stairs had been rendered useless, a wall had come down, a ceiling was about to collapse, and an air conditioner set in a rear second-floor window had been blown out and sent flying across the rear alley.[36] On the other side, Team B had succeeded in destroying the porch wall between 6219-21. Another explosive was hurled through the fortifications of MOVE's front porch, blowing out much of the front of MOVE's house. At this point Sgt. Connor peered into the MOVE house and saw what appeared to be a body, possibly with a severed head.[37]

Goode, Brooks, and Sambor all claim they had no prior knowledge of what the two "insertion" teams were actually going to do. The mayor told the commission that prior to May 13, all he knew was that the teams were supposed to poke three-inch holes into the walls; he wasn't even aware that explosives were going to be used for this limited purpose. He further testified that he didn't learn of the extensive damage that was done to the four homes by much more powerful explosives until *after* May 13, "from reading news accounts of what happened."[38] The managing director told the commission that the mayor's memory once again seemed faulty, since he had told Goode the night of May 12 that explosives would be used to insert tear gas. But like Goode, Brooks maintained he had no idea that heavier explosives were going to be used and also only learned of them subsequent to May 13. But after the demolition teams were finished, Brooks had been invited by Sambor to come to 6218 Osage, directly across from the MOVE house, and have himself a look. Which he did, with binoculars. The commission asked Brooks if anyone had told him, or if he had asked anyone as he gazed at the destruction, how so much damage had occurred. Brooks replied that no one told him and he didn't ask. Perhaps a little stunned themselves by this, the commission asked again: "We have a photograph that shows the front of the [MOVE] house pretty much blown away. Were you aware at any time during the day of May 13, that explosives had been used that were powerful enough to pretty much destroy the front of the house and blow through a brick wall in the front?" Brooks' reply: "I was not."[39]

Police Commissioner Sambor also testified that the destruction wreaked by Teams A and B came as a complete surprise. He could not explain why neither team sought his approval before using the powerful explosives. But Sambor once again was about to be exposed by his subordinates, who weren't about to be the fall guys. This in fact was a pattern in the aftermath of May 13, with angry police publicly proclaiming through their union that they would not allow the principal authorities to get away with dropping all the blame on their shoulders.

In this instance, several subordinates testified that Sambor knew full well what kinds of explosives were going to be used.

For example, Sgt. Connor, leader of Team B, told the commission that on the night of May 12 and then again in the early morning hours of May 13, Sambor was present at meetings where these explosives were discussed, including the use of a hatch charge to blow out the common wall between 6217 and 6219.[40]

Perhaps sensing the vulnerability of his position, and also wanting to make it appear that there were no differences between how he and his subordinates saw the situation, when asked by the commission if he considered the explosions a violation of any order he had given, either directly or indirectly, Sambor replied it would be if "it was done without any reason or purpose."[41] But there very well could have been a good reason, added Sambor. "[F]or example, one of the things that I heard . . . is that . . . one explosive was used to get people out of a situation where they were pinned down. Now, if in fact that is accurate, then I would consider the use of any means to extricate personnel who are pinned down by hostile fire to be appropriate."[42]

What Sambor is referring to is the claim by Connor and Team B that they had come under fire from MOVE as they attempted to proceed from 6217 to 6219, and that Connor himself was knocked down by some kind of projectile. But even if this were true, the fact remains that the teams were equipped with all these explosives with the obvious intent of using them, *with* Sambor's knowledge and consent and whether or not they ran into some resistance. For example, Team B detonated at least one and probably two major charges before this supposed shootout with MOVE, blowing a three-by-four-foot hole in a porch wall. And Team A almost totally destroyed 6223 and blew out a major portion of the front of the MOVE house.

The effort to place the blame on Lt. Powell, Sgt. Connor, and the other team members for the use of explosives that were not supposed to be present or used goes hand in hand with the effort to convince the public that none of the principal decision makers such as Goode, Brooks, and Sambor really had anything fundamentally to do with how MOVE children ended up being in the house; how "emotionally involved" cops from the 1978 confrontation ended up being on the May 13 assault teams; or how these assault teams ended up being equipped with powerful military weapons not normally found in city police department arsenals.

Operating here is the well-known and well-worn gambit of "deniability," in which secret plans and policies are developed in such a way as to include the option for the higher-ups who are actually responsible for them to deny any such responsibility. The U.S. public and entire world were treated to a heavy helping of "deniability" at the end of 1986, when Ronald Reagan and members of his National Security Council tried to distance themselves from the "Irangate/Contragate" crisis. In the case of the massacre in Philadelphia on May 13, 1985, Mayor Goode—even though he had earned and assiduously cultivated a reputation as a "hands-on" administrator—chose also to distance himself physically from the scene, thus enabling him to claim that he didn't know and therefore could not be held responsible for all that went down there.

Many of the commission's major conclusions are designed to lend legitimacy to this notion that much of what happened on May 13 was the result of certain individuals like Powell and Connor deciding to do whatever they liked because they weren't properly supervised. The commission, for example, criticized the two "insertion" teams, saying that they "violated acceptable safety standards and imperiled human life by enhancing and misapplying explosives of such force that the results were completely different than those contemplated by the assault plan."[43]

But in the eyes of the commission, the authorities (in this particular case especially Sambor) are guilty of nothing more than compounding the teams' incompetence "by allowing the unit to operate without adequate command or control.... Through the default of his superiors, the lieutenant [Powell] assumed unrestricted discretion in selecting and employing explosives which were excessive under the circumstances." Similarly, in examining why powerful military weapons were on hand, the commission concludes that "so great was the latitude given the police planners that they were allowed to augment the department's arsenal with military weapons...not normally available to municipal police departments."[44]

In sum, despite all the evidence to the contrary, evidence which the commission hearings themselves played a role in uncovering, the commission resolutely maintains and wants the public to believe that there was no real plan, no real line of command or communication, no real intention on the part of the authorities (MOVE's intention, of course, is another matter) to kill anyone—just a big mess. Much, much better that the people believe their leaders are incompetent fools than calculating assassins.

But there is also still much, much more to be told, all of which only further demonstrates that this was the premeditated murder of eleven Black rebels whose only real crime was their determined refusal to accept the master's command that they bow and scrape and remember to keep their place.

3 | The Bomb

By mid-morning of May 13, the shooting and explosions had ceased, but the Squrt guns continued to pound the house and roof for five hours with nearly 640,000 gallons of water.[1] By mid-afternoon two simultaneous but very different kinds of efforts were underway. On the one hand, community activists and others pleaded with Mayor Goode to stop the police operation. On the other hand, the mayor and his associates prepared to continue it.

Louise James no longer lived at 6221 Osage, but her son, Frank, and brother, Vincent Leapheart, did—and both were inside on May 13. She arrived on the scene in the morning and roved from one police barrier to another, beseeching all who would listen to do something to end the assault. "The police should never have gone in," she said. "How can you reconcile sending storm troopers in, tear gas and six hours of water over some goddamn complaints from the neighbors? How can that be reconciled with the taking of life?"[2] Louise James also attempted throughout the day to meet with Goode to talk about finding a way to end the confrontation, but was rebuffed. "I sent messengers and they don't respond," she said, referring to the mayor's office. "I don't know at this point whether my sisters and brothers and my son is dead. Either they're [the police] letting water stream in on dead people or on people who are living who will soon be dead. Now, either way you cut it, that's a terrible thing."³

A delegation of community activists and clergymen did succeed in meeting with Goode at City Hall early in the afternoon. These were people who also had witnessed the attack during the morning and had formed themselves on the spot into a group called the Citizens Committee for Humanity and Justice. One of them explained that they took to Goode

> a six-point proposal for a peaceful resolution to the crisis on Osage Ave. Among those things was for the mayor to come out personally and speak to the people inside the house; for them to immediately stop the water from going into the house; immediately stop the shooting; to pull the policemen back to eliminate the threat, the immediate threat that was being imposed on the MOVE members to set an atmosphere that was conducive for negotiations and for discussion and some sort of peaceful resolution.⁴

But Goode

> denied all of those requests except for one, and that was to allow a delegation of four people to go near the MOVE house and try to talk to them personally. . . . He refused to go himself. He refused to have any city official go with them. Those people that did go to the MOVE house were at least three quarters of a block away, could not see the house, could not see anybody in it, were probably out of earshot of anything going on inside the house. And they spoke through a bullhorn for about five minutes, making requests, trying to get some response which was obviously impossible to get under those circumstances, with all the police around the building and everything. . .⁵

But even as this delegation was attempting to make contact with MOVE, Mayor Goode was demonstrating once again that a peaceful resolution was the farthest thing from his mind. At a City Hall press conference at roughly 3 p.m., he told reporters, "We intend to evict from the house. We intend to evacuate from the house. We intend to seize control of the house." When asked how he intended to do that, Goode replied, "We will do it by any means necessary."⁶

Even as he spoke, the "necessary means" were being discussed at the command center in Walnut Plaza by Managing Director Brooks, Police Commissioner Sambor, Fire Commissioner

William Richmond, and other city officials.[7] The smoke and tear gas grenades, the explosions set off by Teams A and B, the approximately 640,000 gallons of water, and the ten thousand rounds of ammunition had failed to silence MOVE.[8] It was more than evident now that all of MOVE's fortifications and preparations had been necessary, even if these were unable ultimately to withstand the magnitude of the assault.

Of particular concern to the authorities and police was the strategically placed front rooftop bunker, which was still standing. Central to MOVE's philosophy is reverence for and preservation of life. But if attacked, they say they will defend their own lives, and with arms if necessary. The police claim they were fired upon by MOVE. There is no hard evidence to substantiate this, and the police would obviously have their own motives for making such an allegation. But given MOVE's belief in armed self-defense, it is possible that at least some of those inside 6221 Osage did fire back, although such a confrontation would have been decidedly one-sided, with MOVE's four guns going up against the formidable arsenal assembled by the police.

In mid-afternoon the police and authorities gave some thought to the possibility of dislodging or lifting the bunker with a crane. But this option was quickly abandoned, supposedly due to major logistical problems – the streets were too narrow, there were too many obstacles such as trees, etc. But Paul Geppart, the head of the construction company to whom the police had spoken on May 8 and 9 about the possibility of using a crane, testified before the commission that while he couldn't guarantee the police anything, he did tell them he thought he could perform the task from behind the MOVE house, on Pine Street.[9]

Further, Sgt. Albert Revel revealed at the commission hearings that Lt. Powell told him he had received a phone call from Geppart a few days before May 13, and that while he could not provide an ironclad guarantee, Geppart thought he could deal with the bunker by placing a crane on Pine Street at a cost of $6,500. Powell informed Sambor who said he would check with Goode. Revel testified that the crane option was subsequently dashed because Goode would not okay the $6,500.[10]

Clearly the main consideration here was not the city budget, since a $6,500 expenditure was hardly going to lead to bankruptcy. The crane operation could at least have been tried and then if it didn't succeed something else could have been attempted. But Goode and the other officials preferred another method for dealing with the bunker and MOVE – a bomb. They also preferred dropping it right away, although they could have maintained the standoff, even could have waited overnight to see what might develop and then consider again the possibility of negotiations and some kind of peaceful resolution.

But according to Managing Director Brooks, this option really didn't exist. He told the commission that

> we had a very difficult situation, because we knew there was a labyrinth...of tunnels....And if that was the case, that there were probably some escape routes.
>
> Secondly, we knew that it was very difficult to secure that area. The alley there is very narrow behind those houses. There was no place to set up the typical kind of searchlight business that the Police Department normally does with great care. You would have had to change the people. And there were many other things of that nature that made it difficult. Plus, neighbors were already in the street, agitating to get back into their homes.[11]

Some of the neighbors *were* agitating for the confrontation to be stopped and to be allowed to return to their homes. All the rest of what Brooks said is false. Even Police Commissioner Sambor, who no one would accuse of having a "wait and see" attitude toward MOVE, told the commission that it wasn't essential to try to finish the job before nightfall. Illuminating the alley after dark? Sambor said it was no problem and never told Brooks otherwise. Rotation of the stakeout officers? Also no problem, said Sambor; in fact, it already had been worked out with the appropriate tactical commanders and could have been implemented if deemed necessary by Brooks or other authorities. As for the upset neighbors, Sambor indicated they didn't present a serious problem. He simply would have used "the Civil Affairs and other personnel, to have them explain at the various barricaded situations the reasoning for waiting until the next day."[12]

There remains the question of the "labyrinth of tunnels" that Brooks said the authorities knew were there and could be used by MOVE to escape. But after the massacre no tunnels were found. It is highly unlikely that this was the result of bad intelligence, given the constant surveillance of the MOVE house in the weeks and months prior to the attack. Much more likely is that the authorities knew there were no tunnels and simply invented them as part of their propaganda campaign to portray MOVE as wild and dangerous. But even if the tunnels had existed, Brooks' statement reveals a central truth: MOVE was not going to be allowed to escape if the authorities had anything to say about it, either through tunnels or by any other means. Some or apparently even most of the MOVE people in the house had somehow managed to survive everything thrown at them so far. It was therefore time to bomb them – and there was no time to waste.

Every one of the officials and police involved in developing the assault plan insisted in the days immediately after May 13 that using a bomb was never part of the original tactics, that it was a last-minute idea. Unfortunately for this contention, several months later information was made public that facsimiles of MOVE's roof had been repeatedly blown up in preparation for the August 8, 1984 confrontation, that is, as much as a year *before* May 13, and that various officials, including Sambor, had been involved in repeated consultations with explosives experts. The entire "Kirk plan" for August 8 was well known to Sambor and others, and many of its major elements had already come into play on May 13. Now it was time for another – the bomb.[13]

The MOVE members inside 6221 Osage were not warned about the bomb; they were not to be given any last chance to surrender. But residents on the north side of Pine Street, who for reasons that are not totally clear had not been forced on May 12 to evacuate, were now warned that a bomb was about to be dropped and were ordered to stay indoors. The police in 6218 Osage, the house directly across from 6221 and which had been rechristened "Post One," were also withdrawn moments before the bomb was dropped, as were all other cops from Osage and the south side of Pine.

These withdrawals from the immediate area around the MOVE house would suggest that the bomb they were about to drop was a powerful and dangerous one. But the authorities denied they had anything more in mind than using a relatively mild and definitely safe "entry device" to achieve the limited goal of dislodging the front bunker and poking a hole in the roof through which more tear gas could be thrown. Mayor Goode said he had been told a hole would be blown in MOVE's roof, but denied knowing what would be used to do this, or that the method of delivery was going to be by helicopter.[14] But both Brooks and Sambor say that Goode absolutely did know. Brooks testified he had called the mayor at about 5 p.m., with Sambor standing next to him, and after having been apprised that they wanted to use a helicopter to drop an "explosive entry device" on the MOVE roof, the mayor had paused for about thirty seconds and then given them the go ahead.[15]

Sambor testified that he had asked Lt. Powell of the Bomb Disposal Unit if he could build this "safe entry device." Powell replied that he could, said Sambor, and then told the police commissioner that the bomb would contain Tovex (TR-2), a blasting agent developed by Du Pont Corporation and used in underground mining operations. As further evidence that dropping a bomb was not a last minute decision, Tovex was among the explosives tested for use on the MOVE house in the days leading up to the August 8, 1984 confrontation. But the bomb dropped on May 13 contained more than Tovex. It also consisted of more than three pounds of C-4.

C-4 is a very powerful and closely restricted military plastic explosive. A U.S. Army field manual describes C-4 as being "ideally suited for cutting steel, timber and breaching concrete." U.S. troops used C-4 in the infamous Claymore mines during the war in Vietnam. Compared to an equal amount of Tovex, C-4 is roughly 80 percent more powerful, and even has more explosive power than an equivalent amount of dynamite.[16] A California physicist states that the purpose of C-4 "is to break things apart, blow things to pieces... It's designed for destruction."[17]

As early as May 14 there were reports in the Philadelphia media that the bomb contained C-4. But Sambor maintained it had nothing in it but Tovex. Lt. Powell also professed ignorance of the C-4 and discounted its possible use, claiming that his Bomb Disposal Unit didn't possess any.[18]

But according to William Stephenson, a detective of the Philadelphia Police Department who kept a log of the events of May 13, at 3:40 that morning, before the assault had been launched, Lt. Powell and Sgt. Connor were explaining the attack plan to the staff who were present, which included Police Commissioner Sambor. According to Stephenson's log, Powell and Connor said their teams would use shape charges containing C-4 on the walls of the MOVE house.[19]

Apparently, then, C-4 was so much a part of the assault plan that it was even being used by the demolition teams in the morning. But Sambor claimed he had no idea who Stephenson was and couldn't recall Powell or Connor talking about C-4. But press accounts continued to indicate the use of C-4 in the bomb and various officials and cops soon started pointing fingers at one another, each trying to distance himself from the bombing and its results.

Then, one month after the bombing, tests were conducted using only Tovex on plywood piling positioned a short distance from a group of metal cans, one of which contained gasoline.[20] In a memorandum, Sambor had to report: "Various levels of gasoline were used; the Tovex was moved closer to the cans; shrapnel and fragmentation objects were employed; placements were made to cause the violent concussion of the gas cans. In *none* of these tests were we able to cause an incipient gasoline fire using Tovex in the quantity reportedly used on May 13, 1985."[21]

This led Sambor, in an obvious attempt to save his own neck, to claim, "I will not be satisfied that the composition of the device is that which has been reported...until further tests are conducted..."[22] Yet another result of the testing was the revelation that the amount of Tovex used on May 13 was *twice* as heavy as Lt. Powell had reported, weighing over four pounds instead of two.[23] But much more damaging was the fact that there clearly was something else in the bomb besides Tovex.

By August of 1985 it had become completely impossible for the city to deny the existence of C-4 in the bomb, so officials switched gears and sought another way out. By this time, Leo Brooks had resigned as the city's managing director. Testing the limits of everyone's credulity, Brooks said his reasons for leaving were personal and had nothing to do with the MOVE confrontation. This, even though it was just in 1984 that he had given up a thirty-year career in the army and his rank of major general to become the city's second highest official. But the new managing director, James White, took up exactly where Brooks had left off. Announcing that C-4 had been used in the bomb after all, he then maintained that this had been the work of an individual officer, William Klein of the Bomb Disposal Unit. Klein had been designated by Lt. Powell on the afternoon of May 13 to build the bomb and, according to Managing Director White, it was Klein who put the C-4 in the bomb without anyone else's knowledge.[24]

Klein "confessed" to this, even though the initial media reports on May 14 had cited police department sources as confirming the use of C-4, therefore indicating that Klein definitely was not the only person to know of it. Similarly, Detective Stephenson's log chronicling the events of May 13 recorded that, "17.28 State Police Helo [helicopter] & Frank Powell on board gets into position. On board is a satchel containing 2½ lbs. of plastic explosive C-4 which is dropped on the roof of MOVE."[25]

Nevertheless, the official picture presented is of Klein discussing the bombing mission with Powell, Sambor, and Brooks on the afternoon of May 13 and then going off on his own to add C-4 to the Tovex – and in this account, only adding 1¼ pounds. Klein claimed he didn't tell his BDU chief what he was up to because he believed Powell was wrong in his assessment that Tovex would be powerful enough to dislodge the bunker and blow a hole in the roof. Klein also said there just wasn't enough time to tell Powell of his intentions.

But no sooner had Managing Director White told this tale than it began to unravel, as some of the principal players once again began to finger each other. Klein's attorneys as well as the police union for whom they worked, the Fraternal Order of Police, were incensed that as things were developing, Klein was going to face further scrutiny and even possible prosecution for his "confession." The attorneys and police union wanted a deal that Klein would not have to testify at the commission's public hearings, would not be prosecuted, and that top officials would stop trying to place the blame for "everything that went wrong" on May 13 on lower echelon cops like Klein. Some of their demands were met, but subordinate officers continued to be offered up as scapegoats.

Angry attorneys for Klein therefore revealed that Sambor and Brooks knew on May 13 and probably for months before about the planned use of C-4.[26] Attorney Robert Mozenter stated, "I am telling you there were discussions about C-4 before the bomb by people other than Klein and Powell in the presence of Brooks and Sambor. Klein didn't take it upon himself without checking with his superiors..."[27] Mozenter also corroborated the testing of various explosives in preparation for the assault on MOVE since August 1984, and that use of plastic explosives such as C-4 was definitely discussed during that period.[28]

The futile attempt by Philadelphia's top officials to put a big distance between themselves and any knowledge of the C-4 is due not only to the fact that the presence and use of this powerful military explosive serves to expose their intention of doing much more than dislodging a bunker and poking a hole in the roof. Because once the inevitable next question is asked – where did the C-4 come from? – the intentions of some other very interesting people are exposed as well.

C-4 is a highly restricted military explosive and its transfer to civilian agencies is illegal. C-4 also cannot be purchased commercially anywhere in the U.S. Powell's initial claim that his Bomb

Disposal Unit had no C-4 was altered in Klein's subsequent "confession" to the existence of a block of C-4 which he used to make the bomb. According to Klein, it "was the only block I knew we had. And it was old and ratty. We use it for K-9 dog bomb training so that they know what it smells like. I don't know where we got it; it's been there for a while."[29]

Lt. Powell and his superiors apparently expect the public to believe that the head of the Bomb Disposal Unit wasn't aware that his officers used C-4 to train police dogs. No matter. The truth is that his unit and the entire Philadelphia Police Department did have C-4 – and a lot more than Klein's "old and ratty" block. All these denials of having a large stock of this explosive are easily understood once the actual supplier is revealed: the FBI.

The FBI and other federal agencies had been paying attention to MOVE since it came into existence in the early '70s. Shortly after he became mayor and during the same period that he was being briefed by subordinates about MOVE, Wilson Goode met with the FBI, the Secret Service, the U.S. Attorney's Office, and the U.S. District Attorney's office to elicit their opinions on how to deal with MOVE.[30]

More, the FBI participated with the Philadelphia Police Department in the actual planning of the assault in the days leading up to May 13. According to police records and Sambor's testimony before the commission, three FBI agents attended a strategy session on the morning of May 9 in Sambor's conference room, and again on May 11. Sambor testified that he had no idea how the FBI came to be there, but another top cop later testified they were there because Sambor had invited them.[31]

Also at the May 9 meeting were Fire Commissioner Richmond, the deputy police and fire commissioners, the captain and inspector of the stakeout unit, detectives Benner and Boyd from the Major Investigations Division, Capt. Shanahan of Civil Affairs, Lt. Powell, and others – in essence, the city's "brain trust" responsible for developing the tactical plan for May 13.[32] At this meeting, according to Sambor, "the entire plan in general had been discussed and walked all the way through."[33]

The FBI's approval of the plan was sought and received. The FBI agents present certainly had the qualifications to pass judgment on the plan's soundness. Two were expert SWAT tacticians, the other an explosives expert. Sambor testified that the agents approved "The gas, the water, the smoke, the lateral entries through the walls, tactical positioning of the officers, the outer perimeter, the inner perimeter, the evacuation, the coordination with other departments..."[34]

Sgt. Connor also testified that it was federal authorities who assisted the police department in obtaining the antitank gun and other high-powered military weapons that were used in the assault. On the afternoon of May 9, as a strategy session in Sambor's conference room was going on, Sgt. Connor arranged for these weapons to be picked up. Authorization for this came from the Federal Bureau of Alcohol, Tobacco and Firearms (ATF), which is under the jurisdiction of the U.S. Treasury Department. The authorization, said Connor, was verbal, hence conveniently there is no written record of it. Said Connor of the authorization, "It was verbal approval from *Washington* through the Philadelphia office [of the ATF]."[35] This was a revelation almost completely omitted in news coverage of the hearings.

There is also reason to believe that federal agents were at the scene of the massacre itself. The chief inspector of the Philadelphia Police Department told the commission he seemed to recall that federal agents were at the command center in Walnut Plaza.[36] Sambor, once again exhibiting the plague of amnesia that swept through the ranks of Philadelphia's top officials whenever they were asked a sensitive question, could only tell the commission, "I'm trying to recall whether or not there were some of them at the scene as observers and I don't recall whether they were or not."[37]

Finally, it was the FBI which in January 1985 delivered close to thirty-eight pounds of C-4 to the police department and its bomb squad.[38] In sum, the footprints of the FBI and other federal agencies are all over the May 13 assault and massacre of MOVE. Yet not one federal agent was called by the commission to testify at its public hearings, and almost nothing is known about the commission's private interviews with any of these agents.

The commission's actual relationship with the FBI is revealed by the hiring of Neil P. Shanahan as its chief investigator. Shanahan was himself an FBI agent for twenty-one years, and at the time of his retirement in 1983 was supervisory senior resident agent of the FBI's suburban Philadelphia office in Landsdale, Pennsylvania. Shanahan was considered an expert on "domestic terrorism." Another commission investigator, Clyde E. Berry, was a former special agent with the Federal Bureau of Alcohol, Tobacco and Firearms and another antiterrorist expert. Before joining the ATF, Berry was a member of the Philadelphia Police Department. And there is the commission's explosives expert, James R. Phelan, who until 1983 was one of the FBI's principal bombing and counterterrorist specialists.[39] One of Phelan's pupils was none other than the person given the "honor" of dropping the bomb on MOVE, Lt. Frank Powell.[40] Further, one of the commission members, Neil J. Welch, was special agent in charge of the FBI's Philadelphia office from 1975 to 1978, and was once a candidate under the Carter administration to head the FBI.[41]

The commissioning of such people to investigate the events of May 13, including the role of federal agents, is a clear case of hiring a team of foxes to guard the chicken coop. But as blatantly transparent as this was, it was born of even greater necessity: the commission had the critical if burdensome responsibility of trying to cover over the federal agencies' tracks because these led inexorably to higher and higher levels and established that the decision to silence a group of Black rebels did not rest ultimately with a group of Philadelphia cops and politicians.

The kinds of contortions the commission had to put itself through in its effort to cover these tracks is graphically illustrated by its ready acceptance of the FBI's fantastic claim – rather shamelessly stolen, it would seem, from the scriptwriter of Officer Klein's story that he put the C-4 in the bomb on his own – that one of *its* agents had forked over the C-4 to the Bomb Disposal Unit on *his* own, that is, without the FBI's knowledge or approval.[42] This agent failed to tell his superiors of what he did, the commission reports, because he feared losing his job.

Since the FBI didn't know about this agent's treachery, the commission continues, it is to be excused for having given the commission "inaccurate and untruthful accounts of that agency's involvement in events related to May 13, 1985."[43] This refers to the FBI's earlier insistence that it had no involvement in those events. Of course, the commission fails to explain why the FBI's claim of having no knowledge of the C-4 should be taken at face value, especially in light of the many other ways in which the agency was involved in the planning of the MOVE massacre.

The FBI agent also told the commission in private that he "never had to keep any kind of records of anything" regarding the C-4. And the Philadelphia bomb squad also failed to keep any record of "delivery, inventory or use of the C-4, or any other explosives under their control." The commission is then forced to conclude, not at all unhappily, that, "Because of the absence of record keeping by the FBI and the Philadelphia Police Department, all the facts of C-4's use on May 13th may never be known."[44]

Unfortunately for the commission and those it is trying to protect, too much is already known about the use of C-4 on May 13, including its devastating effects. As previously noted, on impact the bomb threw off a heat wave of 7200 degrees F., melting tar roof materials into flammable liquid and turning wooden debris into flying kindling. Moments afterward, a fire started on the MOVE roof, eventually consuming the entire house and sixty-one others.

In the fire's immediate aftermath, the city authorities scrambled wildly to dissociate themselves from it and to blame it on MOVE. Mayor Goode even refused to call the bomb a bomb, preferring less lethal-sounding terminology such as "concussion device." Said Goode: "We've talked a great deal about dropping a bomb as if a decision was made to – quote – bomb a house. That is not the case. The decision that was made was to use a device that would...extricate...[the bunker] from that house....That worked...but what happened was, a fire took place after that... and also there was something in that house that caused the fire to just go up very quickly."[45]

Police Commissioner Sambor also bristled at the notion that the bomb was a bomb, and insisted along with Goode that the "entry device" and the fire had no relationship to one another, as he elaborated on the mayor's theme that "something else" caused the fire. The device was not incendiary, claimed Sambor. It was the MOVE people in the house, he said, who deliberately poured flammable liquids on their house and adjoining ones as well, thus causing the fire and its spread. "There would not have been any fire if it had not been assisted by some sort of inflammatory material," he declared, adding, "...from what we have been able to determine, inflammable liquids had been poured there by MOVE residents."[46]

But neither the police nor anyone else has produced one shred of evidence to support this accusation. On the other hand, there is plenty of evidence indicating that it was the bomb itself which started the conflagration. One demolitions expert told the *Philadelphia Inquirer* that C-4 "will start things burning.... There's a tremendous fireball that comes off it."[47] Charles King, a fire cause-and-effect expert hired by the commission, testified that the fire was caused by the bomb.

According to King, the flying, hot kindling created by the bomb made contact with gasoline cans on top of MOVE's roof. MOVE had two gasoline-powered generators in the house, one to run the sound system and the other, as part of their preparation for the confrontation MOVE thought was coming, was to be used to pump water out of the basement. King believes the flying kindling penetrated these cans, located about ten feet from where the bomb detonated, and ignited gas vapors.[48]

King also indicated that the heat generated by the bomb was so intense, particularly because of the C-4 in it, that a fire could well have started even without the presence of the gasoline cans. He testified that "Any time you use any explosive...there's always the possibility of a fire. When you put a military explosive of C-4, which is extremely hot and produces more fragmentation, that's enhanced."[49]

Even the commission was forced to conclude from King's testimony that the bomb caused the fire. It also agreed with the finding of its explosives expert, James Phelan, that the bomb contained much more C-4 than was originally claimed by Officer Klein, and that the bomb's ability to fragment wood, brick, and metal was therefore greatly enhanced.[50]

The existence of these gasoline cans on MOVE's roof was well known to the authorities. An Associated Press news photograph taken on May 2 depicted a MOVE member hoisting a gas can up to the roof. Also, police aerial surveillance photos taken on May 12, just one day before the assault, showed the gas cans on the roof,[51] and news photos taken on May 13, before the fire, also depicted at least three gasoline or kerosene cans on the roof.[52] A student helicopter pilot, Bruce Johnson, flew over the house on the morning of May 13 with a stakeout unit officer, Richard Mealey. Mealey said he didn't remember seeing any gas cans, but Johnson certainly did: "The cans...were pretty visible. They were almost obvious," so obvious that Johnson didn't even feel it was necessary to point them out to Mealey.[53]

But none of this prevented Brooks or Sambor, on the last day of the commission hearings, from denying they ever had any knowledge of the gasoline cans. Some of the very same people who right after May 13 were accusing MOVE of starting the fire by soaking the whole neighborhood with gasoline now turned around and claimed they were not even aware of the gasoline used by MOVE for their generators—an incredible political somersault obviously arising out of their need to argue, after they couldn't pin the blame for the fire on MOVE, that "lack of information" led them to underestimate what effect the bomb would have.

Mayor Goode did admit to the commission that on May 13 he believed there was at least a possibility of gas cans on the roof. But this is hardly to his credit, since it amounts to a confession that even though he knew of the great dangers of dropping a bomb, he went ahead and told his subordinates to do it anyway.[54]

Similarly, both Goode and all the other major planners of the assault were well aware that the MOVE house was filled with combustibles. For example, Sambor and Brooks conducted an inspection of the house in the early afternoon of May 13. Because the morning explosions and heavy weapons firepower had already blown out and laid bare parts of the house interior, Sambor and Brooks as they stood across the street in Post One could see parts of tree trunks and other wood materials MOVE had used as part of their fortifications. And of course police surveillance in the weeks and months prior to the bombing had also helped to establish what was in the house.

In short, despite all their vociferous and pious claims that their aim was to preserve life and not to destroy it, the authorities dropped on a house full of people, including five children, a powerful bomb which was capable of starting a raging inferno.

However, when the fire began it was not inevitable that it would grow into a monster capable of devouring the MOVE house and a whole neighborhood. It could have been put out shortly after it started. But it wasn't. From the time the bomb detonated at 5:27 p.m. until approximately 6:10, the fire was considered small by firefighting standards and had not spread beyond or below MOVE's roof. At any time during those forty to forty-five minutes the two Squrt guns located on Pine Street, each with the capability of pumping one thousand gallons per minute, could have extinguished the blaze. Nor could it be argued that using the Squrts posed any danger to firefighters because they would be fired upon by MOVE, since these snorkel guns were a full block away and strung up on cherry pickers that could be operated remotely. There had been no perceived danger to firefighters all during the morning hours when the Squrts pounded the MOVE house with hundreds of thousands of gallons of water. Further, no one thought there was any problem with turning on these Squrts just five minutes before the bomb was dropped to divert MOVE's attention and provide the state police helicopter with protection.

Why, then, wasn't the fire put out when it was safe and still relatively easy to do? The reason, according to Sambor, was that the fire had to be kept burning long enough to destroy the front bunker. "I wanted to get the bunker. I wanted to be able to somehow have tactical superiority without sacrificing any lives if it were at all possible."[55] And according to Fire Commissioner Richmond, Sambor recommended letting the fire burn and Richmond concurred.[56] Mayor Goode claims he first became aware of the fire about twenty minutes after the bomb detonated, while watching the scene on his television. He thought he also saw water being poured on the fire, but when he realized it was just "snow" on his TV screen he became alarmed and immediately called Managing Director Brooks and told him to have the fire put out.[57]

Brooks claims he had already called Sambor via radio a few minutes before he got Goode's call and had told the police commissioner to have the fire extinguished. Brooks testified he said to Sambor: "we have – you have accomplished your mission. . . . You have punched a hole in the roof. You have destroyed the face of the bunker. Why don't we put the fire out?" Then, according to Brooks, Sambor left the radio to go put the fire out.[58]

Sambor does not deny receiving a phone call from Brooks, and claims that he passed along the order to Fire Commissioner Richmond. But Richmond categorically denies that he ever received an order from Brooks, Sambor, or anyone else to put out the fire.[59]

Goode says he acted decisively once he realized he was watching "snow" rather than water; Brooks argues that he didn't even wait to hear anything from Goode and acted resolutely on his own; Sambor blames Richmond; Richmond in so many words calls Sambor a liar. Each tries yet again to absolve himself while implicating his associates, as no one of course wants to bear the responsibility for letting an entire Black neighborhood go up in flames. But the truth is that none of these officials really did anything decisively to stop the fire. To the contrary, there continued to be decisions made to let it burn.

For instance, by 6:15 p.m., about forty-five minutes after the bomb had detonated, the fire began to travel below the roofline of MOVE's house. There were more than 150 firefighters on the scene, manning thirty-seven pieces of equipment.[60] But as the blaze began to move downward, the first command the firefighters received was to train their hoses not on the burning MOVE house but on the nonburning one next door. The decision, then, was *to limit* the fire to the MOVE house rather than try to put it out altogether,[61] in the obvious hope that the flames could accomplish what the other components of the assault had so far failed to – the elimination of everyone in the house.

There then followed a bizarre series of events. No sooner had the firefighters trained their hoses on the house next to MOVE's, 6219, than the police ordered them to stop. Then at 6:30 p.m., with both the MOVE house and 6219 now in flames, the hoses were turned on again, but only for short intervals and then once again turned off.

At the same time, police who had returned to Post One after leaving it briefly because of the bombing, sat with their weapons trained on the MOVE house – and laughed. A police videotape filmed at 6:30 p.m. from a second floor window of Post One shows the tip of a stakeout cop's weapon fixed on the flaming MOVE house. In the background one cop is heard to say, "That's the last time they'll call the [Police] Commissioner a mother-fucker." This remark was followed by robust laughter of approval from other cops.[62]

As the police laughed and the firefighters did little or nothing, the fire spread through the MOVE house and then to adjoining ones. At 6:54 p.m. the first fire alarm was sounded, but the fire-fighting efforts continued to be too little, too late. And once again there was an effort to blame this failure on the victims themselves. Officials in the days immediately after May 13 would claim that the firefighters were hindered in their efforts to quell the blaze at this point because MOVE members were firing on them.[63] But there is absolutely no evidence for this accusation either, and the fire commissioner testified at the hearings that he did not know of a single instance where a firefighter was the target of gunfire from MOVE.[64]

It does appear, however, that the police attempted to make firefighters think they had better stay clear or risk getting caught in a gunfight. For instance, at approximately 6:40 p.m., Deputy Fire Commissioner Frank Scipione entered Post One to get his first look at the fire from in front of the MOVE house. According to Scipione, as he began to observe the blaze a police officer next to him pushed his head down while another shouted that MOVE members were on the roof. Scipione was then ordered to leave Post One for his own safety, leading him to believe, he said, that firefighters would be exposed to gunfire if they attempted to stretch hose lines directly onto Osage Avenue, which at that point was the only effective way to attack the spreading blaze. "I made the decision that that would not be a likely location for us to try and attack the fire. . . because there would've been a gunfight between people who they said were on the roof and themselves and there would be no way that firefighters could operate in that position," reported Scipione.[65]

It is difficult to know whether Scipione really believed this, but in any case it was impossible at that point for any MOVE members to still be on the roof – or to be there and still be alive. The roof had become a flaming oven. Just as Scipione entered Post One, the smaller bunker on the rear of the roof fell into the house, and the larger one in the front would do so just a few minutes later. From where on the roof, then, could MOVE members be firing? The police themselves knew there was no one on the roof at that point, and that surviving MOVE members had been forced to retreat to the rear of the house or into the basement. Sambor himself admitted this before the commission,[66] and Detective William Stephenson's log also reads for that time: ". . .MOVE believed to be hiding in rear of 6221."[67]

Finally, once the front bunker fell in a few minutes before 7 p.m., what officials had been insisting all along was the key tactical objective had now been achieved. Yet there was still no serious effort to stop the fire. Managing Director Brooks explained why. There was great concern, he said, that MOVE members might escape under the cover of the smoke and steam created when the fire hoses were turned on. The police in fact were complaining that the conditions created by the water were hampering their efforts to keep MOVE clearly in their sights. Said Fire Commissioner Richmond: "I think the fear was that under this smoke and steam MOVE members would exit, to either exit shooting, one, or two, relocate and shoot from those new positions."[68]

The bottom line, then, is that MOVE was to be kept trapped inside an inferno. And so intent were the authorities on completing nothing less than a search-and-destroy mission that they ended up letting the houses on both sides of Osage Avenue, half of Pine Street and part of Sixty-second Street go up in flames to deprive MOVE of even one inch of safe quarters.

But even with all of this, the mission was not yet quite completed. As the fire raged out of control, the people in 6221 Osage

Avenue had only one way out: from the basement into the adjoining garage in the rear of the house, then through the tiny back yard and into the alley. They tried desperately, repeatedly, to get out. But they didn't make it – and it was more than the fire that stopped them.

4 | The Alley

The six dead adults are:

James Conrad Hampton (Conrad or "Rad" Africa)	Age 36
Theresa Brooks (Theresa Africa)	Age 26
Raymond Foster (Raymond Africa)	Age 50
Rhonda Harris (Rhonda Africa)	Age 30
Frank James (Frank James Africa)	Age 26
Vincent Leapheart	Age 54

The five dead children are:

Tomaso Africa	Age 9
Katricia Dotson ("Tree")	Age 13-15
Zenetta Dotson	Age 12-14
Delicia Africa	Age 11-12
Phil Africa	Age 11-12

The two survivors are: Ramona Johnson Africa and Birdie Africa, who were ages 30 and 13 at the time of the attack.[1]

How did these eleven people die? According to Birdie Africa, the women and children had been in the basement during the morning siege. They managed to survive the explosions and gunfire, and by huddling under blankets soaked in water to withstand the effects of the tear gas. But by 7 p.m. the blankets were no longer useful as the basement became blistering hot and smoke choked off the shrinking supply of oxygen. By that point the surviving men had moved through the blaze above and joined the others in the basement.

Moments later police radios crackled with reports that MOVE members were coming out of the back of the house through the garage. More police officers rushed into the back alley to augment stakeout sharpshooters already positioned on the rooftops and inside houses on the south side of Pine Street directly across the alley from the MOVE house.

Mayor Goode told reporters at a quickly called press conference that three adult MOVE members had fled into the alley and were firing at police. Shortly after midnight Goode announced that the MOVE members who had been spotted in the alley were "still on the loose."[2] These "roving gunmen" were then used as the explanation for why firefighters had to be withdrawn from the area for some length of time and could not fight the spreading blaze.

Sambor, Brooks, and Richmond also said that emerging MOVE members were firing at police and that their whereabouts were undetermined. Sambor once again introduced the phantom tunnels, suggesting that the three perhaps had used them to make good their escape.[3]

Mayor Goode also claimed that the police behind the MOVE house did not return fire. But some of those police also talked quite extensively to the press later in the evening and told a much different story. For example, the *Philadelphia Daily News* reported on May 14 that cops told of three MOVE people being shot to death in a gunfight that broke out as MOVE exited the rear of the house. On May 17 the newspaper elaborated further on the initial account:

> Late Monday night, police sources told the *Daily News* that three men came out of the MOVE house about 7:20 p.m. and began firing at stakeout officers, who returned the shots, killing the MOVErs. Officers left the bodies of the men in the alley behind the MOVE house, according to police sources. . . .
> Stakeout officers in the Pine Street houses saw a gunman come out of the MOVE house and open fire. "Everyone started shooting. It became a 100 percent bona fide shootout," one police source said. Three other men were behind the first gunman in the doorway of the MOVE house.

Stakeout police saw the first gunman "blown back" into the house by a barrage of bullets and assumed that they also hit the other three MOVE men, sources said.[4]

Mayor Goode rushed to dismiss these reports as "inaccurate," and after all eleven bodies were carted off to the city morgue the city's health commissioner declared, "We have x-rayed each of the bodies, and at this time, we see no evidence of bullet fragments."[5]

But in the following days of conflicting explanations and hostile outbursts at press conferences, it became clear that police had fired at exiting MOVE members. It also seems likely that the original police reports of having left three dead bodies in the alley are also accurate and later were covered up with denials. These denials may have resulted from the fact that two of the bodies were probably children and not adult "gunmen." According to both Ramona and Birdie Africa, MOVE children were definitely among the first attempting to get out. Both Ramona and Birdie Africa also said that none of the exiting adults were armed.

As more news accounts appeared about police shooting and killing several MOVE members in the alley, officials scrambled to come up with their own explanations. At a press conference on May 16, Mayor Goode categorically denied that police fired at emerging MOVE members. At that same press conference, Police Commissioner Sambor gave three different accounts. Sambor first said, in direct contradiction of Goode, that police had returned fire. He then qualified this by stating he thought police had fired but that this was unconfirmed. Finally, Sambor completely reversed field and said that police had *not* fired their weapons at all in the back alley.[6]

At the same time, police officers who just several days earlier had been boasting to the press of MOVE members being "blown back" into the house, also did an abrupt about-face and started to recount how they tried to bring MOVE people to safety through flames, smoke, and bullets. At the commission hearings several months later, police officers uniformly maintained that their only concern in the alley was with saving MOVE lives, that they had tried to coax the MOVE people out of the burning house even at the risk of their own lives, and all they received in return was a hail of hostile gunfire.[7]

One stakeout officer, William Trudel, who had been positioned in a Pine Street house across the alley from the MOVE house, testified that Ramona Africa, one male adult, and three of the children came out; that he and another officer in the house held a "conversation" with her, telling her to keep coming, that they wouldn't shoot. Trudel also claimed that he and the other officer stayed at their post even though it was going up in flames, shouting to the MOVE people to come their way to safety. Despite their efforts, Trudel said, they were fired upon by the male adult but didn't fire back.[8]

Three other officers positioned at the west end of the alley, toward Cobbs Creek Parkway, told a similar story. They said they saw several MOVE members emerge, first Ramona Africa, then Birdie Africa, and then an adult male. According to police officer Michael Tursi, the MOVE man, with one hand on Birdie Africa and another on a rifle, fired directly at them but missed. They also did not fire back. They then lost sight of him and kept their eyes on the other two.

When they saw Birdie Africa fall into a large pool of water caused by the flooding, one of the officers turned to another and said, "Now we have no choice. He either drowns or we save him." The other responded, "Go ahead, I got you covered."[9] And with that the police claim they rescued Birdie Africa while they kept a close watch on Ramona Africa until she was taken into custody.

But overwhelming evidence points to a much different and murderous chain of events: police gunfire kept MOVE members trapped inside the basement and garage when they made an initial effort to leave; when some of the MOVE people finally made a desperate effort to exit because the conditions had become unendurable, some were forced back into the house by police bullets while others were shot to death and their bodies were then probably thrown back into the fire to destroy the evidence; it seems almost certain that children were among those gunned down and thrown back into the fire. This chain of events is established by the accounts of Ramona and Birdie Africa; from information in Detective William Stephenson's log, which is corroborated by a fire department battalion chief; and from information that came out during the commission hearings, including vital ballistic and forensic evidence.

Upon being captured in the alley, Birdie Africa was taken to a hospital and treated for second- and third-degree burns. While there, he was kept under close guard which included K-9 patrol dogs roaming the hospital grounds, perhaps by some coincidence the same ones who had been trained by Lt. Powell's bomb unit to sniff out C-4. Since the night of May 13, Birdie Africa has had no contact with any members or supporters of MOVE. Upon leaving the hospital he was placed under the custody of his born-again Christian father, Andino Ward.

Birdie Africa gave his initial account of what happened in the alley to police and fire investigators on May 15, just two days after the assault, and then gave several more accounts later that month. Although the press knew what Birdie Africa told investigators in his initial interview, coverage was at best minuscule and mostly buried. For example, on May 16 the *Philadelphia Inquirer* devoted five lines at the end of a full-page article to report Birdie Africa's account that as the house began to burn, a MOVE adult was shouting to the police, "The kids are coming out!"[10] It was not until a month later that more of Birdie's account came out in public. On June 30, the *Philadelphia Inquirer* reported that in his discussions with these investigators, Birdie Africa had maintained that in addition to Ramona Africa and himself, Frank James Africa, Conrad Hampton Africa, and probably all five of the other children had tried to get out but were forced by police gunfire back into the rear and garage area of the burning house.[11]

Five months later, on October 31, 1985, in a videotaped session that ran over two hours, the testimony of Birdie Africa before the commission was broadcast on Philadelphia television. By this time his father had renamed him Michael and had cut off his dreadlocks. He clearly was uncomfortable and intimidated as he sat between his father and the commission's chairman, with his father's attorney and a camera crew also bearing down on him. If he had been given the chance to speak more freely, probably even more of the truth would have come out. Still, his testimony before the commission remained markedly consistent with what he had told the other investigators months earlier.[12]

Birdie Africa described desperate efforts to escape the inferno. Conrad Africa and the other adults were yelling that the kids were going to come out of the garage. Conrad Africa wrapped one of the children, Tomaso, around his waist, crawled to the garage door and unbolted it.[13] As they started out into the yard shots rang out. Birdie Africa described how the gunfire sounded: "It was a do-do-do-do-do-do, like that...like bullets were going after each other." He was asked a number of times if Conrad Africa was armed, to which he always replied "no."

Conrad Africa was forced to close the garage door. Inside, the smoke threatened to suffocate everyone trapped in there. When Conrad Africa handed Tomaso to Rhonda Africa, Birdie's mother, the young boy, who had been crying, fell silent. Tomaso Africa was apparently either dead or dying from the smoke and heat. Rhonda Africa slapped him several times on the back but he failed to respond.

They had to get out. The heat alone was causing their skin to peel. The adults began to yell, "The kids are coming out! The kids are coming out!" The children were also crying, "We want to come out! We want to come out!" At this point several people just rushed out into the yard.

Ramona Africa's account of what happened is identical to Birdie's. In a three-hour conversation on May 21, 1985 with a lawyer, Angela Martinez, Ramona Africa explained that as the basement and garage filled up with smoke the MOVE members decided that all of them would surrender and that an adult, Ramona herself, was selected to go first in case the police were still firing.[14] Ramona Africa was to yell, "We're coming out. We're not armed!" She dashed out, believing the others were following.

She darted through the small yard and driveway, at the end of which was a wall about four feet high with a three-foot-high hairpin fence extending up from it. Birdie Africa says that behind her were at least three of the children: Tree, Phil, and himself, and then apparently Conrad Africa, who brought up the rear and made it at least into the yard. When Ramona Africa reached the wall she grabbed Tree and Phil and pulled them up to her. According to Birdie Africa, "She was putting Phil and Tree up in the alley. . . . And then she told me to run. And then she tried to get me and I didn't make it. Then I fell and I kept running again. And I tried to climb up the wall parts, and that is when I fell and then I fainted."[15]

Thus according to the accounts of both Birdie and Ramona Africa, as well as the accounts of police who themselves were in the alley, at least five people came out of the garage. Birdie Africa had one other crucial recollection. The last time he saw Tree and Phil Africa they were running west down the alley toward Cobbs Creek Parkway. What happened to them, and to Conrad Africa? What happened to others who may have tried to leave, and also to those who perhaps never came out?

A dozen police officers told commission investigators that they were trying to bring the MOVE people to safety. Despite the gas, the explosives, the guns, the bomb, and the fire, they were now trying only to save the MOVE members' lives. But despite their efforts and the attempts of the authorities to erase what happened in the alley, the truth has emerged: people attempting to surrender were gunned down in cold blood.

There were apparently some eyewitnesses besides the police. One person who was at a barricaded street corner recalled that as the fire was beginning to spread, "There was this one person that ran out there and said that there were two kids lying in the backyard dead already. It was a white man. If I could see him again I could remember who he was...He was a media man...he ran out like he was in shock...he said a cop told him this. He said a cop said that there were two kids in the backyard dead."[16]

There is also the testimony of Detective William Stephenson, who brought his log with him to the commission hearings. Stephenson told the commission that he had not been encouraged by fellow police officers to testify – a polite way of saying he had been threatened. He indicated that there would be and already had been attacks on his reputation.[17] Among the press people covering the hearings, word was spread that Stephenson was a "flake." This was clearly designed to discredit his testimony, and the *New York Times*, for example, did not report on any of it.

None of this is surprising, since Stephenson's log reveals that stakeout unit Sergeant Donald Griffiths had shot a MOVE member at the rear of the MOVE house.[18] The *Philadelphia Daily News* wrote that the log "quotes a sergeant in the police Stakeout Unit as saying he 'downed' a member of the radical group in an alley behind Osage Avenue.... "[19] The newspaper also reports that sources said that "Griffiths fixed the time of the shooting at about the time 'the girl and the child were coming out' of the MOVE house."[20]

Stephenson's log goes on to explain what Sgt. Griffiths was doing on May 16, as a crane dug through the remains of the MOVE house. The log reads that Griffiths "is in the rear of Osage Ave., 6221, and is pointing to an area that he states, I dropped an adult male from the MOVE property who fired at me when the female and child escaped."[21]

Griffiths and the Fraternal Order of Police have issued vehement denials and have claimed that Griffiths' words were twisted. Griffiths testified before the commission that although he was on the scene on May 16 when excavating was taking place, and although he did point to a spot where he thought the crane should dig, what he actually told the operator was to dig out the spot at the back of the MOVE house where he had seen a MOVE member who had "dropped out of sight."[22]

Stephenson continued to maintain he was sure of what Griffiths said. Stephenson also wasn't the only one to hear Griffiths' remarks. John Skarbek, a battalion chief in the Philadelphia Fire Department, also was at the scene on May 16 and recalled Griffiths directing the crane operator to dig at the spot where Griffiths had said, "I got one back there" or "I shot one back there."[23] It is also important to note that while no bodies were found after Griffiths had told the crane operator where to dig, the press reported that a search of that same spot two days earlier had unearthed body parts—a clenched fist and a forearm.[24]

Griffiths' open boast of having "downed" one of the MOVE members was very much in keeping with the mood and soaring morale of the police in the days immediately after the massacre. Griffiths, for example, was not the only cop on the scene on May 16. Stakeout officers swarmed over the hot wreckage on Osage Avenue, even though it was supposed to be a protected and sealed-off crime area. Many of them could hardly contain their glee, and at least one of them, who said he had been grazed by a MOVE bullet, combed through the debris like a wartime GI, looking for a souvenir.[25] Many talked openly about their disappointment over the outcome of the 1978 Powelton Village confrontation and the "much better" results of May 13. Said one cop, comparing the two incidents, "I kind of figured it was going to be the same kind of siege as it was before. I'm glad they went in there and did something this time, rather than sit back and let it go on and on."[26]

It was in this heady atmosphere of victory and conquest that many cops found it all but impossible not to brag about what really happened in the alley. By the time the commission hearings rolled around these officers obviously had gotten the word to button up, but some of the truth continued to squeeze through the cracks and helped to substantiate the testimony of Birdie Africa, as well as that of Stephenson and Skarbek, and Ramona Africa's account.

There was the testimony, for example, of Officer William Stewart during the public portion of the commission hearings. On the morning of May 13, Stewart had the task of protecting one of the "insertion" teams with his silenced .22-caliber rifle. Stewart explained that if he noticed anything that might hinder the team, "I was to take it out."[27] The commission then asked Stewart if that meant, as an example, shooting out a light bulb if one happened to go on. Stewart replied yes, and then added, "or if they [MOVE] came out"—a clear indication that from the very beginning of the assault any emerging MOVE members were to be shot on sight.[28]

Stewart also told the commission that on the evening of May 13, he was on Pine Street when he heard Sergeant Griffiths yell that MOVE was coming out, and that he then heard "low, muffled shots." This was part of the attempt to establish that the shots came from MOVE and not the cops' automatics. Stewart said he saw Birdie Africa taken into custody on Pine Street and then moments later came Police Commissioner Sambor who told him to come along with him because MOVE was coming out. Stewart then grabbed a submachine gun from a police equipment truck "for Sambor's protection," but claimed that he and Sambor never went into the alley.[29]

But all of this is in stark contradiction with what Stewart told a commission investigator in an interview just one month earlier, statements from which were read at the public hearings themselves. When asked by the investigator if he had heard gunfire on the night of May 13, Stewart replied, "Oh, yes, automatic fire." When asked who was firing these weapons, Stewart responded, "Police officers. All the Stakeout officers were running into the alley. They all had Uzi submachine guns."[30] When next asked by the investigator if he had gone into the alley or driveway at the rear of the MOVE house, Stewart said he had and that with him was Police Commissioner Sambor! The two were proceeding down the driveway toward the MOVE house, he explained, when there was a burst of automatic machine gun fire and lots of police officers all over the alley. According to Stewart, Sambor then retreated for his own safety.[31] Sambor's presence in the alley explains how he could disagree with Goode about whether the police fired at MOVE members. It also explains why he then decided just a few minutes later at the same press conference that the police didn't fire after all.

It isn't clear why Officer Stewart gave the commission investigator this highly damaging information. Perhaps it had to do with the efforts of lower-echelon officers and their union to strike back at top officials for trying to make them the scapegoats—scapegoats, that is, for certain tactics that were being criticized. No cop or any official was being accused of murder. It also isn't clear why Stewart radically changed his testimony just one month later. Perhaps, like Detective Stephenson, he had been "encouraged" to do so by sources unknown.

In any event, his testimony places the police commissioner

himself in the alley at the time that Sambor's officers opened up on MOVE members as they tried to escape their burning house. Stewart's statement also sets the time that he and Sambor were in the alley as being *after* Birdie and Ramona Africa were taken into custody, which strongly suggests that the automatic gunfire could have killed the others, including children, who were still in the alley at that time, as well as forcing those who remained in the basement or garage to endure a fiery death.

There is also important evidence that the bodies of those slain in the alley were thrown back into the burning basement or garage in order to cover up their having been shot. The May 17 *Philadelphia Daily News* had quoted police sources as saying that after three MOVE members had been shot in the alley their bodies were *left there*.[32] Birdie Africa remembered seeing the two children, Tree and Phil, running west down the alley toward Cobbs Creek Parkway. But after the assault, the bodies of all the dead MOVE people, including those of Tree, Phil, and Conrad Africa, were reported by the authorities to have been found *inside* the foundation line of the collapsed MOVE house.[33] It is highly improbable that these three turned and ran back into the flaming house. The only ones in the back alley who had the opportunity and the motive for destroying evidence that MOVE people were shot to death, especially when it turned out that at least two of these were probably children, were the police.

This also helps to explain why no effort was made to extinguish the fire for more than two hours after the MOVE members began their attempts to get out. During this period, one of the fire engines whose Squrt gun was intermittently spraying the back alley was ordered to stop and was removed from its position.[34] According to Fire Commissioner Richmond, firefighters didn't actually start to put out the fire in earnest until 9:30 p.m., and, significantly, no one had to give them the order to do so.[35] By then the firefighters could see that the cops had relaxed and that it would be okay for them to proceed. By then the cops were relaxed because they thought that everyone and all evidence in the basement and garage had been destroyed.

But a significant amount of ballistic and forensic evidence substantiates the conclusion that at least three MOVE members were shot while others were trapped in a flaming hell by police gunfire and burned almost beyond recognition.

The city's health commissioner had reported that no bullet fragments were found in any of the x-rayed body parts. But it was disclosed several months later that there were bullet fragments in the bodies of Vincent Leapheart, Rhonda Africa, and in one of the children, Delicia. These fragments were found by Dr. Ali Z. Hameli, who headed a team of forensic pathologists hired by the commission.[36] Dr. Hameli was among the scientists who traveled to Brazil in 1985 to identify the remains of Nazi slaughterer Josef Mengele.

At the request of Dr. Hameli, the FBI conducted laboratory analysis of the bullet fragments. Though the FBI's report was evasive, it did conclude that the fragments were consistent in their composition with 00 buckshot or bullet cores, and consistent with a sample of 00 buckshot belonging to the Philadelphia Police Department.[37] This type of buckshot is fired from 12-gauge shotguns, which were in the police department's arsenal and were used on May 13. On this point Detective William Stephenson's log contains a telling entry: "Approx (30) Thirty 12 Ga Fired Shells are Recovered from the Rear yard of 6228 Pine St. These belong to police."[38] 6228 Pine Street was the location of one of the main police posts, and its yard is just across the alley and only two houses west of MOVE's.

Double-ought buckshot consists of very small pellets which when fired at close range can blow a person to pieces. It is also possible for these pellets, as well as other types of high-powered ammunition, to have entered and exited the bodies of some of the MOVE members without leaving a trace, especially since the bodies were severely burned and mutilated. Over 90 percent of Tree's body, for instance, was never recovered. The single largest portion found was a segment of her hip and thigh.[39]

Dr. Hameli's testimony before the commission also disclosed other steps that were taken to try to cover up the massacre. For example, on May 14, the first day of digging for the bodies, the fire department had requested the presence of a representative from the Philadelphia Medical Examiner's Office. But this office refused to come to the scene until bodies were actually found, which was not until late in the afternoon. But by then the excavating crane had been lifting up debris which resulted in the further dismembering of bodies and the commingling of remains.

The standard procedure in a case like this is not to yank out bodies with a crane, but to carefully remove debris layer by layer so that the precise location of each body can be accurately recorded. Even with the crane it took the city two full days to pull out all of the bodies and body parts. The longer the bodies remained in these hot ruins, the longer they "cooked." Thus physical evidence was being destroyed.

It is also customary in the search for bodies to place stakes at spots indicating where they are found and what their relationship is to other bodies. But with the bodies of the MOVE members this was not done. Photographs were taken, but the precise locations of the bodies again were not indicated and instead were reconstructed from "memory" two months later.

The City of Philadelphia was not lacking in the expertise or the equipment to do these things as they should have been, nor was it experiencing a momentary lapse of responsibility. There were bodies which at one point were in the alley and at another point were back in the garage and basement. And there were bodies with police bullets or bullet fragments in them. By further mutilating the bodies and obscuring the precise location of where they were retrieved, the authorities were attempting to erase evidence of what caused the deaths.

Once the bodies and body parts were turned over to the Medical Examiner's Office, there were more efforts to cover up the massacre. The bodies were stored at a temperature of 56 degrees F. But Dr. Hameli testified that the ideal temperature for preserving remains is 34 degrees F.[40] By the time Dr. Hameli and his colleagues began to examine the remains in July of 1985, this 22 degree difference had caused the bodies to deteriorate at an accelerated rate and resulted in the hardening of tissue and the growth of mold and fungus on them. While under the supervision of the Medical Examiner's Office, the bodies were literally rotting away.

Toxicology tests conducted by the Medical Examiner's Office to measure levels of carbon monoxide in the bodies were too few and too late to be of any definitive value. Carbon monoxide is a poisonous gas which is released during a fire and adheres to the blood cells and cuts off the flow of oxygen. Determining carbon monoxide levels can therefore help to determine whether or not people have died as a result of fire.

There is also the matter of the x-rays taken by the Medical Examiner's Office, which were said to contain no evidence of bullets in any of the remains. But the office took x-rays only from a flat front and back angle. They did not take lateral x-rays which pinpoint objects more accurately. The Medical Examiner's Office told Dr. Hameli that these x-rays were not taken because of faulty equipment. But using the same equipment, Dr. Hameli was able to take lateral x-rays, in which suspected embedded bullet fragments were clearly discernible.[41]

Dr. Hameli concluded that the cause of death of the children was homicide. He quickly added, however, that he felt this was due to the actions not only of the city authorities, but also the MOVE adults. In a similar manner, the commission concluded that the deaths of the children "appear to be unjustified homicides." But the commission didn't attempt to assess who was responsible for these homicides, leaving it for a grand jury to investigate—and also leaving it open that the MOVE adults themselves will be found responsible.[42] In fact, at one point in the hearings Fire Commissioner Richmond said that when the commission apportions out blame for the deaths of the children it should save a "big block" of it for the MOVE adults. That, a commission member replied, was an "absolute given; there's no question about that."[43]

Dr. Hameli also testified that he was unable to determine the precise cause of death of the adults. The choice was between homicide or *suicide*. Even the buckshot pellets found in the bodies of two of the adults did not constitute conclusive evidence in his view because they were not found inside vital organs. The commission also studiously avoided coming up with a definitive cause of death of the adults. This left open a possible determination in the future that the adults were perhaps not only responsible for the children's deaths, but somehow responsible for their own deaths as well. Indeed, in its findings the commission strongly intimates that such a determination would be quite just. The commission reminds everyone that three of the adults who were killed had outstanding arrest warrants against them, and then adds, "This fact was announced to them by the Police Commissioner in the morning and they had a legal obligation to surrender to the police at that time."[44] If you don't surrender you have no one to blame but yourself for being killed. Or as District Attorney Edward Rendell put it, the MOVE people committed suicide. The district attorney and the commission of course neglected to mention that what happened in the back alley showed why any notion of surrendering was quite out of the question.

The commission added that since the lone surviving adult, Ramona Africa, had also been named in an arrest warrant, she too had the same "legal obligation" as her dead comrades. In fact, while as of the beginning of 1987 not a single city official or police officer had been indicted for anything that happened on May 13,

1985, Ramona Africa was immediately dragged away in hand-cuffs, held on over $4 million bail, and subsequently charged with twenty-one counts, most of them felonies. Among these was the charge of assaulting the police![45]

The testimony of one of the police officers who took Ramona Africa into custody on May 13 speaks volumes for how both she and all MOVE members are perceived by the forces of law and order, and why eleven of them are now dead. He said that when he looked at her, his mind flashed back to his days in Vietnam and he therefore searched the severely burned woman to see if she was wired with explosives.[46]

As for the lone child survivor, in a symbolic insult to MOVE's belief in natural foods and as a way of beginning his re-entry into "normal society," Birdie Africa's nurses decided on a special prescription for him – McDonald's burgers.[47] Birdie Africa, of course, had already gotten a taste of the real America.

5 | Mr. Mayor: Frank Rizzo

1900, New Orleans – Two Black men, Robert Charles and Leonard Price, were harassed by police as they sat on the steps of their home. As the police attempted to beat Charles, he killed two of them and escaped. A white vigilante mob of ten thousand set out to find Charles and lynch the jailed Price.

For five days the vigilantes destroyed Black property, plundering stores and homes. A Black woman was killed in her sleep, several Blacks were beaten unconscious, and a Black schoolhouse was burned to the ground. On the fifth day Charles was found and burned out of his hiding place. But not before he killed eight of the vigilantes – making him a folk hero among Blacks.

1910 – In the early 1900s Jack Johnson became the first Black heavyweight champion. Not only a great boxer, Johnson refused to kowtow to whites and further enraged them with his outrageous lifestyle and his open romances with white women. Former champion Jim Jeffries was called out of retirement and thrown up against Johnson as the "great white hope." But it was hopeless – Johnson beat him severely.

The myth of the natural superiority of whites also took a severe beating, leading in the fight's immediate aftermath to white rioting and vigilantism throughout the U.S. Gangs attacked Blacks, especially those who refused to hide their pride in Johnson's victory. The debunking of the myth of white superiority was seen as so serious that the roughrider himself, Theodore Roosevelt, called for an end to boxing in the U.S.

1917, East St. Louis – As the U.S. entered World War 1 to "make the world safe for democracy," a wave of racial turmoil swept the country. One of the starkest outbreaks occurred in East St. Louis. Mobs of whites enraged by the employment of Blacks at a local factory that was on strike invaded the Black community, set fire to hundreds of homes, and massacred hundreds of Black men, women, and children. One white army officer who witnessed the rampage said that he saw members of the Illinois militia and East St. Louis cops shoot Blacks, and also saw the mob board up the windows and doors of houses before setting them ablaze. Over six thousand Black people were left homeless.

1919, Houston – A Black soldier, recently returned from fighting in Europe, was murdered by a white officer. Upon hearing of this, other Black World War 1 veterans armed themselves and descended upon Houston. In the ensuing confrontation, fourteen whites including one police officer were killed before the vets were disarmed, immediately placed in secret confinement, and months later taken to trial in total secrecy. Thirteen of them were executed and buried in an unmarked grave whose location was also kept secret. Dozens of others were sentenced to death, but public outcry led to the commutation of their sentences.

1921, Tulsa – On May 30, a white woman accused a young Black man, Dick Rowland, of attacking her. The local newspaper roused a white mob with headlines such as, "To Lynch Negro Tonight." Armed Black men went to the jail offering to protect Rowland, but the sheriff refused. Then as whites attempted to disarm a Black veteran a gunfight broke out. When the fighting moved away from the jailhouse the Tulsa police deputized scores of whites, many of whom had been part of the lynch mob.

The Tulsa National Guard was mobilized and in the early morning hours of June 1 the wholesale looting and burning of Black Tulsa began. The National Guard and the Tulsa police carried out mass arrests at gunpoint, as Blacks continued to resist with arms. Then, still in the early morning hours and portending what would happen in Philadelphia nearly sixty-five years later, a plane dropped dynamite on Black neighborhoods.

Over four thousand Black men, women, and children were herded into internment camps. Once released they were forced to carry passes or identification cards marked "Police Protection" on one side and with personal information on the back. Anyone caught on the street without a pass was subject to arrest. As many as three hundred Blacks were killed, more than seven hundred Black families were forced to leave Tulsa, and another one thousand Blacks were forced to live in tents throughout the winter.

1943, Detroit — On a Sunday night, white mobs began attacking Blacks as they emerged from downtown movie theaters. Vigilantes roamed Woodward Avenue, beating Blacks and stopping and burning cars. Blacks were beaten right on the steps of City Hall as police watched.

Blacks counterattacked against whites traveling through the ghetto. Police then cordoned off the Black area and invaded it, moving through the streets in squad cars and randomly shooting "suspected looters." In some cases Black youth were ordered to run and not look back, and then were shot in the back. Twenty-five Blacks were killed in the course of this pogrom, seventeen by the police. Nine of the vigilantes were also killed.

1961, Monroe, N.C. — A white mob attacked freedom riders engaged in nonviolent protest. The Monroe NAACP under the leadership of Robert F. Williams came to the defense of the freedom riders. For several days carloads of whites attacked the Black community of Monroe but were driven back by armed Blacks. State troopers were brought in to surround the Black community and suppress the self-defense squads. Williams eluded the police dragnet but in the days that followed he and four others were indicted on trumped-up charges of kidnapping a white couple. An intense FBI and Royal Canadian Mounted Police manhunt was carried out in the U.S. and Canada, forcing Williams to flee first to Cuba and then to China. The charges were kept hanging over his head for more than a decade.

1969, Chicago — Black Panther Party leaders Fred Hampton and Mark Clark were assassinated in a predawn raid on a Black Panther house. The raid was staged from the front and rear, following a carefully developed plan. Armed with shotguns and automatic weapons, the assassins burst through both doors simultaneously and executed Hampton and Clark as they slept.

1969, Los Angeles — Four days after the Chicago execution, three hundred cops launched a full-scale military assault against Black Panther headquarters in L.A. At the end of a five-hour gun battle, four Panthers were wounded and the leaders were jailed. In a two-year period ending February 1970, twenty-eight Panthers had been killed nationwide and scores were in prison facing trial.

1971, Jackson, Miss. – On the pretext of searching for a fugitive who was wanted in Wisconsin, FBI agents and Mississippi state troopers surrounded and attacked a farmhouse occupied by members of the Provisional Government of the Republic of New Africa (RNA). In the ensuing shootout, one of the attackers was killed and another wounded. All those in the house were held on charges including murder and sedition in the state of Mississippi. Imari Obadele, the president of the RNA, was also arrested on the sedition charge, although he was not even at the scene of the confrontation. Dubbed the RNA-11, these Black nationalists were ultimately convicted of lesser charges and several spent more than a decade in jail.[1]

Clearly, the MOVE massacre was not an aberration, not atypical, not a "mistake." Throughout U.S. history there have been countless attacks and atrocities committed against Black people, and especially against those who, like MOVE, refuse to remain silent or to curry favor with their tormentors. The attacks mentioned here are but a small sampling. Well into this century, these would take the form of pogroms – white reactionaries murdering Blacks and pillaging their communities, either whipped up and covertly supported by the police and other agencies of the armed state or acting openly and in concert with them.

In more recent decades, while continuing to build, incite, and unleash a white reactionary social base behind which it hides its own role, the state has also persecuted and murdered Blacks, especially Black revolutionaries, more openly. Such was the case with the Black Panthers, with Attica in 1971 when the rebellion of revolutionary prisoners was crushed by Governor Nelson Rockefeller, and of course with MOVE in 1985. And while these attacks have taken place with horrifying regularity throughout U.S. history, it is also true that they have intensified in times of national crisis, as in the periods of the two world wars and in the 1960s. In the period 1917-1919 and also in 1943, for example, there were various other pogroms sparked by Black migration from the south into urban areas in conjunction with the world wars. The MOVE massacre takes place in the midst of another such period of national crisis and presages another round of intensified repression.

But there is also something markedly different about what

happened in Philadelphia on that day—the massacre of eleven Blacks was presided over by a Black mayor, and there also was a Black managing director and a large number of Black bureaucrats in the city administration. The fact that Wilson Goode was in charge created a great deal of confusion and uncertainty in the Black community, not only in Philadelphia but nationwide, about how to respond to the events of May 13, and enabled many authorities and large sections of the mass media to claim that what occurred on that day could not be interpreted as racially motivated.

The massacre, of course, was nothing if not racially motivated. People were murdered because they were Black and incurably rebellious, and the sixty-one homes that burned down were certainly not in a white neighborhood. On the other hand, it is true that significant sections of the country's Black upper crust either overtly supported what was done to MOVE or, by their resounding silence in the massacre's aftermath, strongly implied their support. And there were those among the Black middle and working classes who also supported the events of May 13, albeit with some misgivings and criticisms about particular aspects of the operation.

If the assault had been carried out under the administration of a white mayor, the response of these sections clearly would have been different. But a Black man sat in the mayor's chair. Blacks had also been elected mayor in other major cities—Atlanta, Chicago, Detroit, Los Angeles, D.C.—and with that came the hope and promise that as Blacks were elected to high office and gained more political power, things would really start to get better for the vast majority of Black people.

From this perspective, any exposure or criticism of Wilson Goode's role in the massacre was viewed as gravely detrimental to the strategy of "Black empowerment." Goode was a major representative and symbol of this strategy—he even had been seriously considered as a possible vice-presidential candidate on the 1984 Democratic ticket—and therefore had to be defended, either by upholding his role in the massacre or, at the very least, by trying to establish that it was others and not he who should bear the blame for what happened.

But for millions of other Blacks in Philadelphia and across the country, both from the working and middle classes, the MOVE massacre produced shock and outrage, and has led to considerable controversy and debate about the value of electing

Black officials and the entire strategy of "Black empowerment." One young Black said: "I'm kind of ashamed to say this but I'll just let it all hang out – I was one of those people who voted for Jesse Jackson. I really thought that voting for him would do some good.... Well, I was wrong and these massacres in Philly teach us a good lesson about who we can trust and expect to 'save' us. It looks to me that it's going to take what you call a revolution to solve the problem."[2]

By no means everyone has reached that conclusion. But the MOVE massacre – indeed, the whole eventful history of MOVE and the uncompromising, rebellious stand which it continues to adhere to even in the aftermath of this massive assault – has reflected and in many important ways concentrated the debate among Black people in the U.S. about how to move their struggle forward, and particularly around the question of whether this involves working through and ultimately embracing the present social order (although with certain reforms, especially those that improve the economic and social status of Black people), or viewing the present system as fundamentally oppressive and unworthy of salvation – essentially the question of "we want into the system" versus "we want out of it." The history of MOVE is therefore one that needs to be examined, if only briefly, for the important lessons it contains.

The focal point of MOVE's activities when it was founded in 1972 was Powelton Village, an area of West Philadelphia bordering Drexel University and the University of Pennsylvania. Powelton Village was a predominantly middle-class, racially mixed neighborhood, and during the turbulent 1960s was a major center of progressive and radical circles and teemed with political life. The *Philadelphia Inquirer* wrote of Powelton Village that it was "a determinedly anti-authoritarian community, accustomed to suspicion of officialdom. For example, following the burglary of FBI records from the bureau's media office on March 8, 1971, agents swarmed through Powelton Village looking for suspects. For months FBI agents maintained a heavy surveillance in the neighborhood, looking unsuccessfully for those who had stolen the documents."[3] The authorities and police therefore kept a constant and watchful eye on this area. But of even greater concern were the large and volatile ghettos spread throughout the city. The authorities lived in daily fear of a Black uprising, and attempted to whip up and play on the same fear among various sectors of the city's whites.

The man selected to control radicals, hippies, and especially the city's seething ghettos was Frank Rizzo. Nicknamed "Supercop" and "the Cisco Kid" (after a popular TV cowboy of the time), Rizzo came out of a tough, predominantly Italian section of South Philadelphia where racism ran wide and deep. He always wanted to be a cop and during the '60s he rose through the ranks of the Philadelphia Police Department, first to deputy police commissioner, then to police commissioner in 1967, earning respect and admiration along the way from other cops and city officials as a no-nonsense guy who knew how to deal with troublemakers.

Rizzo first came into the local and even national spotlight in 1964. On a hot summer day of that year, a white motorcycle cop tried to break up a quarrel between a Black man and woman sitting in a car in North Philadelphia's ghetto. As traffic backed up and a large crowd gathered, the cop tried to get the woman out of the car but she fought back. Moments later someone from the crowd came to her aid and others started moving in.

Other police had also moved in by this time and the woman was finally forced into a paddy wagon. But before the police could clear the area, bricks and bottles started flying from rooftops and doorways. A long, hot weekend of rebellion in the ghetto had begun. The police commissioner was momentarily out of town and the task of trying to quell the rebellion fell to his deputy commissioner, Rizzo. His plan was a frontal assault down the ghetto's major avenue to sweep everyone off. He would arrest when he could, shoot "if he had to."[4] But Rizzo never got to carry out his plan. It was overruled at the last minute by the returning police commissioner, who feared that some of his men would be cut down by snipers hiding on the roofs and upper floors of buildings lining the avenue. Rizzo got the chance to go into battle just a few hours later, but by then it wasn't a question of trying to control just one street. The rebellion had fanned out over a large area, and no sooner would one part of it be "pacified" than it would break out with even greater intensity somewhere else. By the time it ended late Sunday night, more than two thousand Blacks had participated in the rebellion, which included heavy property damage and many smashed store windows as people helped themselves to large amounts of goods.

Several hundred people were injured, including fifteen cops, but the police commissioner justified his approach by noting that no one had been killed. But Philadelphia's mayor accused him of backing down and argued that a more forceful approach at the start of the rebellion would have prevented its spread. Rizzo couldn't have agreed more and accused the police commissioner of being a "phony faker."[5]

Immediately after the 1964 rebellion, the police department began to develop elaborate contingency plans in case of another outbreak. His star now clearly in the ascendant, Rizzo played a major role in developing these plans. The main problem, according to one of his biographers, was one of logistics:

> how to get men to a given location in the shortest possible time and keep them mobile enough to be able to move to another point on a moment's notice.
>
> Frank Rizzo...borrowed a tactic the French used in World War I, when Paris had been saved from the advancing German armies by French soldiers who were taken by taxis to the staging area for the Battle of the Marne. Rizzo's strategy for "saving" Philadelphia was to rent buses capable of carrying fifty armed policemen at a time. The buses were equipped with police radios so they could be summoned instantly, thus providing strong back-up force for the various district commands. The department later purchased three of its own buses, which Rizzo used extensively.
>
> "You have to have superior force," Rizzo explained. "Even if you don't have it, you can fake it. Like you can station a busload of cops in a conspicuous place. Or you can move the same busload around to various places. This way you create the impression that the cops are everywhere. It's possible to make fifty policemen look like a thousand if you handle it right."[6]

To protect cops from rooftop sniper fire, Rizzo helped to develop a special team of sharpshooters armed with high-powered rifles equipped with telescopic sights. This was the birth of the stakeout squads that were to play such a major role in the MOVE massacre. To improve surveillance and reconnaissance, the police department worked out a deal to lease helicopters from Philadelphia International Airport. Rizzo wanted the city to give the department its own helicopters, but he was turned down. If he had gotten his way, the city wouldn't have had to borrow a state helicopter to bomb MOVE in 1985. Rizzo also wanted but didn't get two bullet-proof personnel carriers, at about $30,000 each. These have wide rubber wheels instead of traditional tracks, and cover themselves with foam if hit by

Molotov cocktails.[7]

But Rizzo got most of what he wanted, including the green light to use his highly trained and well-equipped troops wherever and whenever he deemed it necessary. In August 1966, tensions in the ghetto were again running high and there were rumors of armed Black militants "looking for trouble."[8] Rizzo mobilized eighty heavily armed cops backed by a reserve contingent of one thousand and raided four meeting places of the Student Non-Violent Coordinating Committee (SNCC). One of the raiding parties "found" some dynamite, which SNCC's national director, James Forman, said had been planted by the police. Stokely Carmichael, SNCC's national chairman, came to a church in North Philadelphia and told the large crowd gathered there: "The next time Rizzo tries to march 1500 cops into our community, he's not going to get away with it."[9]

In November 1967, just ten days after he had been promoted to police commissioner, Rizzo unleashed his squads on thirty-five hundred Black high school students who had gathered in center city to demand courses on Black history and culture. Students were chased literally for blocks as they tried to escape, and many were severely beaten.

Rizzo defended the action, but many who witnessed the attack were angered. Said the president of the Board of Education: "There were no threats of disorder when all of a sudden 200 uniformed cops charged and went right through the crowd, whacking kids on the head...even while they were running away...."[10] Said the assistant to the city's school superintendent: "They just beat the shit out of those kids who offered no resistance. It was a real stampede. I had seen police brutality before but never at this level."[11]

In August 1970, Rizzo's men conducted simultaneous raids on three headquarters of the Black Panther Party. Panther members were forced out of the buildings and into the street. If it is true that one picture is worth a thousand words, then a news photograph of these raids stands as an excellent summation of the Rizzo years and what they represented: the photo shows the apprehended Panthers stripped naked and lined up against a wall.

Rizzo's terrorist tactics against Blacks and others were viewed with keen interest in America's major halls of power. In 1968, as many inner-city ghettos were going up in flames, presidential candidate Richard M. Nixon came to Philadelphia to praise its notorious police commissioner – praise similar to what would be heaped on Wilson Goode seventeen years later. Said Nixon: "Rizzo's record had met with the approval of all law enforcement officers across the United States. He has an effective record. I wanted to get his views. As I see it, other cities could use Rizzo's ideas."[12]

Rizzo's "effective record" catapulted him into his first of two terms as mayor of Philadelphia in 1972, the same year in which MOVE was born. Rizzo's mayoral campaign came down to the promise to continue his reign of terror in the Black community as well as against white radicals, hippies, and other "social misfits." According to Richardson Dilworth, a former mayor and the person who as school board president witnessed the attack against Black high school students in 1967: "Every slogan – all the off-the-record talks – they're all based on one thing. Really, he says at all these off-the-record meetings, 'I know how to keep the blacks in their place.'"[13]

But MOVE refused to stay in their place. In fact, their politics of denouncing the system, of challenging and rejecting its authority, stood out all the more in the terrain of the mid-'70s, as the upheavals of the '60s and early '70s began to ebb. The *Philadelphia Inquirer* described MOVE as "railing against anything that smacked of the system. R. Buckminster Fuller, school boards, pet shops, the Rev. Jesse Jackson and Quakers were the targets of MOVE. Its members were disruptive and tumultuous, abrasive and unyielding, hurling obscenity after obscenity at the system they despised."[14] The *New York Times* described MOVE as "preaching to passersby a revolutionary doctrine that would literally give America back to the Indians and abolish all governments 'from here to Peking and Moscow.'"[15]

MOVE and Rizzo were clearly on a collision course. In the early morning hours of March 28, 1976, several MOVE members went outside their Powelton Village house to greet seven other members who had just been released from prison. But also almost immediately on the scene were the police, responding, they said, to a complaint from a neighbor that the celebration was too loud. Soon even more police pulled up.

Janine Africa was among those greeting the returning members. In her hands was an infant, Life Africa, the first child born to MOVE. According to her, the cops "had blackjacks...Next thing I know, they were beating people and had their guns pointed at everybody....The cops were going crazy, swinging . . . they tried to reach over me to get to my husband, with no regard to me or my baby. They pushed me so hard that I fell. Cops stepped all over me and on me."[16]

As a result of this assault, Life Africa was dead, apparently crushed when Janine Africa was thrown to the ground. This was not the only child in those years who MOVE lost to the police. In May 1976, MOVE filed a damage suit charging, among other things, that Alberta Africa suffered a miscarriage shortly after being arrested in April 1975 for protesting medical treatment forced on imprisoned MOVE members that violated their religious beliefs.[17] According to Ramona Africa, "cops held Alberta Africa down . . ., knowing that she was pregnant and kicked her in the vagina til she had a miscarriage."[18] Also, on November 9, 1976, Rhonda Africa gave birth to a boy who died just minutes after. MOVE charged that the baby's death was the direct result of Rhonda Africa having been arrested and beaten by deputy sheriffs on November 5 outside a City Hall courtroom where other MOVE members had just been sentenced to prison.[19] The murder, then, of five MOVE children on May 13, 1985 had its precedents. And not a single cop or anyone else was so much as indicted for these deaths.

Along with these murders and other acts of brutality, the Rizzo administration also pursued various judicial methods in its attempt to bring MOVE to its knees. Between 1974 and 1976, MOVE members experienced some 400 arrests, resulting in bail and fines of more than a half million dollars. MOVE members have asserted that beatings in the courtroom were a frequent phenomenon, with judges doing nothing to stop them. The city zeroed in on MOVE's refusal to allow inspectors inside their Powelton Village headquarters to check for alleged health and fire code violations. In 1976 the city went to the State Supreme Court to affirm its right to force an inspection of MOVE's premises.

A major confrontation was brewing, one that would serve as the political justification and military training grounds for both the confrontation in August 1984 and the assault and massacre in May 1985.

Rumors flew through Powelton Village on May 20, 1977 that the police were on their way to evict MOVE for its refusal to allow inspections. MOVE responded to this threat in dramatic and controversial fashion. Several members stood on a platform that had been erected in front of the house – wearing khaki uniforms, brandishing weapons, and vowing that if attacked they would defend themselves. Nothing like this had happened in Philadelphia before. And not since the Black Panthers stood on the steps of a Sacramento, California government building nearly ten years earlier, shotguns in hand, had such an action taken place anywhere in the country.

It was defiance like this that the authorities could not countenance, particularly because it could serve as an inspiration to others. Two hundred cops were dispatched to the MOVE house. There then ensued something else never before witnessed in the U.S., although things like it are common enough in a country like South Africa. Police surrounded the house and began what would turn out to be a one-year siege of the MOVE headquarters. Police sandbagged apartment windows across from the MOVE house and also established an extensive blockade of several streets around the MOVE house. Within this area were multiple-dwelling homes, Drexel University dormitories and local businesses. People who had to enter the area were frequently stopped, forced to produce identification and to state what their business was.

The Powelton Village community was sharply divided in its stance toward MOVE and the actions of the city. Organizations sprang up in support of MOVE, others against it, and still others who didn't particularly sympathize with MOVE but who were strongly opposed to the police occupation of their neighborhood.

A large percentage of Blacks in the community supported MOVE, as did a significant number of whites. For many of these, MOVE's headquarters became a center of resistance. Challenging the blockade, people would gather there from all over the city, and national Black personalities such as Dick Gregory would visit the house to offer their assistance. Some would run the blockade or take advantage of lulls in the siege to bring MOVE members food and other necessities.

In contrast, there was the Powelton Emergency Rights Committee (PERC), which circulated petitions demanding that the city proceed against MOVE for housing and health code violations. Principally a white group which included people with certain real estate interests in the area, PERC played a key role in trying to push the progressive and radical forces in Powelton Village into the backward political tides that were developing in the late '70s and have reached much higher levels today. Said one of the PERC leaders, speaking of those who were supporting

MOVE: "...there's a phobia toward police operating here. It comes from a rigidity about political beliefs that were held during the '60s but just aren't applicable in the current situation. But people refuse to let go of them."[20]

Ten months into the siege and with MOVE showing not the slightest sign of giving up, the authorities attempted to tighten the screws. The Pennsylvania Supreme Court authorized the city to shut off the water to MOVE's house and to stop deliveries of food to them. MOVE members were to be starved into submission. Nearly five hundred cops assembled in the neighborhood on March 15, 1978. Red snow fences went up at street corners, sealing off any access to MOVE, and the police forced all civilians, including the press, out of the area.

Demonstrations were held, as more people sought to aid MOVE. One group of seventy-five people gathered as close to the MOVE house as they could get and asked the police if food and water could be delivered. When the police refused, about thirty of these supporters defiantly rushed the police lines and attempted to deliver food and water anyway. Nineteen people were arrested and the food was knocked to the ground.[21]

But the attempt to starve MOVE out did not break their resistance. More, the siege had sparked so much anger and mass support that numbers of nervous Black and white civic officials and leaders sought to bring the confrontation to an end through some kind of compromise and before it sparked even further rebellion. One such person was Leon Sullivan, a Black minister and author of the "Sullivan Principles," a set of equal opportunity guidelines for U.S. businesses operating in South Africa which has been roundly condemned by anti-apartheid forces as not going anywhere near the heart of the matter. At Sullivan's behest, civic, banking, and business organizations met with Rizzo administration representatives to work out a compromise. The city also hired someone to help mediate with MOVE and by May 1978 an agreement between the city and MOVE was hammered out.

The terms of that agreement have been disputed ever since. Officials claim that one proviso called for MOVE to vacate permanently their Powelton Village house within ninety days of the agreement. MOVE says it never agreed to this. When the ninety days passed and MOVE members were still there warrants were issued for their arrest. When MOVE ignored the warrants the police attacked.

The assault began in the early morning hours of August 8,

1978. Six hundred cops surrounded the Powelton Village house, including Rizzo's sharpshooters from the stakeout unit. A bulldozer first destroyed the protective fences MOVE had constructed around the house, then a crane was deployed as a battering ram, punching out the wooden slats MOVE had nailed across the windows. Cops actually went into the house at one point but found no one. All of the MOVE members were in the basement.

Firemen then axed down the wooden slats across the basement windows and turned on their deluge guns. Within minutes water in the basement was so high that MOVE adults had to hold babies, young children and some of their dogs over their heads to prevent them from drowning. Shortly after 8 a.m. there was an outbreak of gunfire that lasted for about two minutes. Officer James Ramp fell dead and other cops and firemen were wounded. Word went out immediately that MOVE had killed a cop.

From 8:30 a.m. to 9 a.m. the deluge guns continued to flood the basement and minutes later the MOVE people climbed out through the basement windows, drenched, shivering, and staring down the barrels of the stakeout unit guns. The women and children went first. The last to come out was Delbert Africa, one of the most militant and well-known MOVE members. Naked from the waist up and with arms over his head to indicate he was surrendering and had no weapons, Delbert Africa was grabbed by one stakeout officer who smashed him across the face with his helmet, grabbed him by his dreadlocks and held him down while three other cops beat, kicked, and stomped him.[22] Since the whole thing was being filmed by TV cameras, other cops pulled the four off Delbert Africa but he says the beating resumed once he was out of public view and in their custody. The police commissioner argued that his men had seized Delbert Africa because as he emerged from the basement he had "a cartridge clip in one hand and a knife in the other."[23]

Delbert Africa's alleged weapons are not the only ones the police claimed they saw. Shortly after the MOVE people surrendered, police entered the basement where they "found" a cache of automatic weapons. They then proceeded to demolish the house completely. Every brick and scrap of wood was torn down and the property was turned into a vacant lot — a symbolic act of "annihilation" by the authorities and a rather thorough way of destroying critical evidence, including evidence relating to who killed Ramp and wounded the others. The destruction of important evidence after the May 13 massacre also had its precedents.

The twelve surrendering adults were all charged with murdering Ramp. In a matter of hours and long before the trial ever started, they were tried, convicted, and sentenced by the authorities and the media, which unleashed a venomous campaign against MOVE and in their headlines branded the twelve as unequivocally guilty. At a press conference on the afternoon of August 8, Mayor Rizzo exploded: "The only way we're going to get rid of them is to get the death penalty back in, and I'll pull the switch myself."[24] Rizzo of course was aware that legalization of the death penalty really wasn't necessary. As one police officer declared, perhaps looking ahead to what would happen on Osage Avenue seven years later: "There's no way the police can win in a thing like this. They should have killed all of them."[25]

Ramp's funeral services were given extensive media coverage. Over a thousand mourners were shown filing into a church to view Ramp, who was laid out in his police uniform with a Marine Corps uniform at his feet. Ramp had recently been promoted to master gunnery sergeant in the Marine Reserves. And the bullet taken from Ramp's body, the police insisted, matched up in ballistic tests to one of the weapons taken from the MOVE basement.

But there were many who didn't mourn for Ramp and who doubted that MOVE was responsible for his death. More, the vicious nature of the assault on MOVE and the beating of Delbert Africa, who as film footage and photographs would clearly show had absolutely nothing in his hands when he surrendered, drove many people themselves into much sharper confrontation with the authorities and police. At around 10:30 a.m. on August 8, a pitched street battle broke out two blocks away from MOVE's Powelton Village house, where a large and militant crowd had gathered, shouting at and cursing the police. Mounted officers started knocking people down, and the cops in turn were pelted with rocks and bottles. Several protestors were grabbed, but other clashes flared well into the night.[26]

In the following days the city braced itself for more protest. Security at the Police Administration Building was tightened, as packages and pocketbooks of anyone entering the building were searched. Plainclothes cops normally assigned desk jobs were ordered back into uniform and into the streets "to cope with continuing civil unrest."[27] On August 17 more than two thousand marched through the streets, protesting Rizzo, the police, and the assault on MOVE – one of the largest and most militant demonstrations in Philadelphia in several years.

Philadelphia's elected Black officials and some other Black civic leaders watched these developments with growing uneasiness. From their perspective of "go slow and work through channels," things seemed to be moving dangerously out of control. On the other hand, many of these same individuals had long been in opposition to Rizzo, whom they saw as a major obstacle to the maintenance and expansion of their economic and social gains and their continued striving for equality of opportunity. In 1967, for example, following the attack on the Black students who were demanding changes in the school curriculum, the leadership of the local NAACP called for Rizzo's immediate removal as police commissioner. Other local and well-known civil rights activists such as Cecil B. Moore also called for Rizzo's firing. Just two days after the attack, some of these leaders organized a meeting attended by eight hundred Blacks who voted to boycott public schools and white merchants until Rizzo was fired.[28]

During the Rizzo administration's year-long siege of MOVE, these Black officials attempted to limit and channel the explosive anger of large numbers of Black people into a campaign to get rid of Rizzo and what they considered other constructive rather than destructive avenues. For instance, in April 1978, a group called the Black Community Coalition for Human Rights, which included Cecil B. Moore, who later became a city councilman, and State Representative David P. Richardson, sponsored a symbolic blockade around City Hall to protest the blockade of MOVE.[29]

In that same month, Black city councilman Lucien Blackwell introduced a bill urging Rizzo to end the blockade of MOVE. Blackwell wanted to make it clear, however, that he was "not challenging Rizzo's right to blockade MOVE . . . I'm saying that his wisdom is short-sighted, and I'm asking him to reconsider." Blackwell's resolution was also critical of MOVE and was designed to protect only the MOVE children who, according to him, were "the victims, not the perpetrators of what we have in Powelton Village."[30]

Then, in the aftermath of the August 8 attack, when the anger of many Blacks reached the boiling point and spilled over into the streets, these Black officials rushed to contain it. Some of them attended the August 17 demonstration, by their own admission to gauge the mood of Black people there.[31] They urged people to vote and to boycott the First Pennsylvania Bank because its president was supporting a city charter change which would allow Rizzo to run for a third term. One of them, Milton Street, told the crowd: "There are two things the leaders of this city understand. They understand when you vote, and they'll understand when you make businessmen understand that you have economic power."[32] Street and other Black politicians on the scene were also upset by the speech of a MOVE supporter and tried to divert attention from her. According to the *Philadelphia Inquirer,* "Some of yesterday's speakers indirectly dissociated themselves from MOVE speakers. As Ms. Knighton, for example, read a long selection from the writings of John Africa. . . . Street and other politicians upstaged her, using a bullhorn and a truck as a speaking platform."[33]

There were also other larger, more powerful forces who were anxious to contain and channel the anger and rebellion. The August 8 attack occurred during the administration of President Carter, with its noisy rhetoric about improving civil rights and "finishing the job" begun by President Johnson and his "Great Society" program. Thus, U.S. Attorney General Griffin Bell was quickly dispatched to Philadelphia, where he met with political leaders from the Black Public Officials Association, a group which had been formed in the immediate wake of August 8. Following this meeting, Bell announced the formation of a federal task force to investigate the extent of illegal police violence in Philadelphia.

Some of these events signalled that the heyday of Frank Rizzo was coming to an end. Praised for years by the powerful – even practically canonized for preventing in Philadelphia the kind of large-scale rebellions that tore apart many inner-city ghettos in the late '60s and threatened to tear apart the very social fabric of the country itself – Rizzo's strong-arm methods were now seen as something of a liability, if only in the short term. As one biographer put it: "The city . . . had become polarized concerning Rizzo and the police, and much of it by his own design. By eliminating the dispassionate middle ground of opinion, Rizzo felt that people would have to choose between law and order on the one hand, and lawlessness and chaos on the other. If you were for Frank Rizzo, you stood up for law and order; if you criticized him, you were a 'coddler of criminals.'"[35]

The *Philadelphia Inquirer,* in its editorial summing up the August 8 attack, said: "Unfortunately, the MOVE confrontation with lawful authority, and the organization's clear defiance of the law, have been blurred by acts and statements in a wide range of contexts by Mayor Frank L. Rizzo and by his subordinates. The effect has been to increase polarization of the city on racial lines with the result that when an incident such as yesterday's tragic events occurs, hatred and mistrust spread through the city. That is not what Philadelphia needs."[36]

The editorial sheds no tears for MOVE and pointedly remarks on their "clear defiance of the law." MOVE got what it deserved (a position the *Inquirer* would certainly maintain after the events of May 13, 1985), but something had to be done about the polarization and the "hatred and mistrust spread through the city," a clear reference to the anger and volatility of the city's Black population.

Neither the *Inquirer* nor the chief power brokers for whom it spoke were suggesting that Frank Rizzo's methods should be permanently retired or carted off to some museum. State violence against those who dare to rebel is always the bottom line. But after more than ten years of the brutal and blatant wielding of the big stick, it was thought to be time for a period of "healing."

A strong alliance began to take shape between some of the city's foremost white businessmen, bankers, and politicians and elements of the city's most privileged Black strata, including and especially certain Black businessmen and politicians. This would give Philadelphia, after a short period of political transition involving a liberal white mayor, its first Black mayor. And in the same manner as Blacks who were elected mayor in other large cities, although in Philadelphia this came later and in a different social and economic climate than that of the late 1960s and early '70s when this strategy was first tried, Wilson Goode was expected to play the critical role of containing the rage always simmering and sometimes flowing out into the open in Philadelphia's vast ghettos, while at the same time encouraging and assisting in the development of the city's Black middle class which, like the Black petty bourgeoisie throughout the country, was becoming increasingly troubled by the steady erosion of economic and social reforms fought for and won over the last two decades.[37] And of course there was still the knotty question of what to do about MOVE, which in the aftermath of "Supercop's" August 8 assault became more defiant than ever.

6 | Mr. Mayor: W. Wilson Goode

The trial of nine of the original twelve MOVE members accused of murdering James Ramp didn't begin until sixteen months after the August 8, 1978 confrontation.[1] Frank Rizzo had been pushed out of City Hall by then, and in his place stood William Green, a white liberal Democrat in the Kennedy mold and son of one of Philadelphia's most powerful politicians.

Green had been a candidate on whom the city's white and Black officials could agree, as he was able to attract votes from both sides of the tracks and could campaign on a platform of healing the city's racial wounds. Also, part of this agreement on Green was that he would include a relatively large number of Blacks in his administration and would bestow the honor of the second most powerful position, managing director, on W. Wilson Goode. Another of Green's noteworthy changes was the appointment as his new police commissioner of the man who had been in charge of the tactical operation against MOVE on August 8, 1978. And one month before Green was inaugurated, in January 1980, the MOVE trial got under way.

Officials claimed that the trial was so long in starting because judges had to weigh many pretrial motions. One of these was MOVE's motion to dismiss the charges on the basis that critical evidence ,which could have aided the defense had been deliberately destroyed when the police leveled MOVE's house. This motion was denied. But more than pre-trial motions and other legal actions, there were important political reasons for delaying the trial's start. For one, the delay put a comfortable distance between the stormy passions and demonstrations of August 8, 1978 and the trial itself. The authorities were counting on being able to conduct the trial, and to arrive at the predetermined verdict of guilty, without stirring up another hornet's nest. The delay was also designed to give police who participated in the attack and constituted the bulk of the prosecution's witnesses a chance to work out and synchronize their courtroom stories.

When the trial finally did begin, it proved to be one of the lengthiest and most controversial in the city's history. Angered by the court's refusal to dismiss the charges, and displaying their total contempt for the U.S. judicial system, the indicted MOVE members acted outrageously in court, refusing to play by the rules and even doing push-ups and back flips in the middle of the proceedings.[2] They also opted not to have a jury trial, arguing that the jury would only be composed of "racist whites from the Northeast [a predominantly white area of the city] and store-bought Negroes from downtown."[3] Each defendant also acted as his or her own attorney, in accordance with MOVE's beliefs and strong distrust of lawyers.

The defendants' actions, designed to expose the trial as a farce and crude railroad, led to their frequent and none-too-gentle removal from the courtroom. Several weeks into the trial, the judge told the defendants they could answer only yes or no to his question of whether they would abide by the rules. When they responded with "We'll do what's right," they were expelled permanently from the courtroom and tried *in absentia.*

With the defendants banned, the judge ordered court-appointed counsels to proceed with the case, even though the defendants insisted they did not want to be represented by them. The attorneys took the matter to the State Supreme Court, which returned an unusually quick response mandating the lawyers to ignore the defendants and try the case. Only two of them did so; the others called no witnesses and presented no evidence.[4]

But despite these judicial maneuvers, the trial itself was anything but a smooth affair. A major problem was that the police witnesses apparently needed even more than sixteen months to get their act together. As they took the stand, they contradicted themselves and each other, revealing information highly damaging to the prosecution's case.

Officer Samuel Hatch Jr. testified, for instance, that on August 8 he and other police were on the first floor of MOVE's house when firefighters were dispatched to cut a hole in the floor through which MOVE members in the basement were supposedly urged to come out and surrender. According to Hatch, MOVE responded by shooting: " . . . gunshots were fired up through the floor from the basement. I observed wood chips flying up from the floor and bullets striking the ceiling."[5] But on cross-examination it was revealed that Hatch in prior statements to his superiors had never reported any such occurrence. Hatch also testified that one defendant had a knife on him when arrested. But this, too, Hatch had never mentioned before.

Similarly, there was the testimony of police department cameraman John Sigmann, whose film footage of August 8 was shown during the trial. The film's narration included the allegation that one MOVE member had a gun when he surrendered. But the film does not show this, nor could it because Sigmann never saw such a thing. He explained that the narration was based not on what he had observed but on what other police officers had told him. The narration was so thoroughly discredited that it had to be struck from the record.[6]

Another cop testified he had taken photographs of the basement right after MOVE had surrendered, and that none of these showed any weapons, even though the police had claimed they discovered a large cache of automatic arms in the cellar. This officer also admitted during cross-examination that he never saw any weapons in the basement.[7] In fact, not a single one of the police department's films or photos showed such a cache or any MOVE members surrendering with weapons.

Further, Walter Palmer, the person the city had hired to negotiate with MOVE and who had talked with MOVE members on the morning of August 8, stated immediately after the assault: "I don't believe any shots came from the house. The cracking sound was to my left and not in front of me. I had my eyes trained on that [the basement] window. You can't hold babies and shoot guns at the same time."[8]

Eight others who had also witnessed the assault corroborated Palmer's contention that no gunshots came from the MOVE house. Three firemen who had been operating the deluge guns and who had been struck by bullets could not say where the shots had come from or that they had seen any MOVE members with guns.[9]

Before they were banned from the courtroom, the defendants argued that this testimony clearly established they had no weapons on August 8 and couldn't have shot Ramp. They explained that there were police in the basement next to their house – a point not challenged by the prosecution – and that when they commenced firing at MOVE they precipitated police gunfire from the streets.[10] As for the automatic weapons, the defendants denied having any weapons on August 8, 1978, and pointed to news photos of Police Commissioner O'Neil crouching near one of the basement windows with a weapon in his hand. The media (and O'Neil) said that the commissioner was retrieving the weapon from MOVE's basement, but MOVE argued that he was putting it *into* the basement. And when the weapons supposedly found in MOVE's house were brought to court, not a single one of the defendants' fingerprints was on any of them, and none of the defendants was charged with illegal possession of weapons.[11]

But the defendants' permanent expulsion from the courtroom prevented them from fully developing these arguments. Further, since only two of the court-appointed attorneys attempted to wage any kind of defense at all after the nine were barred, and since the MOVE house had been completely leveled right after the confrontation, much critical evidence about how Ramp actually died was never brought to light.

This, combined with the fact that the defendants had already been tried and found guilty by the authorities and media, made the outcome of the trial highly predictable. All nine defendants were found guilty of murdering Ramp, of attempted murder, conspiracy, and seven counts of aggravated assault on other police officers and firefighters. The prosecution had made no effort to identify any particular defendant as having fired the fatal shot, and the four women defendants were found guilty even though the prosecution had called no one to the stand to claim that they had been seen even holding a weapon, as was claimed of some of the men.[12]

On August 4, 1981, almost three years to the day after the police stormed MOVE's Powelton Village headquarters, presiding Judge Edwin Malmed delivered the sentence: thirty to one hundred years for each of the defendants. Judge Malmed then defended the harsh sentence: "In my opinion, any thought of rehabilitation of these defendants would be absurd. They have persisted in setting their own bizarre codes of conduct without regard for the laws of the commonwealth or the rights of others, and I don't think their attitudes will change."[13] In these few carefully chosen words, Judge Malmed revealed the political essence of this lengthy and stormy trial: MOVE cannot be moved. Their behavior is "bizarre," they are intransigent, unrepentant, and beyond redemption. Their total disregard "for the laws of the commonwealth or the rights of others" can therefore only give rise to the "lawful right" of the authorities to try to eliminate MOVE, and in so doing to send an unmistakable message of intimidation to Black people and anyone else about whom it may also be said that "any thought of rehabilitation . . . would be absurd."

This same message was also contained in the very different ending to the trial of the cops who almost beat Delbert Africa to death on August 8, 1978. One of these four, Lawrence D'Ulisse, was never even charged and would be one of the "1978 veterans" who would be sent against MOVE again on May 13, 1985. As for the other three, presiding Judge Stanley Kubacki intervened in their case just as it was about to go to the jury. Judge Kubacki argued that the case, which had already been moved out of Philadelphia to the predominantly white suburbs of Dauphin County, should be thrown out because he was convinced that even if the jurors brought in a verdict of guilty it would be overturned by a higher court.

He then acquitted the three, agreeing with their attorneys that the cops were simply acting in self-defense when they attacked Delbert Africa. In a written opinion, Judge Kubacki stated he believed the cops were "fighting for *their* life" on August 8, in an atmosphere of "battlefield pandemonium."[14] The three had testified that they felt fully justified in beating Delbert Africa because they believed he was armed – even though published newspaper photographs clearly showed him carrying no weapons and trying to surrender.

But this didn't trouble Judge Kubacki, who said, "It is possible that the officers did use excessive force in subduing Delbert Africa. But that is mere conjecture. The officers had seen their friends and fellow officers gunned down minutes before. They knew Delbert Africa's physical prowess and could not know whether or not he was armed. . . . the entire world saw photographs of the defendants striking Delbert Africa. But it is not enough for the Commonwealth to show the striking. It must prove that the officers did not think their actions were necessary.... "[15]

And that was that. Nine Black radicals were sentenced to long prison sentences for the murder of a police officer, although there was absolutely no evidence to substantiate the conviction. Three police officers were acquitted of the charge of almost beating a Black radical to death, although there was plenty of evidence to substantiate a conviction. And all of this took place under the "new deal" administration of William Green and Wilson Goode, neither of whom had any difficulty in accepting these verdicts as a just outcome of the 1978 attack.

Nor did the attacks on MOVE end during this administration. Many members continued to be harassed and arrested, including Vincent Leapheart who the authorities believed to be MOVE's leader, John Africa. The authorities found and arrested Leapheart in Rochester, N.Y. and charged him with bomb-making. But they didn't succeed in this particular case as the jury refused to believe the testimony of the prosecution's main witness, Donald Glassey, a former MOVE member who had turned informant.[16]

In 1982, as MOVE members began to live at the Osage Avenue home of Louise James, the radical group stepped up its efforts to secure the release of the nine members jailed for the death of James Ramp. This included several legal appeals, all of which were ultimately denied. Also, according to Wilson Goode he met at least fifteen times with MOVE members while he was managing director. They provided him with documentation of how the nine had been convicted without any kind of evidence, and prevailed upon him to use his influence to help secure their release. They also wanted the city to provide them with a house, since it was the city that had destroyed the one in Powelton Village. But nothing came of any of these efforts.

In 1983, William Green did not run for a second term, thus opening the way for the election of Philadelphia's first Black mayor. Adding to the appeal of Wilson Goode's bid in the Democratic Party primary was Frank Rizzo, who stepped forward to challenge Goode. In one of the city's largest voter turnouts for a primary election, Goode won the nomination, securing roughly 7 percent more of the votes than Rizzo and carrying 97 percent of the Black and 23 percent of the white votes.[17] Goode then rather easily defeated his Republican opponent in the general election, garnering 55 percent of the vote. One survey indicated that he carried 98 percent of the Black and nearly 28 percent of the white vote.[18]

On inauguration day in January 1984, the new mayor declared that in America "dreams can come true."[19] At any rate, W. Wilson Goode's dream had come true. Born in 1938, one of seven children of North Carolina sharecroppers, Goode moved to Philadelphia with his family as a teenager. A biography produced by his office reads: "Goode completed his undergraduate studies at Morgan State University and then spent four years in the United States Army as Lieutenant in the Military Police. Following his discharge, he earned his Master's Degree in Governmental Administration from the University of Pennsylvania's Wharton School."[20]

Goode held a number of jobs, including as an insurance claims adjuster and probation officer. As executive director of a non-profit organization, the Philadelphia Council for Community Advancement, Goode established himself as a tireless and efficient administrator. He came to the attention of the state's governor, who appointed him in 1978 to head up the Public Utilities Commission, where Goode got some tough on-the-job training in crisis management when the nuclear reactor at Three Mile Island nearly blew up. According to his office biography, Goode's handling of the crisis "earned him enormous public recognition and respect," and he then moved on quickly to become Philadelphia's managing director and four years later its mayor.[21]

Goode took office in the same year that Jesse Jackson was running for President; the first Black astronaut was launched into space; the first Black woman was crowned Miss America (albeit not for long); and another of the nation's major cities, Chicago, also elected its first Black mayor. For elected Black officials and other Black leaders who represent the interests of the country's most privileged Black strata, these events are viewed as proof positive that it has been possible to make progress even in the midst of the hostile Reagan years, and that the electoral road in particular holds great promise for further economic and social progress. Said one Black official of Goode's victory and the growing number of Black mayors: "The election of Black mayors, like the integration of the schools, is all part of the same movement – the end of exclusion. The basic movement of black people since the end of slavery is to be included... Goode's election is an expression of empowerment."[22]

This statement reflects one side of the historic and continuing debate among Black people in the U.S. about the road forward – "we want in" versus "we want out." There are many Black people, for instance, who disagree strongly with the view that the basic movement of Blacks since the end of slavery "is to be included," and who argue that while a small number have been able "to make it" to some degree, the large majority of Blacks still find themselves in the same or even worse economic and social conditions. While this is true, it nevertheless is also the case that in recent years the "we want in" side of the debate has gained considerable currency, and there is no question, for example, that in a city like Philadelphia, as a *New York Times* article documents, a significant number of Blacks "have broken through to important positions" in economic, political, academic, and cultural life.[23]

In the enthusiastic words of William H. Brown III, one of Philadelphia's influential Blacks, "You see people in key positions that were almost unheard of 15 years ago. . . . You're not surprised today to see a black in top corporate management."[24] As the *Times* article also indicates: "The bureaucratic structure that helps hold the city together, from the Mayor down to clerks, is largely staffed by blacks." Or, in the words of another of the city's Black leaders: "You cannot realistically examine the city and not see those thousands of black social workers and cops and bureaucrats who are holding it together."[25]

At the same time, people like William Brown III are acutely aware that the number of Blacks in Philadelphia and nationwide who are achieving economic security and influence in many walks of life is still relatively very small compared to the Black population as a whole. In attempting to sum up the situation of Blacks in Philadelphia and nationally, Brown claims that "There is no question that over all, when you take all the pluses and all the minuses, blacks as a group are better off than they were 15 or 20 years ago."[26] But Brown himself seems to be aware that his arithmetic has gone haywire, for he also notes that there is a growing gap between Black "haves" and "have-nots": "You're seeing more of a class division now than you did before, and the division between the two groups is widening."[27]

The *New York Times* also notes that large numbers of Blacks in Philadelphia, like large numbers of Blacks in most of the country's big cities, still "find themselves in mean circumstances. Nearly a third live below the poverty level, more than double the proportion of whites . . . In some ways, the city's blacks as a group appear to be regressing: Their median income of $11,369 a year, according to the 1980 census, was 37 percent less than that of the city's population as a whole. Ten years earlier, it was 32 percent less."[28]

The *Times* further notes that income trends reveal a widening gap between the most successful Blacks and the much larger group of Black poor: "Nationally, the proportion of black households earning more than $35,000 a year, in constant 1983 dollars, nearly doubled from 1967 to 1983, rising to 11.1 percent from 5.9 percent. At the same time, a bigger group, earning less than $10,000, also grew, rising to 42 percent of all black households, from 40 percent. Figures for Philadelphia...show a similar pattern."[29]

Added to this is the fact that residential segregation in Philadelphia has not only remained extremely rigid, but has even worsened: "In 1970, the typical Philadelphia black lived in a neighborhood where 74 percent of his neighbors were black. By 1980, the figure exceeded 80 percent."[30] Unemployment for large numbers of Blacks in the city has also worsened, as labor-intensive industries once concentrated in the city either have shut down or moved to the suburbs, making them inaccessible to the unskilled, poor Blacks trapped in the ghettos.

At the same time, the situation for middle-class Blacks in Philadelphia, as well as nationwide, has grown increasingly contradictory. For example, more Blacks in Philadelphia now own their homes than ever before, and as the *Times* observed, a number of these homeowning Blacks "seem anxious to point out that solid black families, the kind made famous in the comedy routines of Bill Cosby—a Philadelphian—abound here, confounding a welfare-family stereotype that many of them have come increasingly to resent and deplore."[31]

But there is another, very important side to this picture of the Black middle class of Philadelphia, as well as nationwide. For while it is true that these petty bourgeois strata have been able to achieve certain economic and social progress as a result of the civil rights struggle and the concessions made by U.S. ruling circles (who actually saw it in their interests at that time to help build the Black middle class and even create new elements within it), it is also no less true that because of continued and deeply embedded discrimination in the U.S., many middle class Blacks find themselves facing major obstacles to further progress. Their rising expectations are being thwarted and their frustration is growing, particularly within professional and intellectual strata. More, an increasing number of the economic and social reforms won during the '60s and early '70s are now being taken back, and many middle-class Blacks as well as many Blacks in better-paying, working-class occupations are also discovering that their status does not at all protect them from the attacks and misery that have marked the condition of Black and other minority peoples throughout U.S. history. Their relatively secure and stable status, for example, did not protect the 250 people who were burned out of their Philadelphia homes on May 13, 1985, a fact not lost on large numbers of other middle class Blacks across the country.

Of course, it also remains true, as William Brown III has worriedly noted, that there is a growing gap between Black "haves" and "have-nots," and a growing class polarization within the Black community overall. This was very much in evidence in the immediate aftermath of the MOVE massacre, as different forces reacted in sharply different ways and as a battle broke out for the support and allegiance of these forces – expressed by the efforts of Mayor Goode and the authorities to suppress dissent among large numbers of lower- and middle-class Blacks, which included the muzzling and bribing of those Cobbs Creek residents who counted themselves among the opposition.

The principal response of elected Black officials and certain other Black leaders in the massacre's immediate aftermath was silence. An aide to Jesse Jackson said the 1984 presidential candidate wanted "to consult with Mayor Goode before issuing a statement."[32] The same response came from Black mayors' offices in Chicago, Detroit, Atlanta, and Newark – all declining comment through aides. A similar silence descended upon other such Black leaders – from the heads of various civil rights organizations to congressional offices to corporate and foundation boardrooms.

The reason for this silence is that most of these individuals approved of the attack on MOVE, with some quibbles about tactics and especially those that led to the fire's spread. To denounce the assault would have thrown into question their own ability to "respond effectively" and to wield the power of the state against those, including and especially those Blacks, who are viewed by that state as rebellious and dangerous. At the same time, because these individuals claim to represent the interests of all Black people, including the millions who were enraged by the massacre as well as the middle-class Black families who lost their homes and almost all earthly possessions as a result of the assault, they found it politically inexpedient to proclaim their approval.

Such approval should come as no surprise, for it represents

only the most recent and one of the sharpest expressions of what Blacks in positions of power are expected and required to do by the country's principal, and principally white, powerholders. As stated in the *Revolutionary Worker*:

> Every prominent Black official owes his position to his promise to suppress rebellion in the inner city. Mayor Washington joined in the hunt for Puerto Rican FALN nationalists in Chicago. Mayor Tom Bradley of Los Angeles presided over the "Olympic fascism" that descended on Blacks and Latinos last summer. Coleman Young sent squads of armed police into Detroit's high schools and declared a 10 p.m. curfew for youth – all clearly to terrorize (not protect) minority youth. The virtue of these men (in the eyes of the broader ruling class) is their ability, *as Blacks*, to involve the more privileged and conservative strata of Blacks in such suppression – all in a way that white mayors were often unable to do in the 1960s and early '70s.[33]

But if these Black powerholders remained silent in the face of the massacre, there were many other voices raised both in protest of the murders and in denunciation of these powerholders' complicity. The cries of "Murderers! Murderers!" that had been heard at the police barricades on May 13, 1985 soon took organized expression. Meetings of protest were held in Philadelphia and several other cities. On May 20, an ad hoc group which included the Reverend C. Hamilton Robinson, representatives of the Consumers Party, individuals supportive of MOVE, and others rallied outside City Hall to condemn the bombing and to gather signatures on a petition of protest. On May 25, a street corner rally in West Philadelphia was held under the sponsorship of the Revolutionary Communist Party, with people then marching in a show of solidarity to a home of MOVE supporters that was under heavy police surveillance.

On May 30, approximately one hundred protestors chanting "Goode is a murderer!" marched with eleven cardboard coffins from North Philadelphia to City Hall for a rally. Coordinated by the Citizens' Committee for Humanity and Justice, demands included that city officials be suspended without pay, that an independent citizens committee be set up to investigate the events of May 13, and that bail for Ramona Africa be drastically reduced. One of this rally's organizers said that May 13 "was more than a tragedy. It was a criminal act, and the people responsible have to be brought back to justice."[34]

In Washington, D.C., a National Committee of Inquiry into the Philadelphia Crisis, involving noted Black intellectuals and political figures, conducted a hearing to investigate what had happened in Philadelphia. One of the organizers explained why he felt the inquiry was necessary: "I became upset by the awesome silence, the silence of confusion...that appeared to say – once again – that it is all right in America to commit a holocaust against poor, black, radical people...There is reason to fear the awesome precedent set by Philadelphia."[35]

In June, the Provisional Government of the Republic of New Africa held a day-long hearing on the massacre, taking testimony and investigating charges that city officials were guilty of murder, arson, and genocide. Black poets also held public readings of their works which expressed many thoughts and emotions over the MOVE bombing. (A year later, a collection of these poems was published in Philadelphia.) There was also the formation of a Philadelphia Investigative Commission, involving representatives in Philadelphia from the Black United Front, the Afro Cultural Preservation Council, the National Foundation of African American Historical and Patriot Society, National Black Artists, and United Black Veterans, which held a series of public meetings soliciting testimony about the events of May 13.

A statement by Black poet Sonia Sanchez caught the tenor of those who were denouncing the complicity in the massacre of elected Black officials and certain other Black leaders: "Why are we silent, why are people not in the streets? Because they [MOVE] were dirty? Tell me about dirty, and I'll tell you about America.... In the 1960s, Malcolm X called us chumps for being silent at the bombing of churches. It seems we are populating the kingdom of chumpdom again...if we do not brand them as murderers at worst and as traitors to humanity at least. And treat them accordingly."[36]

Frightened by these organized protests and the widespread outrage they reflected, the authorities attempted to control the damage and minimize the rebelliousness and radicalization the massacre was giving rise to. For example, the widely publicized surveillance of a West Philadelphia home of MOVE supporters had the intended effect of deterring people from linking up with those close to MOVE, out of fear that they too might come under police scrutiny. Also, while collecting signatures on a petition protesting the bombing of MOVE, a representative of the Consumers Party was arrested on some twenty charges, including inciting to riot and disorderly conduct, and was held for seventeen hours.[37] The media attacked the credibility of the Philadelphia Investigative Committee because its chairman, Reverend C. Hamilton Robinson, had called Mayor Goode a murderer.[38] Further, Robinson, who operated a storefront in North Philadelphia which used city funds to cover operational costs for the social services he provided, soon found the money withdrawn, forcing him to shut down the storefront.[38] Other Black organizations and individuals, holding city contracts or in other ways tied to the Goode administration, refrained from publicly criticizing the mayor or the city because they feared official retribution. Sentiments existed among still others that if Goode went under, a whole network of Black civic and social organizations tied to the administration would go with him.

But there continued to be those who protested the massacre and fought to break through the wall of silence the authorities were attempting to erect around the events of May 13. Of particular note in this regard was the campaign by Black and other activists around "Draw the Line," a statement which organizers wanted to run in one of Philadelphia's major newspapers. Signed by more than one hundred people representing a wide range of political viewpoints and including many Black activists and people of all nationalities, the statement read in part: "When Black elected officials use their positions of power to attack Black people, or to cover up for or excuse such attacks, they are no friends of ours and don't speak for or represent the interests of Black people. In the past, lines were clearly drawn on this question. Those who attacked Black people were counted among our enemies. This line must be firmly drawn again. Murder is murder, no matter whether those responsible are Black or white" (see Appendix B for full text of statement).

In response to the authorities' efforts to suppress dissent, one of the organizers for "Draw the Line," Carl Dix, said:

[I]t's been okay to support the attack on MOVE and then call into question different parts of how it was carried out. But what's been out of bounds, what's not been allowed, was people saying straight-up that the whole murderous attack on MOVE was a criminal event that should be called out and condemned. They've worked to create a situation where if you go by what they're willing to publicize, you would think that there's nobody who seriously questions it, and that everybody kind of goes along with it, and has secondary objections here and there to raise. And from their end that's pretty important, because they're aware that there's a lot of rage simmering, especially in the Black community, but not only there.[39]

In fact, even before this simmering rage took organized form, and as the rubble of MOVE's Osage Avenue home was still being searched for bodies, the authorities sent legions of police through West Philadelphia's ghetto in a preemptive strike that included a search for other MOVE members and their supporters and the terrorization of many others. But this strike, too, did not go unchallenged.

On May 15, police raided a house on the 5100 block of Baltimore Avenue, with no warning, no search warrant, and to the complete shock of the owner who had made the unwitting mistake of planning to have an apartment added to the top of his building. The cops justified the raid by saying they had received a phone tip that the construction on top of the house might be another MOVE bunker! One tenant awoke to find cops on his fire escape who were attempting to force open his window. "I kept asking who they were," the tenant said, but "they never explained anything."[40] Another tenant said the cops asked him as they rushed in through the front door, "What did the people look like who lived here—did they have funny hair?"

Two days later, May 17, the 5300 block of Girard Avenue in West Philadelphia found itself under a siege that recalled the days of Frank Rizzo. For three hours a section of the street was cordoned off as heavily armed stakeout officers took up positions outside an abandoned rowhouse. This time the police said they had been informed that MOVE members might possibly be around, as two men wearing dreadlocks had been seen entering the uninhabited house.

A search of the house found no one, but by the time the cops had finished a crowd of two hundred had formed, angry at the presence of fifty cops armed with M-16s, shotguns, tear gas, and accompanied by the increasingly familiar and foreboding helicopter.[41] One person shouted, "Here comes the bomb!" Fearful that the neighborhood could become the next Osage Avenue, another in the crowd explained, "We weren't about to let them burn down this neighborhood."[42]

Anyone wearing dreadlocks—the hairstyle preferred not only by MOVE but also by believers in the Rastafarian religion, fans of reggae music, or simply those who like the fashion or identify with Africa or Jamaica – were suspect and, in many cases, literally under the gun. *The Philadelphia Tribune*, a Black-owned newspaper in Philadelphia, reported receiving "a number of calls from people saying they were looked at suspiciously or questioned by police because they wear the dreadlock hairstyle."[43]

One such victim was Amka Uhuru, who told the press how he had been pulled over by a police cruiser and taken into custody as he was walking home: "They handcuffed me and pressed a gun against my neck. All the while, I'm asking them, 'What did I do? What am I being charged with?' And they just took me into their car without even telling me whether I was under arrest."[44] At the station, when he refused to let the police fingerprint him because no charges had been brought, one cop threatened to beat him unconscious. He then allowed the fingerprinting and was released after four hours. The cops' parting words were a warning to "get that stuff off your head."[45]

The two remaining MOVE houses in Southwest Philadelphia also came under this climate of terror, as Mayor Goode threateningly declared on May 17, "I believe that there is a potential for additional violent confrontation between MOVE members and the city. I don't think we've seen the last of MOVE."[46] Then, on May 20, District Attorney Rendell reported that the two homes belonging to MOVE supporters were "under extremely careful surveillance and as soon as there is any evidence of weapons being brought into those locations or threats made by people in those locations, I think that you will see swift action to ensure that problems at those locations do not get out of hand."[47]

But for many of the residents in the two neighborhoods in which the MOVE supporters' houses were located, it was statements like these by Goode and Rendell, and not MOVE, that represented the problem. On August 17, as police surveillance of the MOVE supporters' house on Fifty-sixth Street near Springfield Avenue entered its third month and with no end in sight, the residents of the neighborhood called a press conference which was very different in tone than the one called by Osage Avenue residents two weeks before the massacre.

Working through their block association, the Fifty-sixth Street residents issued a press release which read in part:

> We the concerned neighbors of 56th Street have followed the MOVE situation since Powelton Village (the police attack in '78) and have watched with outrage the massacre on Osage Avenue,

and now Mayor Goode is threatening similar action against a MOVE sympathizer's house.... We will not be used as an excuse for further attacks against MOVE. We have no problem with the MOVE house, they are a welcome member of our street just as anyone else. The only problem we have is with the police watching the MOVE house as well as neighborhood people, and leaving uncertainties. We have also been subjected to low-flying helicopters, causing more tension within our neighborhood."[48]

The residents also made it clear they wanted no part of any action against the MOVE sympathizers, and that if police attempted to take the supporters to jail they would resist and the majority on the block would go to jail with them. One woman explained that she and other neighbors just ignored the cops and refused to talk with them: "I don't talk to them; if they killed children, they'd kill mine the same way."[49]

Mayor Goode and the other city officials also had their hands full trying to handle the situation in the Cobbs Creek neighborhood itself, as anger and divisions there ran deep. The massacre had been carried out in the community's name. Goode insisted over and over that he had to choose between MOVE and residents who were demanding that he rid the neighborhood of MOVE; that he waited longer than many people thought he should, but after the residents called a press conference on May 1, threatening to take matters into their own hands, he had to act.

This interpretation covers over the fact that planning for the attack on MOVE, especially the military planning and including numerous bomb tests, had been going on for well over a year. It also covers over the fact that as part of their political preparations for the attack, the authorities deliberately exacerbated tensions in the neighborhood. On the one hand, they used neighborhood informants to conduct surveillance of MOVE throughout the year leading up to the assault, and to spread terrifying rumors among the residents that MOVE possessed lethal arsenals, had dug tunnels crammed with explosives and were planning to blow up everyone, etc. At the same time, the city gave the impression that it really didn't care what happened on Osage Avenue and that it didn't really intend to do anything about MOVE.

Predictably, the result of this two-pronged tactic was the rapid build-up of tensions to nearly hysterical proportions, which the leaders of the block association worked to mold into an anti-MOVE crusade. But this was not entirely successful, and another indication that the May 13 assault was not really based on some kind of overwhelming grassroots demand is that while some neighborhood residents did support an eviction of MOVE, there were others who did not. Even Clifford Bond, the head of the block association, had to admit that many in the neighborhood would not sign his anti-MOVE petitions and did not want a confrontation.[50] One resident who opposed the association's attacks on MOVE was labeled a MOVE sympathizer and banned from meetings.[51]

Goode and the other authorities also found themselves after the events of May 13 in the untenable position of trying to explain why, if they really assaulted MOVE because of residents' demands to save the community, they destroyed it instead. Comparisons were being made to Vietnam and South Africa, and many of the residents were not merely stunned by the destruction of their homes but infuriated.

Clifford Bond did his best to rally the residents around Mayor Goode and the "necessity" of the massacre: "Even though there isn't a 6200 block of Osage left, I say we are still a unified block, and I am still their block captain."[52] As for Goode, Bond said, "I don't want to see him go. He was just in a precarious situation and we have to support him."[53] Bond also commented that "I don't want to cause any undue problems that are not necessary. I don't want to be part of any propaganda. I just want to be a victim."[54] Milton Williams, who lived on Osage Avenue and helped to organize protests against MOVE, said he had "no bad feelings. It just got out of hand . . . I'm not blaming the mayor. I'm not blaming anyone."[55]

But for many residents, any notion that the block was still a block or that no blame should be apportioned was at the very least absurd and in fact criminal. One enraged Osage Avenue resident said the authorities might soon have a "MOVE II on their hands." As she stared at the rubble that once had been her home, a Pine Street resident said: "This is so horrible. They handled this like a war zone." Another Pine Street neighbor commented: "It's the most devastating thing I've ever seen. . . . They wanted MOVE to leave, but not at this expense. . . . I just don't understand how you drop a bomb on people. That's warfare."[56]

For the authorities this was a dangerous situation. Since the assault had been carried out in the name of the people, it was essential for the neighborhood to continue to proclaim its support. Thus over the next several months, Goode and his associates conducted an extensive campaign to maintain and further develop the support that still existed among some of MOVE's neighbors – no easy task in the wake of the devastating fire – and to contain, even silence, if possible, those neighbors who refused to lend their names to what happened on May 13.

A key component of this campaign was to move quickly to address the needs of the 250 people who had lost their homes. As the *Philadelphia Daily News* remarked two days after the massacre: ". . . the city's bureaucracy has begun a hasty shift from a war footing to a vast relief effort."[57] On May 14, Mayor Goode promised the residents that the city would replace their homes free of charge. The leader of the Building Trades Council promptly offered to supply journeymen and apprentices to work for nothing on weekends to help build the new homes by Christmas 1985. Two of the city's business coalitions offered to contribute $500,000 to deal with the residents' immediate needs.[58]

The federal government also rushed to get into the relief effort. The regional administrator of the U.S. Department of Housing and Urban Development set up a special task force to assist in financing long-term substitute housing and permanent replacement housing, even though most of the middle-class residents normally wouldn't qualify for HUD's low-income assistance programs. And on May 17, Samuel R. Pierce Jr., U.S. Secretary of Housing and Urban Development and a member of President Reagan's cabinet, toured the ruins of Osage Avenue along with two senators and a member of the House of Representatives. After the tour, Pierce, speaking at a press conference on behalf of Reagan, said, "The President is deeply saddened by what occurred" and "has asked me to do everything I can" to help.[59] This consisted of $1 million in federal funds to help rebuild Osage and Pine.

At the same time, clergymen and other elements in the Black community, as well as various organizations such as the Red Cross, sponsored a massive effort to collect donations to replace the residents' belongings. Tons of goods were donated, a reflection in part of the tremendous anger that arose over the massacre, as well as sympathy for the burned-out residents. By mid-June over $1.8 million in goods had been collected, and sixty fire stations had to be used to store much of it.

But from the very outset, the authorities cynically used this outpouring of support to control the political damage caused by the massacre. The relief effort and massive publicity given to the burned-out residents were used to bury the fact that eleven people had been murdered. The only *real* tragedy, as far as the authorities and the media were concerned, was the fire and destruction of property, and that was what they wanted everyone else to believe as well. For example, at the press conference conducted by Secretary Pierce and Goode on May 17, the mayor thanked the cabinet member for coming to Philadelphia to help "focus attention on the future."[60] Neither of them would entertain any questions except those centering on what was being done to rebuild the Cobbs Creek neighborhood.

But there was an even more cynical purpose to the city's handling of the relief effort. The burned-out residents were being offered new homes at no financial cost to themselves, but there was a high political price attached: their continued public support for the massacre. They were being "asked" to stifle their outrage and curb their criticisms. If they consented they would have no difficulty in getting their new homes. If they didn't, well, who knows . . .

To bribe the residents into quiescence, the authorities exercised tight control over the distribution of relief goods and money. Goode gave principal responsibility for distribution of the donated money to the United Way. When the residents kicked up a small fuss and requested that seven of their representatives be given a key say in the distribution, Goode ended the matter by allowing them a vaguely defined "input" but no actual decision-making power.[61]

Over the next several months, the authorities and block association leaders also got into a venal game of haggling over just how much the residents' silence was going to cost. There was controversy, for example, over whether the rent for temporary housing for residents would be covered by deducting it from money that was supposed to be donated to the residents. And although the residents had initially been promised by Goode that their new housing would be provided free, there now developed a controversy over whether whatever insurance payments were made to residents would then be deducted from the city's cost of the houses.[62]

Relief goods and money for immediate needs continued to be dribbled out for several weeks, keeping many of the residents in a constant state of worry and uncertainty. It was not until July that the city guaranteed full compensation to all those who lost their homes, clothing and other personal effects, and regardless of any insurance payments they might receive. Goode estimated that the cost for the entire rebuilding effort would be $5 million, which the city, with the assistance of the federal government, would front. Then in mid-July 1985, with trumpets blowing, flags waving, and most of Philadelphia's press corps, as well as the national media, on hand to give the event maximum exposure, the first cement foundations were poured.[63]

But the authorities were uncomfortably aware that they could not rely only on their control of the money and the media to maintain the burned-out residents' loyalty. The neighbors' astonishment, their disbelief, their anger, also demanded the expert services of "mental health workers." One day after the assault, a psychologist at the Hospital of the University of Pennsylvania described what the residents were going through: "This was not an act of nature. This was gunfire and water cannons and bombs. This was as close as we see to war in a city during peacetime. . . . This block was Dresden. It was an incredible horror."[64]

He then explained that in the coming period, many of the residents would suffer from post-traumatic stress syndrome, the very same "disorder" soldiers experienced after returning from combat in Vietnam: ". . . after the crisis subsides and they get back to the normal routine of living, they might find themselves being extremely angry and somewhat bitter about the whole incident and not knowing what to do with it."[65]

There was particularly grave concern about the effects of the massacre on the city's youth. Another psychologist said that, "youngsters might be overwhelmed by it, constantly having intrusive thoughts about the incident."[66] In early June, at a major conference which brought together sixty professionals to analyze the psychiatric needs of the survivors, one of the block association officers discussed the impact of the massacre on the political consciousness of the city's and neighborhood's youth: "Not since slavery have black children been exposed to so much impotence from their parents . . . when the city finally came, they burned the neighborhood down. . . . I'm here to say there are a lot of kids now with little respect for authority, a lot of teenagers with very confused value systems after living through the years of MOVE's madness."[67]

Another neighborhood resident, whose house was far enough away to be spared, described how he and his family were having serious problems living with their guilt: "We see that crater, and we think about what happened constantly. People come by and tell us, 'You got what you wanted and deserved.' That's a heavy guilt trip."[68]

The authorities naturally viewed such thoughts as unacceptable and in need of "fixing." The Consortium, West Philadelphia's community mental health agency, went into immediate action. On May 14, they set up two crisis centers on Cobbs Creek Parkway. The Consortium also immediately dispatched to Sixty-second Street and Pine a mobile van staffed with counselors. Other mental health agencies had already been working with the Philadelphia School District for several months prior to the assault, "to counsel neighborhood children who have been disturbed by MOVE's presence." Now, in the massacre's aftermath, the Schools Superintendent announced the district would provide a comprehensive program of psychological and counseling services for students as well as their parents.[69]

One specialist in conflict resolution explained that the conservatism of the Cobbs Creek neighborhood remained a basic strength for the government, but that careful attention was required: "These are not your usual victims. They are strong Black people who have succeeded in the world. That strength must be taken into account. They are also angry and outraged, and that anger has to be legitimized."[70]

The head of the Consortium explained what "legitimizing anger" means. It was necessary, he said, to find the ways to give the survivors "opportunity to vent their feelings." Various programs had to be designed, such as providing transportation so that residents could continue to be immersed in religious activity. Discussions had to be organized by mental health professionals to get people "to talk with some control over what goes on." When asked what was the purpose of this "control," he responded that it was to funnel the residents' anger into "constructive channels, and to avoid non-constructive behavior like some kind of hostile action toward police."[71]

Key national Black figures were also working overtime to "avoid non-constructive behavior" such as hostile action toward the police, and to funnel the anger of Blacks in Philadelphia and nationwide into official government channels. Not surprisingly, a chief firefighter was the Reverend Jesse Jackson, who over the years has gained considerable experience in trying to hose things down in the ghettos, as for example during the Miami rebellion in 1980.

Jackson came to Philadelphia in early July 1985, appearing at a fundraising benefit for the burned-out families. Jackson, who had also visited Philadelphia in June and had met with Goode, again met with the mayor during his July visit. That same day, Jackson also met with Ramona Africa because, he said, there were some questions in his own mind about what had happened on May 13. Jackson then told the press that in his meeting with the sole adult survivor of the massacre, he asked her if MOVE had set fire to their own house.[72]

Jackson "balanced" questions like these with some criticism of the May 13 operation, including his belief that the police had overreacted. But the heart of Jackson's message was for people to calm down and to have faith that the authorities would eventually get to the bottom of what happened through carrying out various lengthy and thorough investigations. First and foremost was to be the Philadelphia Special Investigation Commission (PSIC), appointed by Mayor Goode himself. Aware, however, that many people might question the credibility of a commission of the mayor's own choosing, Jackson called also for federal intervention, either through a grand jury or through an investigation promised by Congressman John Conyers and his House Judiciary Subcommittee. Said Jackson: even if the Goode-appointed commission "is vigorous, and earnest and concerned, as I'm sure it is, because there are very credible people on that committee who have long-standing reputations, that does not forego the fact that a grand jury also has its own kind of obligation and the federal government has its own kind of obligation to deal with this tragedy and come forth with a credible conclusion."[73]

"Due process," then, was the watchword to be inscribed on the authorities' banners – certainly not for the first time in U.S. history when it has been necessary to contain people's rage and divert them from independent and militant action. And to Mayor Goode's own hand-picked commission fell the rather questionable honor of being the first line of defense, by attempting to find, as Jesse Jackson stressed, a "credible conclusion."

7 | The Hearings

The eleven members of Mayor Wilson Goode's Philadelphia Special Investigation Commission were chosen with considerable care. Not surprisingly, for the critical post of chairman Goode chose William H. Brown III. A former chairman of the U.S. Equal Employment Opportunity Commission, an affluent attorney, and one of Philadelphia's major Black figures, Brown was a key player in Goode's 1983 mayoral campaign, to which his law firm also contributed financially.[1]

In addition to Brown, Goode selected five other Blacks for the commission. Charles W. Bowser campaigned unsuccessfully for mayor in 1975 and 1979, paving the way for Goode's own campaign and election in 1983. Former chairman of the city's Urban Coalition and member of the executive committee of the National Urban Coalition, Bowser personally contributed to Goode's campaign, as did various members of his law firm.[2]

The Reverend Audrey Flora Bronson is pastor of a West Philadelphia church, a retired professor of psychology, and was cited in 1984 by the West Philadelphia Chamber of Commerce for "educational and religious contributions to the community." Charisse Ranielle Lillie is associate professor of law at Villanova University Law School, a former deputy director of Community Legal Services, and was a trial lawyer with the U.S. Justice

Department's civil rights division during the Carter Administration. Julia M. Chinn is a well-known Cobbs Creek activist and president of Cobbs Creek Town Watch. The Reverend Paul Washington is a well-known Episcopalian rector who in March of 1985 received the Whitney M. Young Jr. Community Service Award from the city's Urban League.[3]

The white panelists were M. Todd Cooke, chairman and chief executive officer of one of Philadelphia's largest financial institutions; Msgr. Edward P. Cullen, director of Catholic Social Services for the Archdiocese of Philadelphia; Bruce Kauffman, a former justice of the Pennsylvania Supreme Court and senior partner and chairman of a prestigious Philadelphia law firm which also donated to Goode's campaign; Henry S. Ruth Jr., who succeeded Leon Jaworski as Watergate special prosecutor in 1974, and whose law firm contributed heavily to Goode's campaign; and Neil J. Welch, special agent in charge of the FBI's Philadelphia office from 1975 to 1978.[4]

These were the people handpicked by Mayor Goode to conduct what was supposed to be "a thorough, independent and impartial examination of the events leading up to and culminating in the death and destruction of May 13th."[5] This is the group — composed of executives, lawyers, academics, church leaders, and former judges and government officials — which Chairman Brown described on the opening day of the public hearings as "a true citizens' commission."[6] Brown's definition of "citizen" is reminiscent of Greek and Roman days. Then, too, the authorities defined "citizen," and all the privileges that go with that designation, in a manner to exclude all slaves. And just as the great democratic forums of those days consisted only of such citizens, so too did this "impartial, independent" and "true citizens' commission" fail to select even one representative from Philadelphia's lower classes and ghettos.

Chairman Brown also claimed his was a "true citizens' commission" because it was "neither police nor prosecution. We are not accusatory. Instead, we are investigatory. We find the facts and report them to you, the people.... By the time we conclude these hearings, you, the people, will be able to judge for yourselves how this terrible day in May came about. You will be the ultimate jury in this case."[7] But this is just more demagogic rhetoric. Even the way the hearings were set up revealed that the public's role was to serve not as jury but as passive and unquestioning spectator.

The hearings were held in an auditorium with eight hundred seats, four hundred of which were reserved for the public, and also were televised live by Philadelphia's public network – thus giving the appearance of being open and aboveboard. But in reality these hearings were conducted in a tightly controlled and closed atmosphere. For example, on October 8, 1985, when the hearings got underway, the welcome mat was laid out by squads of police who took up security positions outside the auditorium – a task simplified by the fact that the auditorium was right next to police headquarters. These officers were joined by sheriff's deputies and members of the city's political police, the Civil Affairs Unit, the same group which had spied on and was continuing to spy on MOVE members and supporters. Anyone who entered the auditorium was subject to search and made to walk through metal detectors. Cameras, shopping bags, and some other personal items were forbidden.

The strong police presence and security measures arose from the commission's demand that the hearings be carried out with the "proper decorum," which meant that the public could attend the hearings but was expected to sit quietly and not express disagreement with the proceedings. But some people decided to express their disagreements anyway. On the first day, several protestors stood up to denounce the hearings and to argue that MOVE people had been murdered. Chairman Brown ruled them out of order and quickly called a recess. All who spoke out from the audience from that point on were removed by the police, their names were taken down, and they were threatened with arrest if they returned. The commission also ordered the television cameramen not to show the protestors, in a conscious policy, as the *New York Times* noted the following day, to discourage any further protest.[8] But the audio had not been cut off, enabling thousands to hear if not to see this "impartial" commission engage in blatant censorship.

The heavy air of intimidation that hung over the hearings, the censoring and removal of protestors, the striving for a "proper decorum" – all were important elements in establishing the appropriate political atmosphere for the mayor's panel to carry out its actual role, which arose not from a citizens' mandate or some "democratic impulse," but harsh necessity. What was required was a commission that would criticize the "excesses" or "mistakes" of May 13 – particularly those associated with the bombing and the fire – while at the same time upholding the effort to eliminate MOVE. The commission could not attempt to condone every aspect of the assault, because that would further inflame rather than mollify the many who were already infuriated and would throw even more people onto the side of those who were condemning the events of May 13.

Months before the hearings began, the authorities and others were publicly discussing and determining the commission's task. Edwin Guthman, the editor of the *Philadelphia Inquirer*, stressed in a signed article that the commission had to "search exhaustively for the truth and let the chips fall where they may. Then the mayor must take whatever actions are indicated."[9] This of course assumes that the mayor himself is innocent. Representative William H. Gray III, the Black congressman for the district which includes Osage Avenue, wrote a letter to Commission Chairman Brown saying that "by the best available data" the decision to drop the bomb "may represent a case of gross negligence."[10] Here Gray does not call into question the legitimacy of the whole search-and-destroy mission against MOVE, and he suggests that only negligence was involved in the bombing, not murder. This is exactly the position the commission would take nine months later.

On July 4, Acel Moore, the associate editor of the *Philadelphia Inquirer*, wrote that the "plan to evict the MOVE members was ill-conceived, poorly planned and poorly executed. The police botched the job from the beginning to end, and those who are responsible for the planning should be held accountable."[11] Here again the terms are being set around poor planning and poor execution, not premeditated murder. Moore also added that if Birdie Africa's testimony to commission investigators about what happened behind the MOVE house was true, it "means police disobeyed orders to fire only when fired upon."[12] But Birdie Africa's testimony means much more than that, and here too the effort is to focus attention on "excesses."

Nevertheless, the fact that Acel Moore even mentioned Birdie Africa's testimony is significant, because it represented one of the first and only times in that period that the existence of such testimony was publicly acknowledged by people in positions of power and influence. For more than a month the media sat on Birdie Africa's highly damaging remarks, and when they finally did publicize them it was part of the same effort to focus on "excesses," "mistakes," and scapegoats.

By July 2, a week after Birdie Africa's testimony was publicized, both Police Commissioner Sambor and Fire Commissioner

Richmond were being publicly criticized, even while Mayor Goode was being upheld as a symbol of law and order. A headline in the *Philadelphia Tribune* read, "Sambor rumored on way out."[13] The article states it was Sambor who decided to drop the bomb, neglecting to mention that Goode had given him the go-ahead. A key city official was also quoted as saying it was important for Sambor to resign because "the longer he sticks around the tougher it's going to be for the mayor."[14]

The fingerpointing and scapegoating intensified in mid-July, when the Fraternal Order of Police filed suit to block the commission. They contended the whole investigation might be a "witch hunt" aimed at them.[15] Their suit was quickly dismissed, and they just as quickly appealed, as the FOP spokesman angrily spilled out the truth to the press. He said the commission was not truly independent, but "an advisory commission advising him [Goode] and beholden to him."[16]

By the end of July, it was fully apparent that Police Commissioner Sambor had been marked for sacrifice. The City Fire Marshal released an official report on the bombing and fire. It documented that the fire had in fact been started by the bomb and not by the MOVE people. The report ignored the official police story that the roofs had been drenched in gasoline, noting that the bomb appeared to have ignited a container marked "gasoline" which was sitting on the MOVE roof. Then, when on August 6 the city's new managing director, James White, disclosed that the bomb contained the powerful explosive C-4, and not just Tovex as the police had been claiming all along, Sambor's days were clearly numbered.[17]

The fact that one of the city's highest officials and one of the principal planners of the May 13 assault was being pushed to resign is a powerful indication of just how difficult it was to control the damage caused by the massacre and fire. As the commission's public hearings neared, even Mayor Goode came under increasing criticism. The *New York Times* reported that some of his staunchest and most influential backers were considering not supporting him for another term as mayor unless he acquitted himself well at the upcoming hearings.

Thus, on the one hand, a commission had to be created. Explanations were needed; a believable justification for the deaths of eleven MOVE members and the destruction of a Black neighborhood was required. To this end, scapegoats and even the major decision makers themselves were to be criticized and blamed for "excesses" and "mistakes." But on the other hand, holding such public hearings was a risky business. The hearings meant that those who ordered the assault had to hold themselves up to some public scrutiny. Further, the commission, which had previously interviewed witnesses in private, could not control what these same witnesses would say once they were before the camera. The public was thus treated to the spectacle of these authorities going after one another, as private career-saving agendas conflicted with the overall need of the power structure to produce a credible justification for May 13.

But while there was some falling out among these officials, the bottom line for all of them was unity on the need for a cover-up: no one was to be accused of murder. There was also complete unity on the need to underscore the message that was delivered on May 13, the message of a mid-1980s America hurtling towards world war and demanding obedience on the home front: rebellion is impermissible and will be met with maximum force. "MOVE dared to go up against us—look what happened to them."

The commission attempted to carry out its task by continuing the attacks on MOVE while portraying their murderers as merely inept and incompetent. One of the first witnesses was Joseph O'Neil, Mayor Frank Rizzo's police commissioner and the commander of the police assault on MOVE in Powelton Village in 1978. The hearings were designed to have the Powelton Village assault and the death of Officer James Ramp brought up first so that MOVE could be depicted from the outset as cop killers. O'Neil of course said nothing in his testimony about the considerable evidence indicating that Ramp probably was killed in police crossfire.

Instead, O'Neil portrayed the Powelton Village assault as a model of moderation and thoughtfulness. He said police tried patiently to negotiate with MOVE, and when that failed they launched their assault only with the greatest care and with the safety of the MOVE people always uppermost in mind. As an example, O'Neil said that when police used a battering ram on the MOVE house, they would let the people inside know each time they were about to try to smash in. O'Neil also testified that he decided against the use of tear gas because of its possible harmful effects on the MOVE children.[18]

At this point a protestor stood up in the auditorium to take on O'Neil and the commission: "This is ridiculous!. . . . You're such concerned police . . . where was all that concern when y'all killed four babies?. . .This ain't just a whitewash. What it is, it's part of taking that massacre even further than it went before. You continue the very same lies. Murderers, murderers, no more!. . .You would think eleven police got killed on that day...murderers, murderers, no more! The line has got to be drawn on this shit!"[19] It was then that Chairman Brown called a recess and had the protestor removed by police. But when he left another person spoke up, and then another.

Outside the auditorium, a press conference was called where representatives of the Committee for Humanity and Justice, the Revolutionary Communist Party, and the Consumers Party criticized or denounced the hearings and condemned the May 13 assault as murder. This press conference and the protests received wide media coverage in Philadelphia.[20]

Inside, the hearings continued with testimony from Civil Affairs cops which was designed to supplement the imagery of MOVE as bent on provoking violence. The cops read into the record the hundreds of arrests on charges ranging from disorderly conduct to riot and possession of weapons involving MOVE members for a period of twelve years. This testimony also came with special effects. The commission asked one of the cops to imitate MOVE's threatening speeches, complete with all the "motherfuckers" — unfit language for Osage Avenue but not for live TV.[21]

A cast of Osage Avenue neighbors was also called in to run down a litany of complaints against MOVE. This testimony provided a good view of the thinking of these Black middle-class residents and how they could be used by the authorities as a pretense to go after MOVE. One of them portrayed the MOVE children as dangerous, just as dangerous, she believed, as Vietnamese children who booby-trapped U.S. GIs (thus echoing the viewpoint of the cop who took Ramona Africa into custody). Others likened MOVE to terrorists, but said nothing of the real terrorism of May 13. The block captain without a block, Clifford Bond, lectured the commission, "It seems to me, if we learn from any of this, that all governments in large cities should be aware of the potential of terroristic groups and the inability of the city government to deal with it. So these are the things that I think you need to begin to watch very closely, because terrorism is right at our back door here in the United States."[22]

Of course, some of the testimony of police, neighbors, and also officials from various city agencies disclosed in an unintended fashion the systematic persecution of MOVE and just how conscious was the decision to assault MOVE on May 13. There was, for example, the testimony of one of the Osage Avenue residents who participated in the meeting with Mayor Goode in July 1984: "We met with him and asked him what he was going to do . . . and he said that he was working on a legal way to get rid of the MOVE people, he said, because he wouldn't go in there and have to go back a second time. When he went in there he would make sure that it was legal and right and we would not have any MOVE because if it was done the right way the first time we would not have MOVE."[23]

The testimony of Civil Affairs and Major Investigations Department cops also revealed the extensive surveillance of MOVE for a long period and right up to the massacre itself. There were also the remarks of bureaucrats of different city agencies, such as the Department of Licenses and Inspections which had received complaints about MOVE but which, according to their testimony, the department didn't respond to.[24]

The point of this sort of testimony was to portray the city government as inept, bungling, and "paralyzed" by MOVE, but during the hearings it also came to light that these agencies in fact had played a key role in assisting in the assault on Osage Avenue as well. The Department of Water, for instance, inspected the sewers for supposed escape tunnels before May 13 and found none. Even a Civil Affairs cop testified that he also searched for tunnels before May 13 and could not find any – lending further credence to the view that the authorities knew all along there were no tunnels and were simply using their supposed existence as part of their propaganda campaign against MOVE.[25] There was also the testimony of Clarence Mosley, an assistant managing director under Leo Brooks, who in an apparent effort to save his own neck offered the interesting theory that his boss had deliberately left town the weekend before May 13 to "throw off the enemy," that is, to give the MOVE people a false sense that no assault was impending.[26]

The commission also ended up having its hands full with two former MOVE members, Louise James, mother of Frank James Africa and sister of Vincent Leaphart, both of whom perished in the fire, and LaVerne Sims, Louise James' sister and three of whose children are imprisoned MOVE members. Perhaps the commission felt that letting these two testify would provide it with the appearance of impartiality, as well as giving it a chance to grill these witnesses. But if that was the strategy, it backfired. Louise James stood up to read a statement:

> ...The mayor is wrong.... He was wrong on May 13 when he approved the dropping of a bomb on a row house that he knew to be inhabited by men, women, babies, and animals. He was wrong when he appointed this commission. He is wrong as these hearings get underway and when they are finished he will still be wrong. This is an unchangeable fact, as unchangeable as the fact that eleven voices will never again utter a single, solitary word. No amount of testimony will change either of these facts which is in fact what these hearings are all about. They are about the mayor searching desperately for a hook on which to hang his so-called justification for the annihilation of my family....
>
> Here is a mayor, who is also a Black man, who approves the dropping of a bomb on a row house in a residential area, watches on television as the house becomes a raging inferno, allows the house to burn out of control for an hour without relief of water after permitting thousands of gallons of water to be dumped on the house for six to eight hours without let-up prior to the fire.... He knew that flesh was being seared from the bones of men, that women were being broiled, babies roasting, trying to run away from the fire that consumed them, animals incinerated, everybody in that house burned beyond, charred beyond recognition, and knowing this, this man, this fiend, this mayor of murder, said he'd do it again![27]

Laverne Sims called the commission a "farce, a circus, a ploy," adding that "any time an investigation of any type is held and in its final stages reaches the hands of the perpetrator to make a decision as to the findings—in this instance Mayor Wilson Goode—it is idiotic to believe that perpetrator will find himself, as well as his constituents, guilty and send themselves to jail."[28]

As soon as the two women finished their statements the grilling began: How many members are in MOVE? Was MOVE violent? Did MOVE ever have any weapons? Had MOVE changed its philosophy from one of peaceful change to violent confrontation? When and why did they join MOVE and why did they decide to leave? Some questions the women refused to answer; others they used to expose the history of systematic violence against MOVE by the police, courts, and prisons. When one of the commissioners asked what they meant by "the system," Louise James shot back, "the system, the establishment, *you*."[29] They argued that the portrayal of MOVE as violent was simply an attempt to justify the

May 13 murders, and Laverne Sims pointed out that Mayor Goode "is violent. When is he going to move on himself?"[30]

The second week of the hearings featured the testimony of Goode, Brooks, and Sambor. It was a week of accusation and counter-accusation, as each tried to minimize his own role in the massacre by wagging a finger at the others. The disputes centered on questions of tactics – the use of explosives, what kind of firepower the police had, how long to let the fire burn, etc. It was a sordid scene but also a necessary one because it lent the commission a badly needed air of credibility and left many of those watching the spectacle on television caught up in a multitude of tactical questions and trying to guess which of the three was a liar on *these* matters. The fact that all three were completely in accord with and played major roles in carrying out a premeditated murder, with the knowledge and sanction of the FBI, other federal agencies, and those who inhabit the halls of power in Washington, D.C., was not up for discussion.

Wilson Goode started off the second week's testimony. While still maintaining that as mayor he had overall responsibility for the events of May 13, he tried to put as big a distance as possible between him and those events, and in the process stretched his own credibility to the breaking point. He claimed he never knew that explosives would be used at any point in the police siege, that he thought the sound of explosions in the morning was caused solely by stun grenades. He said he thought the police were only shooting over the MOVE house, not at it. He claimed he had no idea what automatic weapons fire sounds like, even though he had commanded military police. He argued that his order to put out the fire was "interrupted," and Goode blamed his subordinates for misleading and disobeying him, pointing repeatedly to Police Commissioner Sambor as the one who was really in charge on the scene. He admitted he approved of the bomb, but only by "default" by not disapproving it.[31]

Goode's testimony prompted one Black newspaper columnist in Philadelphia to label the mayor a "charcoal-broiled caricature of Richard Nixon lying in his teeth."[32] True, but it was really all that Goode could do. He had to look foolish, duped, and out of touch with what happened on the scene on May 13 in order to wash his own hands of the murderous affair.

The commission was more than happy to help with this masquerade. One of its major conclusions was that "The mayor failed to perform his responsibility as the city's chief executive by not actively participating in the preparation, review and oversight of the plan."[33] It also concluded that "The mayor abdicated his responsibilities as a leader when, after mid-day, he permitted a clearly failed operation to continue which posed great risk to life and property."[34] But at midday, the mayor was before the media declaring his intention to seize control of the house "by any means necessary," and at that very time a lethal bomb was being prepared.

Former managing director Leo Brooks contradicted Goode on several major points. He indicated, for example, that he had personally told the mayor of the plan to use explosives to blow holes in the walls of the MOVE house, and also had told Goode about the plan to use a helicopter to drop the bomb. But Brooks did more than simply contradict Goode's testimony on such tactical matters. He also defended the assault. He testified, for instance, that he had no qualms about blowing holes in the walls of the MOVE house, and stated that police departments all over the country use such entry devices. This is certainly true, and Brooks himself provided an excellent example: the storming of Attica Prison.[35]

He also upheld the bombing and the decision not to put it off for fear that MOVE members might escape under cover of darkness. He agreed that if MOVE people had been in the rooftop front bunker when the bomb was dropped they probably would have been killed. And in a particularly revealing statement about how he and the others viewed the bombing, he said, "the only ugliness is the political implications of the bombing."[36]

Beleaguered Police Commissioner Sambor also did his best at the hearings to place the blame for controversial tactical decisions on anyone but himself, even as he admitted that he approved the details of the plan "to an extent where it can be fairly called my plan."[37] This was Sambor's way of joining Brooks in defending the assault while trying to distance himself from some of its more controversial aspects. Echoing Mayor Goode's argument that a violent confrontation with MOVE was inevitable, Sambor went on to blame the MOVE members for their own deaths for refusing to come out of the house: "It remains a fact that if MOVE members had simply come out of the building, they would be alive today. Property damage would have been minimal and we would not now be gathered."[38] But Sambor failed to mention that MOVE members did attempt to leave their house and were either forced back into the burning building by gunfire, or were simply gunned down, or both.

On the final day of the hearings, November 6, Goode, Brooks, Sambor, and also Fire Commissioner Richmond were called back to clear up "inconsistencies" in and between their previous testimonies. The commission had already provided each of them with the portions of conflicting testimony they were being asked to clarify. But when brought face to face with each other, each of the four stuck pretty closely to his original testimony. In the main, this reflected how serious were the cracks and infighting in the authorities' ranks. There was the question, for example, of who besides Sambor among the major decision makers would have to end up being sacrificial lambs, and the possibility at some future time of indictments being handed down against one or more of them could not be ruled out, as a further demonstration to the public of how justice supposedly was being served.

Thus Brooks now felt he and the others should have had a dress rehearsal (covering over the fact that in many ways, the August 8, 1984 confrontation was that dress rehearsal and that things overall had been well planned). Richmond now felt that his and Sambor's decision to let the bunker burn was a "bad decision" (which was the least he had to say in the wake of a completely destroyed neighborhood). And Goode felt that in retrospect he had relied on experts he now wasn't so sure were experts. (One wonders how much more "expertise" Goode, ever the image of the efficient administrator, thought the massacre required.) The mayor also had what can only be considered the unmitigated nerve to say he was sorry, that he had made some mistakes (but nothing too major, and certainly not the "mistake" of murder), and that he would have to learn to live with the scars.[39] In sum, all preferred to eat a little crow than to admit that on May 13, 1985 they devoured eleven human beings.

The Philadelphia Special Investigation Commission's official report on the events of May 13 was released on March 6, 1986. Actually, a draft of the report was leaked to the press several days earlier, apparently yet another indication of the continuing infighting. Much of Philadelphia's media immediately hailed the report as a scathing and deserving criticism of the city, and particularly of Mayor Goode. There were more than a few suggestions in the press that it might be best if Goode would resign — further proof of how serious was the political damage and fallout from May 13.

The *Philadelphia Daily News* called the report a "stinging indictment" of the mayor.[40] The *Philadelphia Inquirer* characterized it as "a harsh and relentless denunciation of the city's command structure,"[41] and in an editorial wrote that "The MOVE commission's findings have cut like acid through the buck-passing smog over the ruins of Osage Avenue."[42]

Various former Cobbs Creek Park residents were also quoted lauding the commission's conclusions. Clifford Bond, who had been one of those to cry the loudest and longest for the elimination of MOVE by any means necessary, and who could even find justification for the killing of the five children, now whistled a different tune: "It's important that people in power come out and say that it's wrong to drop a bomb on a house and allow kids to burn up.... It was the most blatant misuse of power that I've ever seen in my life."[43] Another former Osage Avenue resident, Howard Nichols, said what the commission and authorities were hoping many others would also say: ". . . because this commission had been empaneled by the mayor himself, I was afraid that it was going to be a whitewash. It's really refreshing to see that there are some professionals in the community who have maintained honesty and integrity. . . . I'm very proud of all the commission members."[44]

But there is more than one way to conduct a whitewash, and people like Howard Nichols fail to realize that it was necessary for the commission to criticize certain aspects of the May 13 operation in order to cover over, and ultimately to justify and uphold, the real crime of premeditated murder that was committed on that day. Even the more seemingly scathing criticisms by the commission abound with key code words such as "reckless," "hasty," "ill-conceived," "irresponsible," "excessive," and "unreasonable." Another displaced resident, also trying to praise the commission, inadvertently hits on an important truth: "These people on the commission are well-educated, they're intellectual, and their reputations were on the line. And so many people could see the negligence throughout the whole system, they had no choice but to place blame where the blame had to be laid."[45] But the only blame they placed, of course, was for supposed *negligence.*

Probably the sharpest charge the commission leveled was that the deaths of the five children appeared to be "unjustified homicides." It is no accident that the commission reserved its harshest words for these deaths. Hundreds of people at the scene on May 13, and millions watching the TV news, witnessed the bombing and burning of a house known to have not only adults but also children inside. Ramona Africa had exposed that the authorities had made no effort to pick up the children before the assault, even though they had plenty of opportunity to do so. And Birdie Africa had testified that when he got outside the burning house other children had, too. But they were later found in a heap of body parts at the rear of the MOVE house, with at least one of the children's bodies containing shotgun pellets.

The deaths of the children angered broad numbers of people, and when the details emerged of how they died even the sentiments of those who were not sympathetic toward MOVE turned to rage and condemnation. The commission thus had no choice but to conclude that the deaths appeared to be "unjustified homicides," or risk creating even further outrage and failing in their task of restoring people's faith in the system – although even here the commission argues that Goode and other city officials merely were "grossly negligent and clearly risked the lives of those children." The point, however, is not that they negligently risked the children's lives – they cold-bloodedly ended them.

In the same vein, the commission claims it does not know what or who is responsible for the children's deaths. This despite the fact that the commission's own expert pathologist testified that buckshot was found in the body of at least one of the children, and even though the commission's own report had to admit that police gunfire prevented MOVE people from escaping the burning house. Further, the commission's call for a grand jury investigation into the deaths of the children – an investigation which by the beginning of 1987 had not taken place in any case – keeps this volatile issue bottled up in yet more "due process." This also leaves open the possibility that a grand jury or some other "impartial" board will find the MOVE adults themselves either partially or completely to blame for the children's deaths. This would be in accordance with the commission's position, stated during the hearings, that the police should have handled the assault as involving hostages – the children![46]

Another commission conclusion that gave rise to considerable commentary, and to the strenuous objections and written dissent of one commission member, Bruce Kauffman, was that racism played a role in the assault. According to the commission, the decisions to use powerful explosives, extensive firepower, the bomb, and then to let the fire burn "would not likely have been made had the MOVE house and its occupants been situated in a comparable white neighborhood."[47]

This of course is true. The assault and massacre of May 13 was of *Black* people, and the message of terror contained in those murders was meant to be delivered mainly to Black people, although in the forthcoming period and as part of "battening down the home front," it is quite possible and even likely that white radicals or revolutionaries in white or predominantly white neighborhoods will also come under all-out assault. But the fact remains that such open displays of terror have been more frequent in the Black community and those of other minority nationalities. These are tied to the much more oppressive conditions that overall are enforced there, and in the future this greater necessity of the authorities to deliver their message of terror in such communities will continue and intensify, even as the general clampdown leads to more across-the-board assaults.

But why did the commission admit that the assault was racially motivated? Principally because it could not avoid such an admission. As already noted, in the days immediately following the assault, the prevailing official wisdom, as expressed widely in the media, was that the events of May 13 couldn't have been racially motivated since they were presided over by a Black mayor, Black managing director, and a city government consisting of many Black bureaucrats. But over the next ten months, including at the hearings themselves, way too much was revealed to continue denying that racism was involved, Black mayor or no. In particular, all the wild and vicious attacks against MOVE leading up to and after the massacre focused on portraying them as filthy and uncivilized savages whom the "civilized" citizenry of Philadelphia had every justification for exterminating.

The charge of racism also appears to be an important component in the effort to exonerate Mayor Goode. A position that has been developed by some forces in the Black community, both in Philadelphia and elsewhere, is that Goode was really a hostage to Police Commissioner Sambor's plan to eliminate MOVE. It was a plan, this view holds, that Goode did not have the power to oppose. It is argued, for instance, that Goode did order the fire to be put out, that Brooks passed along the order, but that whites Sambor and Richmond ignored it and let the fire burn. There also has been some discussion that the police had threatened the mayor's life if he showed up to try and stop the attack, and in a similar vein it also has been suggested that the MOVE massacre was a plot by the "white power structure" to discredit the Black mayor.

It certainly is true that the "white power structure" was behind the events of May 13, in the sense that power in the U.S. remains in the hands of whites who most definitely knew of and sanctioned the massacre. It is also true that people like Sambor and Richmond must have been very aware of what kind of neighborhood they ended up letting burn down in their zeal and determination to silence Black rebels.

But there is also the inescapable truth that Mayor Goode was deeply involved in this planned elimination of MOVE, even to an important degree before he became mayor as the city's managing director. Further, even if all the facts pointing to his complicity and conscious participation in the massacre were to be left aside, even if it were to be agreed despite all the evidence to the contrary that Goode's only guilt lay in his powerlessness to stop this towering crime, all that this would amount to is an admission of the bottom-line bankruptcy of Black electoral politics and the strategy of "Black empowerment." For the plain truth is that with or without the Mayor Goodes – but much more preferably with them because such "Black faces in high places" play a key role in confusing and politically paralyzing many who might not otherwise be paralyzed – the country's armed and other reactionary agents will carry out their "responsibilities," particularly against Blacks, other minorities, and all other rebellious elements.

A prime example of this is what the authorities, including Wilson Goode and other Black officials, had in mind for Ramona Africa. For even as the commission labored to protect the real murderers, these officials, as a major part of continuing their tactic of blaming the massacre on the victims themselves, would put the only surviving adult of that massacre on trial.

8 | The Trial

On January 6, 1986, the City of Philadelphia began its trial of Ramona Africa. The charges against her included aggravated assault – on police officers; simple assault – on police officers; conspiracy – to assault police officers; reckless endangerment – of police officers; riot; and resisting arrest. Conviction on all counts could mean over sixty years in prison. The only surviving adult victim of a murderous assault was to be tried as its perpetrator, while its actual perpetrators were to be portrayed as its victims.

But Ramona Africa had other ideas. Functioning as her own attorney, she attacked the authorities and argued that it was not she who should be judged. When Judge Michael R. Stiles began the trial by reading the charges against her, Ramona Africa retorted that these should be brought against "the people who tried to kill me and my family. You know a bomb was dropped on me and my family. Police officers have acknowledged that they have fired 10,000 rounds of ammunition on me and my family. If that's not assault, if that's not recklessly endangering, if that's not, in fact, murder, even according to the description you have of aggravated assault and conspiracy, I don't know what is."[1]

The authorities had chosen these particular charges with a completely different purpose in mind. In fact, at a preliminary hearing six months before the trial, certain other charges that also had been leveled against Ramona Africa were dropped because they did not conform to this purpose. Dropped, for example, were those assault and endangerment charges which stemmed from police accounts of what happened in the alley as MOVE people tried to escape their burning house. The technical basis for dropping these charges was the court's finding that at the time Ramona Africa ran into the alley, she was no longer acting in concert with other MOVE members who were supposedly assaulting and endangering the lives of police by allegedly shooting at them. But rather than representing some kind of legal fairness, what this did was to eliminate charges that would have focused attention on what actually happened in the alley — and the less said about that the better.

All the charges left standing against Ramona Africa, including several other assault and endangerment charges, pertained only to allegations of criminal acts leading up to and encompassing the morning hours of May 13. The jurors were specifically instructed by prosecutor Joseph McGill not to consider anything that happened after 8 a.m. on May 13, which eliminated, in addition to the events in the back alley, the bombing and the subsequent destruction of the neighborhood.

In this way, any discussion of what really happened on that day was being ruled out of order, while the prosecution was still free to accuse Ramona Africa (and the dead MOVE members) of provoking the authorities and assaulting the police early in the morning. There was thus a great deal riding on trying to get a conviction on these particular charges, since the city would then be in a better position to justify not only its targetting of MOVE in general, but also the specific tactics it carried out on May 13 as a necessary and unavoidable response to MOVE's aggression.

This strategy went hand in hand with a dominant theme of the commission hearings — which had concluded approximately two months before the trial began — that MOVE was the instigator. At the same time, the fact that the trial took place before the commission had issued its report in March 1986 enhanced the prosecution's and judge's position that the bomb, fire, and deaths of MOVE people were not appropriate matters for the jury to consider since these were still being deliberated upon by another body.[2]

The trial also shared with the commission hearings an atmosphere of intimidation. The courtroom and surrounding area were under heavy security. Those attending the trial had to walk through a metal detector and also had to write down their names and addresses on a sheet of paper left in full view of officers from Civil Affairs and the Major Investigations Division. And with the police and press taking up many of the courtroom seats, others, including MOVE supporters, were told they couldn't attend because there was no more space.

The same kind of atmosphere was being created more broadly as well. For example, as the trial began, the Sunday magazine section of the *Philadelphia Inquirer* contained a cover story on John Africa, depicting him as a lunatic messiah with some kind of maniacal ability to turn people against the system.[4] Prosecutor McGill picked up on this theme on the first day of the trial, emphasizing to the jury in his opening remarks that MOVE was "rigid in its resolve to a philosophy which they, in their own words, call revolution."[4] It was a theme that McGill would return to frequently, including in his final remarks to the jury where he called for a conviction of Ramona Africa because MOVE is a "dangerous cult...dedicated to total revolution," and characterized MOVE as "the most dangerous people to deal with."[5]

But Ramona Africa was not daunted by such efforts. Each day, under heavy guard and with her burn-scarred arms manacled behind her, she would enter the courtroom shouting, "Long Live John Africa! Down with this rotten-ass system!" During her trial she argued that it was the authorities who had conspired to murder her comrades and that they had a history of violence against MOVE. MOVE defendants in previous trials had been gagged, beaten, and removed from court for making such statements.[6] But this time the authorities could not afford such overt displays of censorship and brutality. Too much had already been exposed, including through the recently concluded commission hearings, and it was necessary to avoid any public perception of a railroad.

But what was a delicate situation for the authorities provided openings and opportunities for Ramona Africa. In fact, Ramona Africa's handling of her defense caught the authorities by surprise, and the decision to allow her to act as her own attorney proved a disastrous one for them.

In allowing Ramona Africa to defend herself, the authorities had gambled on her being disruptive and easily goaded into courtroom outbursts which would then provide them with a pretext for coming down on her. But she was both confident and defiant, composed yet angry, and never the kind of raving lunatic MOVE members had been built up to be. The sheriff's deputies and other cops who policed the courtroom and the throng of media-types watching over her every move failed to intimidate Ramona Africa. And as the trial progressed, her command over the proceedings and ability to wage an effective defense won her considerable respect, including from those not sympathetic toward MOVE.

Thus the authorities had to swerve delicately between trying to thwart Ramona Africa's determined efforts to put the city on trial, while at the same time trying to maintain the appearance of legal fairness and impartiality. For instance, the prosecution objected to her calling Wilson Goode and Gregore Sambor to the witness stand, arguing that their testimony was not relevant to the case, and that her only reason for subpoenaing them – along with bomb-maker Klein and bomb-dropper Powell – was to focus on the bombing of MOVE, which Prosecutor McGill had already declared off limits. But despite these objections, Judge Stiles did call on Goode and Sambor to testify. On the other hand, Powell and Klein were not called and instead were allowed to plead Fifth Amendment rights against self-incrimination in the judge's private chambers.

McGill repeatedly admonished the jurors to ignore the "trigger words" of "fire, bomb, death." He tried to have the children of MOVE supporters barred from the courtroom, calling their presence a ploy for jurors' sympathies, and also objected to Ramona Africa taking off her jacket because it made the scars on her arms visible.

But while arguing that the bombing, fire, and deaths of eleven people had nothing to do with the charges against Ramona Africa, the prosecutor found nothing objectionable about his own introduction of physical evidence which had bomb and fire written all over it, as he attempted to substantiate the charges that Ramona Africa had resisted arrest and had conspired with other MOVE members to assault the police – a critical component in justifying the massacre. What Ramona Africa was being ordered not to do the prosecution could. For instance, surveillance photographs of the front bunker on MOVE's roof before it was bombed were handed to the jury. This bunker, said McGill, was a "fortress which by itself shouts resistance."[7]

McGill also had a dumpster wheeled into the courtroom containing what was identified as part of the bunker recovered after the bombing and fire. Soot-covered metal and burned, bullet-riddled wood remnants were displayed and inspected for gunports. For days this dumpster was wheeled down the corridor past people waiting to get into the courtroom as a grim and blatant reminder of how a group of Black radicals had been dealt with.

Further, the linchpin in the prosecution's case against Ramona Africa was the charge of conspiracy, which meant that even if no direct evidence could be brought against her, she could still be held accountable for anything that other MOVE members were supposed to have done, even though they were not on trial and couldn't have defended themselves if they had been since they were dead. To establish conspiracy, a tape-recording of speeches alleged to have been the voices of Ramona Africa, Frank Africa, and Theresa Africa, and containing threats against the police and Mayor Goode, was played in court. Most of the tape was unintelligible, but the jury heard what the prosecution wanted them to hear as George Draper of Civil Affairs read aloud from the transcript of the speech, which Draper himself had helped to prepare.[8]

McGill also introduced into evidence a letter which the police claimed they received two days before the assault, bearing the alleged signature of Ramona Africa. She does not acknowledge having written this letter, which also contains various threats against the police and also threats to burn down neighboring houses in the event the police attacked.[9] The contents of this letter, which were not made known publicly until nearly a week after the assault, support the authorities' contention that MOVE planned to burn down the block. The letter also happens to be allegedly signed by the only adult survivor of the assault and therefore could be used as strong evidence against her.

But the prosecution failed to bring out that on Saturday, May 11, the night that the police claim to have received this threatening letter, two stakeout officers disguised as workmen were in the house next door to MOVE attempting to insert spike mikes into the walls. These mikes were intended to determine the exact number of people who were in the MOVE house and exactly where they were located — valuable information for the police when they would attempt to zero in on their targets two days later on May 13. But according to police testimony at the commission hearings, these two made enough noise to alert the MOVE people, who began to shout and bang on the wall to drive them away.

For all the threats that MOVE is said to have made against the police, no harm was done to these two, although there was a clear provocation. The prosecution also neglected to mention that by the time of the trial, the city's allegation that MOVE was responsible for the fire by pouring gasoline on neighboring houses had been thoroughly exposed and discounted. Even the city's fire marshal had contradicted police claims that MOVE had started the fire, and revealed that its actual cause was the bomb.

To strengthen the case against Ramona Africa and the portrayal of victims as perpetrators and perpetrators as victims, the prosecution brought several stakeout unit cops to the stand to testify that they had been fired upon by MOVE on May 13. One of them was Sgt. Connor, leader of insertion team B which had been hurling explosive charges that had blown out much of the front of MOVE's house early in the morning of May 13 and had possibly, according to Connor himself, severed the head of a MOVE member. Connor testified that after he had set off the first charge, he was spun around by an unknown force and then struck in the back by a bullet fired from MOVE's position. The prosecution produced Connor's coverall and bullet-proof vest with a hole in them, along with a bullet said to have been dug out of the vest. Another officer, one of those who went souvenir hunting in the ruins of Osage Avenue, testified that a bullet fired from MOVE's position, six houses away and across the street from where he was located, struck the back of his protective helmet, cut the chain of his gold medal and creased his neck as he was reloading his M-16. A third officer claimed that on May 13 he was almost struck by a MOVE bullet.[10] The prosecution also introduced police department photographs said to have been taken inside one of the police firing positions and which indicated bullet marks on walls which police claimed came from MOVE fire.[11]

This was all the prosecution could muster in its attempt to prove that the police had come under fierce MOVE fire. McGill called no one to testify about the bullet fragments found in the bodies of three MOVE people, or about the ten thousand rounds of ammunition fired at MOVE. The prosecution did also produce melted, bent metal frames and pipelike objects which police identified as once having been two shotguns, a rifle, and two handguns they say they took from the Osage Avenue wreckage. The condition of these objects stood as moot and perhaps unintended testimony to the heat and intensity of the blaze; even the prosecution's ballistics expert said the guns were so thoroughly destroyed that he could not tell if they had ever been fired.[12] And while McGill called an officer to testify that bodies of MOVE members were found lying next to these weapons, thus implying these weapons belonged to and had been used by them, the prosecutor did not call anyone to describe the horribly burned and dismembered condition of most of those bodies.[13]

But the government did not limit its case against Ramona Africa and MOVE to retrieved bunker parts, tape recordings with alleged threats by MOVE members, a threatening letter allegedly written by Ramona Africa, or the twisted remains of a few weapons. Throughout the trial the prosecution attempted to depict MOVE as subhuman terrorists who got what they deserved. For instance, Ramona Africa called various defense witnesses, among them imprisoned MOVE members whom McGill grilled about their views on self-defense, knowing that MOVE would not hesitate to state these convictions and hoping to elicit damaging statements.

But the MOVE witnesses were able to confound McGill, as they used his hostile questioning about their alleged violent past to expose the long history of violent attacks against MOVE. Janine and Phil Africa explained how their three-week-old infant, Life, was crushed to death by police in 1976. Others provided graphic testimony of the Powelton Village police attack on August 8, 1978.

MOVE members also explained their principles of self-defense. They argued it was not they who were violent, but the system; that they would defend themselves if attacked but had no use or respect for weapons, as they said the system did. Said one MOVE member to McGill, "I will use what you believe in to show how dangerous you are."[14] Delbert Africa, who testified about how he had been beaten as he attempted to surrender on August 8, 1978, also commented that if someone came at him with a fist, he would respond with a fist. If he were attacked with a stick, he would fight back with a stick. "If you come at me with a gun," he said, "I'd be foolish to come at you with a feather."[15]

Delbert Africa also responded to McGill's questions about MOVE's possession of weapons by saying that if the prosecutor really found weapons so upsetting he should demand that the gun manufacturers be closed down. He asked why did a group of Black radicals supposedly possessing weapons get the authorities so nervous, while all the atomic bombs that are ready to go off did not? Then when McGill accused Delbert Africa of having issued verbal threats against the system, and of extensive cursing, Delbert Africa replied, "There's nothing more profane than a billy club. No four-letter word ever beat me."[16] Phil Africa added that if he joined the army tomorrow, "you'd want me to fight for your beliefs," and then pointed to the Vietnam War and U.S. invasion of Grenada as examples.[17]

The testimony of Sue Africa, a white member of MOVE, marked one of the most heated and emotional moments of the trial. While prosecutor McGill objected numerous times to Ramona Africa's questions to Sue Africa, both women would ignore him as well as Judge Stiles and would continue to speak. When the judge admonished the women to abide by the court's procedures, Ramona Africa answered, "I know my family was killed because of courtroom procedures . . . what kind of protocol and procedures were used on May 13?"[18]

Sue Africa has been in prison for several years, convicted on charges stemming from the appearance of armed MOVE members in front of their Powelton Village house on May 20, 1977. She testified that for the past three years she had been kept in solitary confinement, and that for the nine months before the trial she had been kept in the hole and denied any fresh air or exercise. She was taken to the hole on May 13, 1985, when guards came to inform her that her son, Tomaso, one of the children inside 6221 Osage Avenue that day, was dead.

Sue Africa asked why was Ramona Africa on trial when Mayor Goode, who she said was responsible for May 13, was still running the city. Why, she asked, should anyone accept what Goode did because he is Black? She criticized the U.S., calling it the "so-called champion of human rights" that dropped a bomb on MOVE. McGill continued to object strenuously; Judge Stiles continued to sustain McGill's objections; and Sue Africa continued to speak over them. She countered, "I had a baby. I was told he was killed . . . I can't sit up here and clinically discuss the death of my son like a piece of paper. [The] murderer who did this is still running the city."[19]

When she stated, "I want to know why the cops who dropped the bomb and made the bomb don't have to come to court to testify," Judge Stiles ordered the jurors removed from the courtroom. Until that point the jurors did not know that Lt. Powell and Officer Klein had pleaded Fifth Amendment rights and that Stiles had ruled they did not have to appear in court. With the jury gone, the judge told Sue Africa that if she refused to abide by court procedures he would not allow her to testify any further and would strike what she had already said from the record. Ramona Africa retorted that the judge, in ordering Sue Africa to submit to the court procedures of the same legal system which legally murdered her son, was telling her to sanction that murder. She also criticized Judge Stiles' role at the trial: "The cops, the whole city of Philadelphia, is trying to wash the blood off their hands and they are using you as the water and you're going along with it." She added, "I'm not on trial. You are. The city of Philadelphia is on trial."[20]

Among those representing the City of Philadelphia at the trial were Mayor Goode and former police commissioner Sambor, whose appearance over vehement prosecution objections was another indication of the continuing inability of the authorities to remove themselves from the ongoing controversy. Ramona Africa's first question to Mayor Goode was, "Are you a liar?" Prosecutor McGill's immediate objection was sustained. But it quickly became apparent why Goode was not permitted to answer this question, as he spun a web of falsehood about how concerned he had been for the safety and lives of the MOVE people. Ramona Africa asked him if he was concerned that innocent MOVE members had been sentenced to thirty to one hundred years in prison for the Powelton Village assault; if he was concerned when he authorized the bombing of the Osage Avenue house, even though he had heard that there might be gasoline in it. She also asked Goode to explain what he meant when he said on the afternoon of May 13 before the bomb was dropped that he intended to evict, evacuate, and seize control of the MOVE house by any means necessary.

In response to these questions, Goode could only attempt to distance himself from the events of May 13, testifying that no one had told him a bomb was to be dropped, that he had only authorized the use of an "entry device" and really wasn't up on the details of the plan since that was the province of the police department. As for his threat to use any means necessary, Goode said all he meant to do was arrest four people, take the children into custody for an examination, and search the house. Throughout his testimony, Mayor Goode demonstrated that he still felt it was better to look the fool than the person who presided over a murderous assault.[21]

Most of the questions Ramona Africa addressed to Sambor were ruled out of order by Judge Stiles, but she continued to ask them anyway: Did he come to arrest or kill MOVE people? What warrants did the police have for the children who were shot in the back alley? What charges were MOVE members wanted on? (Sambor testified that he didn't know.) What were MOVE members not named in the arrest warrant wanted for when a bomb was dropped on them? What charges justified dropping a bomb and burning people alive? Was it Sambor who ordered the MOVE children to be shot, and when is fire used as a means to apprehend anyone?

Sambor's basic response was to blame MOVE adults for the deaths of the children, accusing MOVE of having a history of using their children as a shield against the police. This brought an angry response from Ramona Africa, who asked him to explain – since pregnant MOVE women had been beaten by police into miscarriages; since in 1978 MOVE adults had to hold babies over their heads to keep them from drowning as water was sent pouring into the basement of their Powelton Village home; since the police had trampled to death a MOVE infant in 1976 – how would MOVE ever think that their children could offer any kind of protection from the police?[22]

In a letter that Ramona Africa had sent to supporters during this period, she addressed the same issue. She asked how could anyone suggest that MOVE should have sent their children out to the police on May 13 when "It is *never* suggested that Jews should have turned their babies over to Nazi soldiers instead of resistin em." She also wrote: "This system dropped an atomic bomb on Nagasaki n Hiroshima knowing there are women and babies there. U.S. soldiers burned and pillaged Vietnamese villages, murdering innocent women n children. This system got a history of killing women n babies, so what would make anybody think that we of MOVE would assume that having kids in the house would be any *protection* or make cops less likely to try to kill us?"[23]

Sambor also testified, in an attempt to have his cake and eat it too, that he had not seen the extensive damage done to the MOVE house on the morning of May 13, but at the same time argued that the rooftop bombing was necessary because any more lateral entries were too dangerous since the MOVE house was in danger of collapsing. Similarly, Sambor admitted that he gave his subordinates authorization to go outside the department to acquire powerful weaponry, but then denied he knew what weapons, including an M-60 which was fired from the very same post that Sambor inhabited frequently on May 13, were on the scene that day.[24] When Sambor asserted that MOVE had intentionally provoked a police confrontation, Ramona Africa replied, "Is it your belief that MOVE people could order police officers to come to our house, to shoot at us, to bomb us, and to burn us up alive?" Sambor's only response was to deny the police had done any of that.

Ramona Africa also called Birdie Africa to testify. During the nine-month period between the massacre and the trial, Birdie Africa's father and others had continued their efforts to integrate him into mainstream society. On May 29, the *Philadelphia Daily News* wrote, "Imagine a 13-year-old boy who can't read or write, who has never worn a baseball glove, never had toys, never eaten a Popsicle, never dreamed of what he wants to be when he grows up. Birdie Africa, who has lived in a communal MOVE house since he was 2, left Children's Hospital of Philadelphia yesterday to start discovering all those things – the world as most children know it."[25]

Untold millions of children around the globe undoubtedly would have something to say about the world as they really know it, which has much more to do with hunger, oppression, and early death than popsicles, toys, and baseball gloves. But Birdie Africa was to be brought into a different world, with an eye toward using him against his former MOVE family and Ramona Africa. His name was the first thing to be changed. His father, Andino Ward Sr., would not countenance the MOVE name of Birdie Africa, and he also no longer cared for the name he and Birdie's mother, Rhonda Ward Africa, had chosen as his original birth name, Oyewolffe (Arabic for prince) Momer Puim. Andino Ward renamed his son Michael Moses Ward. "Basically, it's not so much what he wants to be called," explained Andino Ward, "but what I want to call him."[26]

Next to go were Birdie Africa's dreadlocks. As the *Philadelphia Daily News* wrote approvingly, "His close-to-the-head hairstyle now resembles his father's."[27] But his father had to admit that this didn't happen without some difficulty: "It took him a week to accept the idea. For a while he rubbed his head. I told him, 'You miss that hair, don't you?'"[28]

His father also had the task of telling Birdie Africa that his mother, Rhonda Africa, was dead, consumed in the May 13 flames. The authorities offered to provide "counseling" for Birdie Africa free of charge, as he was reported to be suffering from intense nightmares. His father said, "He related one to me where he dreamt the whole world was on fire."[29]

Such nightmares are certainly understandable, but when he testified at Ramona Africa's trial it was apparent that any "counseling" that might have been attempted had not achieved the desired effect of making him more pliable and less resistant to the prosecution's tactics. Birdie Africa remained unrattled as the prosecution fired questions designed to get him to testify against Ramona Africa: "Did you ever hear the words Minister of Defense?" "Do you know what the word bunker means?" "Do you know who built the bunker?" "Did you ever hear the word confrontation?" Prosecutor McGill also asked Birdie Africa if he heard Ramona Africa say on the morning of May 13 that if the police came they would be killed.[30]

The prosecution also claimed that on May 13 the MOVE adults had refused to allow Birdie Africa and the other children to leave. But Birdie Africa testified that when told by the adults to leave the burning house, the children were afraid they might never see the adults again and didn't want to go. Prosecutor McGill also was anxious to make it known that it was the police who had saved Birdie Africa from drowning in the back alley. But to the question of whether the police had in fact performed this heroic act, Birdie Africa replied, "I got up on my own and started running." "And when you ran," asked the prosecutor, "did you fall into the water?" McGill appeared crestfallen when Birdie replied, "No. They grabbed me under here," as he pointed to his armpits and described how the police had dragged him away.[31] And when questioned by Ramona Africa, Birdie Africa repeated the account he had given fire department and other investigators in the immediate aftermath of the massacre: that MOVE people were prevented from exiting the back of the house by police gunfire; that in addition to Ramona Africa and himself, two other children had come out of the house; and that from the early morning hours until their exit, he and Ramona Africa were in the basement and that at no time did Ramona Africa have a weapon.[32]

In her closing statement to the jury, Ramona Africa argued that there was no evidence to convict her of anything, but mounds of evidence of a conspiracy by the authorities to kill MOVE people. She spoke of MOVE's determination to free the nine members who had been imprisoned for the death of James Ramp, of how after all legal appeals had been exhausted they had taken to their Osage Avenue loudspeakers to carry on the campaign. If she was to be found guilty of anything, she said, "I'm guilty of taking a firm stand."[33]

But on Sunday, February 9, 1986, the jury found Ramona Africa guilty of riot and conspiracy, charges for which she faced a possible seven to fourteen years in prison. The riot conviction held that she, along with the other MOVE members who were now dead, engaged in disorderly conduct to facilitate the committing of a felony, tried to coerce official action by demanding the release of imprisoned MOVE members, and planned for the illegal use of weapons. The conspiracy conviction held that she was party to the planning and aiding of the same – in essence, it was a way of convicting her two times for the same alleged offense.

The authorities welcomed the conviction and immediately tried to use it to put the official stamp of approval on their deadly assault against MOVE. The *Philadelphia Inquirer*, in its editorial on the verdict, wrote that the jury held Ramona Africa "accountable in part for MOVE's behavior in subjecting a neighborhood to prolonged abuse – including amplified harangues night after night and flagrant disregard for the basic rights of others. That was a reasonable finding. . . ."[34]

At the same time, the city failed to get convictions on ten other counts, including aggravated assault on police officers and endangering their lives. The three counts of aggravated assault were the most serious and each carried a possible sentence of ten years. The disappointment in not getting these convictions was apparent from the stunned silence of the cops who were in the courtroom when the verdict was read. The *New York Times* wrote of their reaction: "They said her acquittal on assault charges represented a stinging rebuke to police officers who testified that they had been shot at in the confrontation . . ."[35] Another officer, in an overt threat, said that "the government better realize they got to find a way to deal with these people or it's going to happen again."[36]

The failure of the authorities to win these more severe convictions was a reflection of the difficulties they still were having in blaming the massacre on MOVE while covering up their own role. In fact, after rendering their verdict, some of the jurors themselves expressed mixed views to reporters. Some said that the verdict was meant to indicate that both MOVE *and* the police were wrong. Some also felt that MOVE members "didn't come out [of 6221 Osage Avenue] because they feared for their lives."[37] As for Ramona Africa, she told reporters after the verdict was delivered that if the legal system were fair, "I would not have been here in the first place." As she was led out of the heavily guarded courtroom in handcuffs, she shouted to supporters: "Long life John Africa! Down with this rotten-ass system!"

On Monday, April 14, 1986, Ramona Africa was back in court to hear her sentence: sixteen months to seven years in a state penitentiary. Prosecutor McGill praised the sentence, although he also complained that it wasn't severe enough. In expressing his sentiments to reporters, he wasted no words in getting to the heart of the matter: "I would have preferred a more serious sentence, because I think it's important that a message go out to any kind of urban revolutionaries that this kind of conduct will indeed be punished."[38]

But many people did not accept this message, and although the authorities had not succeeded in getting the maximum fourteen-year sentence that Ramona Africa faced, there were many who were outraged that she was sentenced to anything at all. Weeks before the sentencing, people had launched a campaign demanding that she be released. A leaflet issued by an ad hoc coalition called for a rally at City Hall on the day that Ramona Africa was to be sentenced. This leaflet read in part: "May 13, 1985, marks a turning point, a leap, in the repression of Black people in this country. Atrocities of this magnitude cannot go unchallenged. And a key part of this battle is whether or not Ramona Africa walks free. . . . It's key because all along the attempts to justify this massacre have been linked to blaming the victims. . . ."

The call to release Ramona Africa received widespread support and was endorsed by a number of organizations. On the weekend prior to the sentencing, Reverend Paul Washington, one of the members of Mayor Goode's commission, sent a letter to Judge Stiles asking that Ramona Africa be released with time already served. Wrote Washington: "I question at this time, in the light of what Ramona Africa has endured both in her house as well as in jail since that date, if there is still reason to sentence her to a continued period of incarceration."[39] This position was supported by another commission member, Reverend Audrey Flora Bronson. The fact that two members of the mayor's own commission were calling for Ramona Africa's release made it more difficult for Judge Stiles to hand down a more severe sentence. It also provided more openings for even greater opposition, including among those who had previously been hesitant to speak out.

At the April 14 rally itself, two banners were draped on the walls of City Hall, in one of whose courtrooms Ramona Africa was to be sentenced. One banner read, "Free Ramona Africa," and the other, "Murderers! Murderers! No More!" Nearly five hundred people signed a petition that day calling for her release, and in all over two thousand people had signed the petition, which was submitted to Judge Stiles. A group of older Black men and women, some of whom had come to the trial every day, stretched another "Free Ramona Africa" banner across the sidewalk, and hundreds gathered to listen to various speakers.

A Black youth stepped up to the microphone to say: "I'm pretty sure you hear about terrorists every day on your television. What they don't tell you about is things like this. They cry about getting terrorists out of Italy. They cry about getting terrorists out of Great Britain. They cry about getting terrorists out of Germany. But what about here?. . .What about the new world, America? On May the 13th Qadhafi didn't send no Libyans over here to terrorize. It was the man in the blue car, the flakjacket with the utility belt around his waist. He was the terrorizer."[40]

Other speakers addressed themselves to the controversial question of a Black mayor having presided over the massacre of Black people, a point which was continuing to confuse and politically paralyze many. One Black woman said, "I'm sick and tired of people talking about the mayor. He knew what was going down and people better realize that in this city. It was MOVE on May the 13th and it will be us tomorrow."[41]

Inside the courtroom, Ramona Africa spoke for an hour before being sentenced. She said: "I was sentenced on May 13. I was sentenced when hundreds of cops came to my house. I was sentenced when my skin was burned off my body, scarring me for life, when 10,000 bullets were fired in less than 90 minutes, when thousands of pounds of water was forced on me, when I saw my family burned up and shot down in the alley. . . . I'm here simply because I'm a MOVE member and I survived."[42] She also told Judge Stiles that "You would put black South Africans in prison right now for resisting the racist regime in South Africa," and added that just as someone who puts his hand in fire will surely be burned, as long as people are wronged "resistance is inevitable."[43]

As news of the sentence filtered outside the courtroom and into the hallway where hundreds had gathered, anger boiled up and people began to chant, "She shouldn't have got a day!" Nervous police officers conceded the hallway to the protestors but then positioned themselves at both ends of the corridor, apparently to block access to the mayor's office which was just around the corner. Novella Williams, one of the community activists who had pleaded with Mayor Goode on May 13 to end the confrontation peacefully, told reporters, "We don't want Ramona Africa in jail and we're not going to stop until she's out of jail. . . . Those individuals who dropped the bomb, allowed the fire to burn, killed eleven people, must be brought to the bar of justice."[44]

One month later, on May 13, 1986, numbers of people gathered at various places in Philadelphia to mark the first anniversary of the MOVE massacre. At an all-night vigil, at marches and in speeches and verse, the bombing and massacre were strongly condemned. As for the actions of the city officials on this day, while putting on a remorseful face for public consumption, they spent much of their actual time attempting to stop one of the commemorations and heavily policing all of the others. This included the setting up of a "situations room" from which police pegged on a map of the city every movement of the commemorators.

On May 12, the day on which the 24-hour vigil was set to begin in a West Philadelphia park, Mayor Goode revoked the permit that had been previously granted. The vigilers, many of them active MOVE supporters, proceeded despite Goode's provocative act and the threat that police would clear the park. (A federal judge stepped in at the last minute to restore the permit, but by then the vigilers had decided to continue with or without legal sanction.)[45] Strung on trees in the park was a large banner declaring, "Don't Mourn, Organize." At its height the vigil drew about 250 people.

Relatives of MOVE members who had died on May 13 held a procession to Osage Avenue. Some teenagers carried a banner that read, "Long Live MOVE, Long Live John Africa's Revolution." At 5:27 p.m., the time when the bomb had been dropped a year ago, the relatives lit candles and kept them lit for thirty seconds, to mark just how long Mayor Goode said he had paused before approving the bombing. At that very moment a helicopter hovered overhead; its identity remained unknown, but its presence was an ominous and seemingly deliberate reminder of what had happened exactly one year ago.[46]

There was also a march from North Philadelphia on May 13, 1986, ending in a noon rally at City Hall at which numerous speakers denounced the bombing, with opinions ranging from those who considered it a gross violation of people's rights, to

others like a group of poets, the New African Griots, who performed a poem featuring a refrain borrowed from Police Commissioner Sambor as he prepared to unleash the assault: "This *is*
America!" Some speakers criticized those Black leaders who had
failed to speak out against the massacre, and also those Black
clergy who had been sponsoring prayer vigils for Mayor Goode.
Organizers vowed to make May 13 an annual day of remem-
brance in Philadelphia of the bombing and massacre of MOVE.[47]

As for Wilson Goode, while attempting to stop the 24-hour
vigil and sending his armed squads out to keep a careful eye on
the other activities, in a written statement he said of May 13,
1985: "This is a time of healing and renewal."[48] But people's anger
would not abate and, for many, their understanding of what the
massacre signified continued to deepen even as the mayor and
the other authorities continued their efforts to politically disarm
people with their talk about healing and conciliation.

On the occasion of the anniversary, one Black woman from
North Philadelphia said, "They did it to eliminate people who oppose this government."[49] And the words of another Black woman
from North Philadelphia's teeming and volatile ghettos undoubtedly caused shudders not only among city officials but
among other authorities far and wide: "It's not over just 'cause *they*
say it's over. It's *not* over yet."[50]

9 | The Larger Context

In the late 1960s, as the U.S. was wracked by ghetto rebellions, large and militant antiwar demonstrations, and other forms of major political unrest, alarmed federal, state, and local officials moved to strengthen their ability to contain and suppress these outbreaks. In 1966-67, for example, the nation's first SWAT team – SWAT stands for "Special Weapons and Tactics" – was formed in Los Angeles and soon distinguished itself in such forays as the 1969 full-scale assault on Black Panther headquarters, resulting in the wounding of four Panther members, and then in 1974 in the fierce attack on and killing of six members of the Symbionese Liberation Army.

Today, government authorities consider Los Angeles SWAT, which has grown considerably in size and sophistication over the last two decades, "one of the best" of the SWAT squads that now exist in almost every major U.S. city. Thus it is noteworthy that L.A. Police Chief Daryl Gates decided, in the immediate aftermath of the MOVE massacre, to send one of his SWAT leaders to Philadelphia to see what pointers could be picked up. Gates then subsequently reported on *Face the Nation* that his SWAT man came back "very impressed with the professional quality of the tactics of the Philadelphia Police Department."[1]

In point of fact, this was essentially, but not entirely, true. Gates's representative, Lieutenant Dan Cook, certainly didn't disagree with his boss about the need to conduct a massive assault to eliminate members of a radical Black group, but he did express some reservation about a couple of the tactics employed and suggested that the same results might have been more effectively achieved with the use of a tank, since the L.A. SWAT team's own experience had demonstrated that tanks "can open up a brick house like butter."[2] Several other people who are considered experts on police procedures raised similar reservations about tactics. Gerald Arenberg, executive director of the American Federation of Police, a Miami-based national association which specializes in police training and "civil preparedness," said the Philadelphia police on May 13 "just weren't using all the equipment available to any modern police agency. Barricaded subjects with firearms are common in almost any major police department. You bring in an armored car, fire out of its portholes, ram down the doors. . . . You don't burn down the neighborhood."[3]

Such "differences" about the best way to silence MOVE in no way amounted to an indictment of the May 13 operation, and actually reflected a fraternal division of labor. While some like L.A. Police Chief Gates and U.S. Attorney General Edwin Meese III upheld the operation unequivocally (Gates, for example, even praised the controversial use of a bomb as a "sound tactic"), others, while also upholding the goal, used the opportunity to call for more professional, more technologically sophisticated, and less politically damaging techniques. Gerald Arenberg's main fear, for example, was that the May 13 assault and especially the ensuing fire "could set the Philadelphia Police Department back 15 years,"[4] and his and other experts' comments on how less politically costly means could have been employed echoed the views of people like Congressman John Conyers who, appearing on the same *Face the Nation* program as Gates, carped at the L.A. police chief's unalloyed enthusiasm for the May 13 operation and suggested that "there were any number of reasonably forceful alternatives that we could have employed that weren't."

An editorial in the *Chicago Sun-Times* expressed the same concern over how best to deal with groups like MOVE and the prospect of growing political unrest and rebellion. The last paragraph of this editorial urges city police departments to "re-examine their capabilities of dealing with violence prone demonstrators, not in the sure knowledge that 1960s-style disorder will resume, but in the security of knowing, should that need arise, that they have the training and skill to contain the lawless without mass violence, bloodshed and destruction."⁵

But while it can undoubtedly be argued that from the standpoint of protecting the economic and political interests of the prevailing order, there is perhaps never such a thing as *enough* military preparation for dealing with mass rebellion, and that urban police departments therefore must pay greater attention to improving their capabilities in this sphere, it also must be noted and underscored that in the last twenty years since that first SWAT team was formed in Los Angeles, officials on all levels of U.S. government have been engaged in a major effort to strengthen the country's "anti-terrorist" and counterinsurgency apparatus. This nationwide and well-coordinated campaign is being carried out largely in secrecy, including the fact that there has been a significant intensification of this effort over the last few years.

Indeed, many of the same "anti-terrorist" and counterinsurgency tactics and techniques that have been and are continuing to be developed for dealing with "enemies abroad" are now being developed and applied with increasing frequency to try and cope with "enemies at home." And underlying the stepped up pace of these domestic military preparations, as the counterinsurgency experts themselves frequently mention and openly worry about, is the growing possibility in their eyes of civil war in the U.S., concentrated in the nation's ghettos and other urban cores – in the context of all the international troubles the rulers of this country are having.

In this larger setting it becomes possible to understand more fully that the events in Philadelphia on May 13, 1985 did not represent some "tragic mistake" or bureaucratic bungling, or even simply the conscious conspiracy of a few local politicians who should be indicted for murder and thrown out of office, but one of the "first fruits" of a domestic military program that has been years in the making, has been coordinated at the highest levels of government, and has now been intensified in concert with Resurgent America's recently unleashed fascist offensive. It is in this larger context, for example, that it is possible to understand the murder that day of five children. One government expert, in testifying before Congress about the CIA's "counter-terror squads," explained quite well how such an atrocity could happen. He insisted on the need for violent "preemptive strikes" against opponents of the U.S., even if there are incidental "civilian casualties," and he then added that this was true *"whether you are talking about Lebanon or Philadelphia."*[6] In other words, the five MOVE children met the same fate, and essentially for the same reasons, as did the children in the Palestinian camps of Sabra and Shatila in 1982.

The beginnings of the U.S. government's effort to create this nationwide counterinsurgency network can be traced to the late 1960s, when officials fretted over the inability of police departments to handle the antiwar demonstrations and ghetto rebellions. In 1968, a Pentagon task force on civil disorder developed a program to try and deal with these upheavals. Dubbed "Operation Garden Plot," the program called for the extensive use of informants and infiltrators to gather intelligence on U.S. citizens who were in opposition to the government's foreign and domestic policies.[7]

"Operation Garden Plot" quickly evolved into annual training exercises, complete with contingency plans to cope with demonstrations and "riots." These plans were developed for every major U.S. city, and participants in these exercises included key officials from all of the nation's law enforcement agencies, along with representatives of the National Guard, the military, and the intelligence community.[8] The training exercises consisted primarily of joint teams reacting to various scenarios based on information gathered by informants and infiltrators. The object was "to quell urban unrest, and the different war games ranged from minor scuffles with a handful of protestors to serious confrontations between police and large mobs."[9]

By 1970, "Operation Garden Plot" moved from contingency plan to reality. On April 30 of that year, President Nixon announced the invasion of Cambodia, which was met by massive and highly militant demonstrations across the nation. These in turn were met by large numbers of police and National Guardsmen who attacked the demonstrators in strength along a broad front and in a clearly well-coordinated manner. This was particularly evident in California, where Governor Ronald Reagan and his associates had been some of the most enthusiastic participants in "Operation Garden Plot."

On May 26, state police, military, and intelligence officials met secretly in Sacramento to celebrate what they viewed as the success of their efforts against the demonstrators, and to plan for further such efforts. Governor Reagan's right-hand man, Edwin Meese III, addressed the group: "This is an ongoing effort, and is something that despite resistance, despite the activities of some who state this is overreacting, this is an operation, this is an exercise, this is an objective which is going forward...."[10]

Meese in this case spoke the truth. In 1971, Governor Reagan created a special school where law enforcement officials from all over the country could learn the latest tactics for battling civil disorders. To head this school, called the California Specialized Training Institute (CSTI), Reagan chose General Louis O. Giuffrida, a former California National Guard officer and a specialist in military police science. Among his other accomplishments, Giuffrida was one of those to pioneer the SWAT concept, which he likened to the U.S. Army's long-range reconnaissance patrols (LURPs) in Vietnam: "If you know about LURP, then you know what SWAT is – adapted, of course, to domestic needs in an urban setting."[11]

During his ten-year directorship of CSTI, the school trained over twenty-seven thousand officials from every state in the country and from twenty-five other countries as well – clearly demonstrating the close connection between fighting "enemies" at home and abroad. Giuffrida personally taught the California Civil Disorder Management Course, whose topics included: Unrest in Modern Society; Control Force Intelligence; Dissent, Disruptions, and Violence; Contemporary Insurgency; Terrorism; and Mass Arrest Procedures.[12]

At the same time, all during the 1970s and right up to today, "Operation Garden Plot" has continued to exist and remains a major program for the attempted suppression of political disorder or, to use the word preferred by authorities today, terrorism. A 1982 internal Pentagon document still describes Garden Plot as the guide for military response to civil disturbances "in the 50 states, District of Columbia, Commonwealth of Puerto Rico and U.S. territories and possessions, as directed by the President."[13]

But by no means has the U.S. government rested content with its Garden Plot. In 1978, the Carter Administration created a shadowy and secretive organization called the Federal Emergency Management Agency (FEMA). FEMA is supposed to be responsible for coordinating the federal response to natural and man-made disasters, such as floods, hurricanes, and chemical spills. But FEMA in fact spends little of its time and efforts on disasters of this variety, concentrating instead on what are perceived by the authorities as more worrisome and potentially catastrophic emergencies such as civil disturbances, sabotage, and, of course, the ubiquitous "terrorism." To FEMA has also fallen the responsibility of developing the highly secret "Continuity of Government" program, which is designed to ensure that the U.S. government will continue to function during and after a nuclear war. This program includes the creation of facilities buried deep in several mountains, as a guarantee that major government officials and other VIPs do not die along with everyone else. One such stronghold has been built in the Blue Ridge Mountain region of Virginia, about fifty miles from Washington, D.C. While almost nothing has been said of this facility, there have been a few reports indicating that it consists, among other things, of offices, residences, streets with electrically powered cars, and also a lake-size reservoir.[14]

FEMA – headed up since its inception and until 1985 by none other than General Louis O. Giuffrida, the same counterinsurgency expert to whom Ronald Reagan had earlier turned when he was governor of California – has been carrying out various war games that are similar to but also exceed in ambition those connected with "Operation Garden Plot." Every two years since 1978, FEMA has been conducting what are called "Rex exercises." Rex-82, for example, was held in conjunction with a Pentagon war game called "Proud Saber," and had as a major objective the testing of U.S. industry's ability to adjust quickly to full-scale wartime military production.[15]

The next exercise two years later, Rex-84, was shrouded in even greater secrecy than previous ones. From what little it has been possible to piece together, it appears that Rex-84 involved government response to some regional crisis, apparently in Central America, that spills into and intensifies a crisis in the U.S. itself. The "game" centered on a mass of refugees flooding across the U.S.-Mexican border, triggered perhaps by a U.S. invasion of Nicaragua. FEMA's job, with assistance from the Immigration and Naturalization Service, was to apprehend and detain four hundred thousand of these refugees in a six-hour period. The exercise also consisted of holding these refugees in detention camps at military bases across the country, and the rounding up of other protestors and dissidents along with them.[16]

As further preparation for the development of such a crisis, an internal Pentagon document, dated December 1, 1983, indicates how troops could be called out. The document, prepared by the Joint Chiefs of Staff, lists exceptions to the federal law that prohibits the military from operating within the U.S., and gives as its authority for such actions "the inherent legal right of the United

States Government to ensure the preservation of public order...by force if necessary."[17]

In essence, the plan outlined in this Pentagon document involves the declaration of martial law, including the "military assumption of judicial, law enforcement, and administrative functions of local government" which would be accomplished through "coordination between the Defense Department and FEMA at the national and regional levels. [Defense] commanders [with] planning and execution responsibilities are required to coordinate plans and procedures with FEMA."

And as an indication of concern that there be adequate force to carry out this plan, the document also states that "All military forces, Active and Reserve, and the National Guard, when federalized, are considered potentially available."[18] Further, the Army has been developing light infantry units, composed of reserve and National Guard troops, that are being stationed at strategic places around the country and can be used to move quickly into "trouble spots" in the urban cores. According to one military analyst, these infantry units "show a dual viability for urban fighting. There's only a few vehicles for a large number of men; therefore, they'll be walking. And they'll be able to insert an entire battalion into a city in one and a half hours."[19]

Another development that merits close attention is the "Joint Terrorist Task Force" (JTTF), which was formed in the early years of the Reagan Administration.[20] The creation of the JTTF marks the first time that there has existed in the U.S. a nationally coordinated police force, with a centralized command structure and a huge arsenal of sophisticated weaponry at its disposal. The FBI oversees the work of the JTTF, which is composed of a network of federal, state, and local law enforcement officers. The specific personnel and internal structure of this organization, however, are a closely guarded secret.

According to Frank Donner, author of *The Age of Surveillance*, the FBI's transfer of the military explosive C-4 to the Philadelphia Police Department in preparation for the deadly assault on MOVE is typical of the secret cooperation between JTTF and urban police agencies. "Increasingly," says Donner, "there's been intensive collaboration between the FBI and local police forces on threatened terrorist violence, through the Joint Terrorist Task Force," and the C-4 transaction "is definitely part of that kind of operation."[21]

The role of the FBI and other federal agencies, then, was

anything but incidental or "cursory," as Mayor Goode's Special Investigation Commission would have everyone believe. "Operation Garden Plot"; "Continuity of Government"; the Rex exercises; the "Joint Terrorist Task Force"; the entire counterinsurgency apparatus that has been developed over the last several years by the U.S. government, in cooperation and coordination with local police forces – *that* is what lies behind the murder of eleven Black radicals in Philadelphia on May 13, 1985.

It is this which also explains not only why there was such a vicious assault, but also the unprecedented nature of the events of May 13: hundreds of smoke and tear gas grenades; hundreds of thousands of gallons of water; ten thousand rounds of ammunition and the use of sophisticated military weaponry; and then capped off by the dropping of a bomb that ignites a fire which is allowed to burn as people are incinerated or shot as they try to escape the inferno. All of this after the so-called civil rights progress and with a Black mayor. Even a former lieutenant from the New York City Police Department felt compelled to draw the analogy of what U.S. troops did in Vietnam and then to draw the appropriate conclusion that this is the first time such a thing has happened within the U.S. itself: "They destroyed the village in order to save the village.... I can't think of any precedent for what the police did in this situation. It's really unheard of."[22]

Yet another strong indication of what the MOVE massacre represents, and what it foreshadows, is that in its aftermath the collaboration between the Philadelphia authorities and police and the FBI/JTTF and other federal agencies has not diminished or ceased. To the contrary, it has increased markedly. As Richard Poe remarks in his *East Village Eye* article:

> It seems that while the American public has already filed the MOVE bombing in the back of its mind – assuming no doubt that the whole "bungled" operation will eventually be sorted out in a just and reasonable manner – what has in fact occurred is that the Philadelphia authorities have gone on working hand-in-glove with every federal law enforcement agency in the book to ensure that in the future they will have the training, the equipment and the bureaucratic sanction to undertake more such actions, more efficiently, and with a greater degree of interdepartmental coordination.[23]

This question of upgrading training, equipment, and coordination is precisely what lay at the heart of the recommendations formulated by Mayor Goode's own Special Investigation

Commission in its final report published on March 6, 1985.
Among these recommendations were:

> In anticipation of possible crisis situations, such as MOVE's ap-
> parent preparation for a violent confrontation, the Mayor should
> institute a strategic planning process involving all relevant City
> agencies. . . .
>
> The City should promptly establish an integrated system for
> the collection, analysis and appropriate dissemination of relevant
> information relating to crises which affect public health, safety
> and welfare. . . .
>
> Energetic and continuing efforts should be mounted to im-
> prove the training. . .provided officers of the Police Department.
> Training. . .should be required for police officers who may be
> engaged in crisis incidents requiring specialized knowledge of
> firearms, intelligence gathering techniques, cultist or terrorist
> behavior and psychology, barricade or hostage situations and
> others. Such training should utilize not only departmental capabil-
> ities but the resources, where available, of the FBI and other
> appropriate governmental agencies.
>
> The Police Department should maintain a list of agencies and
> individuals knowledgeable in the use of explosives to permit
> ready access to expert views in case of need.
>
> In preparing and monitoring its tactical plans, the Police Depart-
> ment should utilize fully the capabilities and experience of other
> police departments, federal and state agencies and non-
> governmental experts.
>
> The City should maintain and periodically update a list of ex-
> perts who could be consulted on short notice in situations involv-
> ing hostages, cult groups, terrorist organizations, threatened use
> of explosives or other crisis situations. . . .[24]

Mayor Goode and the other Philadelphia authorities did not
bother to wait for these recommendations to be officially published, ten months after the Osage Avenue assault, before they
began to implement them. Apparently it was felt that there was
no time to lose. Just a couple of months after the massacre, Goode
and other city officials moved to establish a "Crisis Manage-
ment/Emergency Preparedness Program," complete with an
Emergency Operations Center, supervised by the city's managing
director, and an Office of Emergency Preparedness with its own
director who also serves as the managing director's principal
assistant regarding all emergency plans and operations.

Strikingly, the language employed to explain this program is

identical to descriptions of the responsibilities of FEMA. According to a "Facts Sheets for Press Briefing" that was published on
March 10, 1986, just four days after the release of the commission's report and with the obvious intention of explaining to the
public what had already been started months before, the scope of
situations the "Emergency Preparedness Program" exists to deal
with includes "severe weather emergencies to hazardous
chemical spills, from hostage takings to other serious incidents
where public safety might be at risk."[25]

Like FEMA, natural and man-made disasters are combined
with very different kinds of "emergencies" such as hostage takings. But also like FEMA, this program and the Operations Group
clearly are much more concerned about one kind of thing than
the other. For example, it is explained that the initial task of the
Operations Group "is the development of a plan for the handling
of any future activities involving the MOVE organization." This
included the continued police surveillance of the home of a
MOVE member, and also, in October of 1985, a highly coordinated operation involving the securing of another house of
MOVE supporters. Elaborate plans were developed for this operation – the Emergency Operations Center was activated, the tasks
of various departments were carefully calibrated and coordinated, etc. – and it was then defined as a success in which there
were no incidents or injuries. In this particular case that was
hardly a surprising outcome, since the residents had already
vacated the house before the operation was carried out. Nevertheless, the operation was important – both as a useful "dry run"
and also as an indication to MOVE and its supporters, and
beyond, that the city had no intention of reining in its attacks.

One month later, the Operations Group got a much better
chance to give the public an indication of what it existed to do. On
the nights of November 20 and 21, 1985, in a predominantly
white section of Southwest Philadelphia, racist crowds numbering in the hundreds gathered outside the homes of a Black family
and a racially mixed couple who had just moved into the neighborhood. In an obvious, and terrifying, reference to the MOVE
massacre, people in these mobs yelled, "We'll evict them . . . and
you know how we evict in Philadelphia," and, "We'll burn them
out." And while one of the families was away, people broke into
their house and wrecked the kitchen, furnace, and hot water
heater. A molotov cocktail was also found on the basement
floor.[26]

The city's response was a meeting of the Operations Group to discuss the situation. It was decided on November 22 that Mayor Goode should declare a state of emergency for the neighborhood in which all persons in groups of four or more would not be permitted to congregate. To implement the plan, a command post was set up in the neighborhood; police were stationed in the area with a "low-key presence"; members of the clergy, in cooperation with a neighborhood group, the Southwest Task Force, were asked to urge the crowds to remain calm and comply with the declaration; and the Crisis Intervention Network was assigned the task of patroling the area and, significantly, to prevent counterdemonstrations. The main idea, according to the Operations Group, was to intervene as minimally as possible and to rely on voluntary compliance with the mayor's declaration. Arrests were to be made only as a last resort.[27]

In a word, the mobs were to be handled with kid gloves and reasoned with. Police, Mayor Goode, and the other city officials stood by as though helpless to do anything, even as newspapers referred to the mobs as "demonstrators" and published the addresses of where members of the two Black families worked, thereby encouraging the "demonstrators" to continue their "protests" all day long. It wasn't long before the words Goode and oreo were being used interchangeably on Philadelphia's ghetto streets, and Black radio stations received many angry calls comparing how Goode had dealt with MOVE and how he was now dealing with the real terrorism visited on the two families by racist vigilantes.[28]

But at this point, some muscle was finally put into the mayor's state of emergency. The target, however, was not those who had been screaming for a lynching, but others who decided to conduct demonstrations to expose what was going on and to offer support to the two Black families. Thirty-four of *these* demonstrators were arrested – the first and only arrests that would be made during the mayor's state of emergency.[29]

Undoubtedly Mayor Goode and the Operations Group have learned such fine arts as who should and should not be arrested at such critical moments while sitting at the feet of FEMA and this federal agency's local clone, the Pennsylvania Emergency Management Agency, or PEMA. During the latter half of 1985 and all through 1986, key members of the Operations Group met with representatives of FEMA and PEMA. This included intensive five-day sessions led by FEMA at the Emergency Manage-

ment Institute/National Emergency Training Center in Emmits-
burg, Maryland. This was followed up in November 1986, also at
FEMA's Emergency. Management Institute, by another five-day
session devoted to FEMA's Integrated Emergency Management
Course, consisting of over two days of lectures, discussions, and
workshops and culminating in a special crisis simulation exercise. According to a FEMA spokesman, this course has been
offered for the last several years and "many communities have requested the course. Los Angeles, Fort Worth, Atlanta . . ."[30]

At the same time as all this has been going on, there also have
been major changes in the functioning of the Philadelphia Police
Department. Formal liaison has been established between it and
the FBI, the U.S. Secret Service, and other federal agencies, as
well as with the Los Angeles Police Department, the Houston
Police Department, and the police departments of other major
cities. It is also planned for members of the Ordinance Disposal
Unit – the bomb squad – to participate in national and international conferences on the use of explosives, and to consult with
outside experts.[31]

Plans also call for the creation of a "special operations unit"
within the tactical division of the Police Department, and officials waste no words in making clear what the function is of this
new outfit: "The purpose . . . will be to operate in teams, and have
the ability and training to take aggressive action against organized
groups and individuals who are engaged in or have the potential
for violent criminal activity."[32]

"Violent criminal activity" is of course today's official
euphemism for dangerous political rebellion. But particularly
noteworthy here is the phrase, "or have the potential." This can
have no other meaning than the intention of launching preemptive strikes against not only those who are deemed to be already
engaged in the "crime" of opposition, but also against all those
whom the authorities may pinpoint as even thinking about such
opposition.

This should come as no surprise. As Mayor Goode said to the
press on the night of May 13, 1985, "What we have going on here
is war." And it is important to note again that these words were
uttered not by some blatant reactionary like Frank Rizzo, but by
an elected Black official who presided over the massacre of
eleven Black radicals and who said in its aftermath that he took
full responsibility for it and would do it again.

This points to the important role that Black officials like

Wilson Goode are playing and are expected to continue to play in the counterinsurgency tactics that are presently being developed and implemented. In the 1960s, the absence of Blacks in key political positions helped to fuel the ghetto uprisings of that period, and also made it more difficult to suppress them. One of the things done in the effort to remedy that situation has been to foster the election of Black mayors and other Black officials who have often been able to fulfill the role of suppressing potential outbreaks among Black people more successfully than the whites who preceded them in these offices. These "Black faces in high places" have been able to diffuse the anger of especially Black people and to disorient many of those who had in the past been in the forefront of opposition to these attacks. These officials have also been able to serve as living examples of the "success" Black people are said to have achieved through traveling the electoral road to "Black empowerment" and as material inducement to divert broader sections of Black people and others down this path.

The response to the MOVE massacre shows that this strategy has had some effect. On the one hand, there have been many in the Black community who have condemned this atrocity and Goode's role in it. But at the same time, there have been others who have said that the massacre should not be condemned because it involved an elected Black official and if he is criticized it will become increasingly difficult to elect more Black officials.

The notion that the MOVE massacre should not be condemned so that more people like Wilson Goode, who claimed full responsibility for this crime, can get elected is rather ludicrous. But to the degree that this strategy can remain effective, the country's ruling forces can be expected to continue to employ it. (The Frank Rizzo's are also kept around, in case the powers-that-be feel the need to reactivate them or forces like them and return to previous methods of suppression.) In this context, the critical importance of understanding, and remembering, what happened in Philadelphia on May 13, 1985, must be stressed. Eleven Black radicals lost their lives in the war to which Wilson Goode referred, and in which he has consciously decided to participate on one side. MOVE has made it clear in its speeches, literature, and actions that it is not preparing to overthrow the existing social order by force of arms. But what MOVE does represent, and what this social order can tolerate today even less than it did in the past, is an indomitable and unrepentant spirit of rebellion.

From this standpoint, it can be appreciated that the murder of eleven Black rebels, rather than being a display of strength is really a sign of weakness. Those who carried out and sanctioned this massacre obviously fear such a rebellious spirit and are aware of its infectious quality and how rapidly it can spread, especially among this society's most downtrodden. For all its horror, then, the MOVE massacre points to a future without such horrors. It therefore must be learned from, and the eleven who fell on that spring day in the city of the Liberty Bell must be honored and not forgotten.

A | Black Activists and Artists Comment on May 13, 1985

Several respected activists and other well-known members of the Black community were asked for this book to share their opinions on what happened in Philadelphia on May 13, 1985. The following questions were submitted to them as a suggested guide for their responses: What do you believe is the principal cause or causes of what happened on May 13? What significance, if any, do you attach to the fact that these events occurred under the administration of a Black mayor? What do you think has to be done to prevent such an atrocity from happening again?

The respondents have expressed themselves in different forms: poetry, excerpts from a radio interview, written replies to the three suggested questions, etc. They are:

Mumia Abu-Jamal, an incarcerated journalist and active supporter of MOVE who is now on death row in a Pennsylvania prison. (See editor's note before his response for more on this case.)

Richie Havens, singer and entertainer who has performed at numerous benefits for progressive causes; appearing in the film *Hearts and Fire* with Bob Dylan; currently working on a television series about opposition to nuclear war titled "Stopping the Unthinkable" and a film project on Jimi Hendrix.

Chokwe Lumumba, National Chairperson of the New Afrikan People's Organization; also an attorney who has defended Black political prisoners and who has faced arrests in Battle Creek, Michigan where he has been active in an ongoing struggle against police brutality and repression.

Florynce Kennedy, attorney and long-time activist; hostess of "The Flo Kennedy Show" on cable television in New York City; co-founder of Black Women United for Political Action and the Coalition Against Racism and Sexism.

Carl Dix, spokesperson for the Revolutionary Communist Party, USA who participated with other revolutionary leaders in a London press conference announcing the formation of the Revolutionary Internationalist Movement in March 1984; author of the article and pamphlet, *Jesse Jackson: The Right Stuff for U.S. Imperialism.*

C. Vernon Mason, civil rights attorney whose cases include defending students who staged a sit-in at Columbia University demanding South African divestment; also represented one of the victims of a racist attack in Howard Beach, N.Y. in December 1986, in which a Black man was killed.

Stanley Vaughan, civil rights activist, member of the Philadelphia Urban Coalition, and one of those who tried to negotiate with MOVE on the afternoon of May 13, but who was not permitted to go to the MOVE house by the police and instead had to speak from a street corner over a bullhorn, not knowing if MOVE members in the house could even hear his voice.

Jitu Weusi, activist and journalist; vice-chairman for administration of the National Black United Front; chairperson for the Committee for a Free Press.

Alice Walker, award-winning author of *The Color Purple* and many other books.

Mumia Abu-Jamal

(Editor's note: Mumia Abu-Jamal is the former president of the Association of Black Journalists in Philadelphia. While working for radio station WUHY, Mumia Abu-Jamal covered the trial of the nine MOVE members who were convicted of murdering police officer James Ramp and were sentenced to prison for thirty to one hundred years. Mumia Abu-Jamal stunned other reporters covering the trial when they noticed that he, like the MOVE people, wore dreadlocks. Abu-Jamal also distributed among reporters *First Day,* a newspaper that MOVE used to publish. Criticisms that he lacked objectivity were lodged, and it wasn't long before he was forced to leave WUHY. However, it was Mumia Abu-Jamal's political stand and activities which caused him to come under fire by certain other journalists.

He also was known to the Philadelphia Police Department because of his increasingly outspoken support for MOVE, and from his high school days as a spokesperson for the Black Panther Party. On December 12, 1981, he was arrested and charged with the fatal shooting of a police officer. Abu-Jamal himself was shot and his supporters have charged that it was the police who did it and that he was severely beaten once he was taken into custody.

The full story of what happened on December 12, 1981 has never been allowed to come out, owing to the fact that Abu-Jamal was stripped of his right to defend himself at his trial and barred from the proceedings. He was thus found guilty of murdering a police officer and sentenced to die in the electric chair. During his ongoing incarceration, Abu-Jamal has been kept in total isolation twenty-three out of twenty-four hours a day. Visits are severely restricted. In fact, a request from Banner Press to interview him in person was denied by a prison official who explained in a letter: "At this time, Abu-Jamal is in disciplinary custody as a result of misconduct behavior. I will not permit an interview until after he completes his disciplinary sentence or agrees to adhere to regulations which would result in the termination of the disciplinary sentence." Supporters of Abu-Jamal charge that he is routinely persecuted because of his refusal to cut off his dreadlocks and disavow his belief in the teachings of MOVE's founder, John Africa.

Mumia Abu-Jamal is currently being held on death row in the State Correctional Institution in Huntingdon, Pennsylvania, awaiting an appeal of his sentence. Here are his written responses to the questions submitted to him.)

Why did May 13 happen? To look at May 13, 1985 as an isolated act of official evil is to fall victim to the wave of propaganda that washed over much of America since that fiery, fateful day. City officials and much of the media have painted a picture of bungling, errors of judgment, and misfortune. Who can forget the idiotic imagery of the Mayor of the City of "Brotherly Love" defending the carnage of Osage Avenue with the words, "Perfect...except for the fire"?

The truth points a far more felonious finger at authorities and exposes such portraits as pure fraud, for the May 13 massacre was not a monumental "boo-boo," in the sense suggested by both the politicians and press. May 13 was no mere "mistake," not a "bad day," nor an incident showing "bad judgment." No. May 13 was an exercise of *deliberate mass murder*, one *planned* and premeditated for *months* beforehand! For *months prior* to May 13, 1985, police tested high explosives at a city facility in its Northeast section. Was it mere "coincidence" that a federal agent of the United States Department of Justice (FBI) would *give* Philadelphia police over *37½ lbs.* of a potent military explosive (C-4)? How about the cop who "happened" to add C-4 to the satchel bomb – William Klein? Was that a "boo-boo"? And what of the commissioners of the Police and Fire Departments? When else will people see such "civil servants" as these, who: (a) start a residential fire; (b) fail to fight it; and (c) use it as a "tactical weapon" of mass murder and destruction? How does one plan, construct, drop, and detonate an incendiary bomb by mistake? How does one barbecue babies by "boo-boo"?

May 13 was an official state terrorism operation designed to *eliminate* the MOVE organization as a direct result of the failure of August 8, 1978. Why failure? On Aug. 8, MOVE members emerged from a deadly baptism of both fire and water, still alive, still committed to the teachings of *John Africa*, and still in resistance to this infanticidal system. May 13 was meant to *stop* MOVE; to *liquidate* men, women, and children of MOVE; to wipe

MOVE off the face of this earth – forever. May 13 was designed to *divert* folks' attention away from the overt injustices of August 8 and the subsequent imprisonment of the MOVE 9 for an aggregate of nine hundred years! The massacre was conducted to still the voice of MOVE; to ignore, by murdering MOVE defenders, the innocence of imprisoned MOVE people. To that end, May 13 too must be counted a failure. For May 13 was a state military attempt to stifle resistance, and resistance continues.

Of what importance was the sitting of a Black mayor over the May 13 massacre? The administration of W. Wilson Goode was launched amidst euphoria in Philadelphia's Black community. On the night of his election, his rhetorical question "Will you help me?" was answered affirmatively by thousands. There was a feeling that, at long last, a Black man, "one of us," had taken hold of the reins of power. That dream died hard, but quite definitely bit the dust on the early hours of May 13. Who knew that when the mayor-elect asked his post-election question it would later refer to help in wiping out and burning a Black family to death? How could a Black man stand by and not merely "allow" but *authorize* the official insanity of May 13? When a Black person serves the interests of this system, how can he serve the needs of his people? Goode answered that question grotesquely.

What of the political fallout? Days after this dreary drama unfolded, America's media set the tone with the May 27 edition of *U.S. News and World Report* observing, "The risk of riots in Philadelphia was dampened by the fact that Mayor Goode is black." Indeed, press reports in race-conscious America strained logic itself to trumpet the fact that because Goode was Black, there was no racism at work on May 13, as the victims were also mostly Black. In a nation historically infected with racism, note its media hypocrisy! Biased news reports lauded Goode's mayoral presence as a triumph over racism; while the very obscenity of the bombing, the fire, and the police automatic gunfire that irrevocably closed the door to escape screamed to the gates of deaf heaven that racism most rank was rampant that day! White cops and firemen launched an urban blitzkrieg against a Black family that would have been unthinkable in a white neighborhood!

It is too soon to predict with any degree of certainty what place history will assign to Goode, but it is safe to say his stature in the minds of Black folk will be less than stellar. History is replete with the foul doings of those who chose the way of their masters rather than the way of the rebel. A treasonous house

Negro betrayed the plans of rebel preacher Nat Turner. Traitorous Black police now lash black flesh during anti-government demonstrations in South Africa. May 13 bequeathed a stench of similar significance to Philadelphia's first "Black" mayor, akin to the shameless opportunism and ambition of South Africa's Gatsha Buthelezi, for both men will be remembered more for their slavish servility to an oppressive system than for the illusion of their service to African peoples. For as Buthelezi's rush to redeem and legitimize the criminal apartheid system evokes shame amongst Africans, so too the politicking by Goode on May 13 marked a point of no return; an act that sacrificed the shattered and smouldering remains of MOVE men, women, and babies on the altar of his ambition. Goode's black skin was a service to this *system, not* to Black folks.

What is to be done to prevent a repetition of this massacre? An early American labor leader said, "Don't mourn—Organize!" That message echoes through the emptiness of what was once Osage Avenue. How to prevent tomorrow's May 13ths? Pull together—unite—come together to resist this system's usurpation of your inherent and God-given rights to freedom, clean air, uncontaminated earth, fresh water, and an untainted, unpoisoned gene pool. People, all peoples on this planet, must be free and unthreatened by a nuclear pistol placed at the temple of the earth's inhabitants. Demand that this system of injustice free MOVE prisoners and all political prisoners from the dungeons of America.

Work for the gifts of God—truth, health, freedom, family and productivity. Resist a system, a way of life, that produces acid rain, toxic waste, poisonous, polluted waters, strangulating air, infertile soil, and ever-deadlier diseases. Quoth MOVE founder, *John Africa*, "It is insane not to resist something that gives nothing but *sickness* to *you, your mothers, your fathers, your babies, your family---*" Resist a system that promises life, liberty and the pursuit of happiness, yet practices dungeons of death and despair, hypocrisy and deceit.

Expose politicians who commit heinous crimes in your name and oppose this system's policies of oppression, here and abroad. Recognize the bitter truth that politicians practice a foul and putrid art, that of prostituting the innate power of the people, and it matters little whether a given politician is Black or white! Of what real import is the color or ethnicity of a politician as long as the corrupt, brutal system remains?

Say "No" to the Three Mile Islands, Bhopals, Love Canals, and Chernobyls that threaten your lives, your health, and the lives of your children's tomorrows! Resist today so that they won't need to resist tomorrow.

Richie Havens

Why must man put up with the will of a few who believe that they know what's best for all other individuals, thereby taking it upon themselves to take up ownership of their fellowmen and their children for generations to come?

Who among us (the general public) think we can force our young into the hands of foreign commands for the CIA and expect them to return home and respect us. . .or love us?!!

The legitimacy of the America we know in the past ('40s-'50s) has somehow disappeared for those who experienced it and its promise. However, young people can in no way imagine or understand that the near past history is in fact the key to the very problems they are now experiencing. They can in no way realize that the words "American dream" were not invented by the constitution but by someone when it was necessary to create an air of hope in some other tragic political situation post-1940s.

The promise not kept is what led to the illegitimacy of the American citizen. The fraud of politics is designed to keep the intelligent American from voting for anyone and by counting on the brainwashed to play the illegal electoral college game. Do you think those who voted for Mondale know that their votes were given to Reagan, before the race even started, via the electoral college backroom, which means that just two percent of the Democrats' votes even counted in the race, in order to create the appearance of the so-called landslide for Reagan? While in fact eighty-two million nonvoters chose not to acknowledge the shameful display of greedy bank and corporate takeover of America, while the C.I.A. drums up high-tech business to create jobs for the new American they are planning to create for the future they plan also for themselves.

KNOW THAT THE RICH DO NOT CARE! (your son to protect their America).

Children cannot imagine that it was any different than it is. We must come to accept this fact and begin to change our approach to their consciousness and what in fact they may well be perceiving of us.

Children are not dumb or deaf. They hear what we say and they see what we do, and although we may not wish to accept it, we know they hate our hypocrisy.

Who or what can make intelligent grownups act as if their children are secondary to a job, the acquisition of groceries, or clothing, or any nonliving thing?

KNOW THAT WE HAVE BEEN BRAINWASHED... i.e., EDUCATION over TRUTH!

Honestly (if you can) ask yourself, is it possible that I have not really taken the time to treat my child as a human being? And if we the eighty-two million outsiders remain apart from our general dilemma, people such as Mayor Goode of Philadelphia can in fact supply a testing ground for whatever new/high-tech/killing machine pays the highest.

What we do know is there is little difference in what the police in Philadelphia did, and what Hitler's SS did in Germany. And I challenge any American to justify those actions.... .Eviction?

(*Editor's note:* The following is a public statement by Richie Havens concerning the sentencing of Ramona Africa on April 14, 1985.)

Today the city of Philadelphia is to sentence Ramona Africa on charges stemming from the atrocity of last May 13th. It would be a tremendous miscarriage of justice if she was sentenced to jail in this case on top of all that has already been done to her. In fact, it was a tremendous miscarriage of justice that she even had to face a trial in this case. Therefore, I add my voice to those calling for Ramona Africa to be released today. As a citizen of the United States, I, Richie Havens, have just begun to recognize the depth to which those who are trying to keep us from a clearer understanding will go to dominate the spirit of the people. The time has come when people must realize that the government of the United States of America does not in fact own our minds, our bodies, or our souls. We do. And the old adage, "You can't beat City Hall" is far from the truth. The people must realize that we are the government and the people who get elected are not. They in fact are representatives of the government (which is ourselves) and most likely are not elected by an actual majority of citizens. We must begin to express our awareness of these facts. We must recognize as truth and fact that the unconsciousness we display is what allows those in office to take advantage of us, the people.

In this land of the free and the home of the brave, how is it that an American citizen can be condemned for her beliefs as Ramona Africa has been? The City of Brotherly Love displays a clear farce, as does the U.S. government in many instances, when it claims that it can condemn others for things it in fact practices wholeheartedly.

This is our legacy unless we think and come to know that it is only by our actions that the truth will actually be displayed. I'm calling upon all conscious citizens to realize that this atrocity is not in fact limited to Philadelphia. It is my hope that we, the citizens of the United States of America, all feel the pain and the shame of what we have allowed to come about through our silence.

I must also say that my faith and belief in the free press has also totally dwindled through this affair because the press has shown that it can be silenced as easily as the people. In sum, I repeat, Ramona Africa has already suffered greatly for no legitimate reason. Let her go free.

Chokwe Lumumba

On May 13, 1985 the United States of America, as represented by Mayor Wilson Goode and the City Adminstration of Philadelphia, bombed the MOVE organization.

This was the second time in history that a component of the American government executed a conventional bombing from the air on a location inside the boundaries of the United States Empire (the fifty states).

The first such occasion occurred with the bombing of the Black community in Tulsa, Oklahoma in 1921. The governor of Oklahoma ordered the Tulsa bombing in response to the Afrikan blood brotherhood's effective organization of the Black community to resist and neutralize white racist mobs and terrorist groups during a red-blooded American lynching spree which was occurring at that time.

The fact is that on both occasions, in Tulsa and May 13, 1985 in Philadelphia, the American government was bombing New Afrikans (Blacks born in America) and their families. This is no coincidence.

Certainly, the American government has utilized other devastating acts of war in America against people other than New Afrikans, and certainly it is capable of air bombing many others who are here and opposed to this regime. Yet the particularly vivid expression of warfare personified by the two abovementioned air attacks most appropriately discloses the real state of affairs between the American government and the New Afrikan population. Indeed, historically there exists no belligerency more constant, intense, and irreconcilably antagonistic than the conflict between New Afrikans and the U.S. Empire (i.e., its civilian armies and its government.)

With the slave trade and slavery the United States and its predecessor European government commenced hostilities against the New Afrikan population and its Afrikan ancestry in one of the most barbaric ways known to the so-called civilized world. These barbaric acts actually led to the formation of the New Afrikan nation in the Southeast Black belt of the American Empire. The nation was born in slavery as Afrikans from many different Afrikan nations became one – united in language, culture, history, political identity, and economic life. The war fought by the nation's ancestors against the slavers became the New Afrikan nation's war.

The nation is quite obviously colonized by the United States, as are so many others in the United States, like the Puerto Ricans, Indians, Hawaiians, and upper Mexico. The methods the United States has used to exploit the genius and labor of the nation, and to separate its people from political and economic control of land in Afrika and to deny it, the nation, its rights to land it developed in America, have consistently been ruthless.

The physical ruthlessness of the United States has only been tempered by the desire to effectively delude the nation's population and to con it into giving up its national rights to self-determination and absolute liberation from the political control of its slavemasters/colonizers. This process of deception is attempted and often accomplished by shifting, from time to time and to some degree, from acts of physical terror to psychological warfare designed to convince the New Afrikan population that they are not oppressed and colonized and that there is no war.

As difficult as it may seem to convince a population which is at the bottom of every national and local statistic of human existence (i.e., employment, health care, infant mortality, education) that it is not oppressed, this feat is to some degree accomplished with regard to some of the New Afrikan population, some of the time. Much time, energy and resources are generally expended by the U.S. Empire for these purposes.

Political phenomena, like Black mayors, are clearly a part of the Empire's cloak and cover. In times past, phony Black leaders were merely appointed by the Empire's political or economic bosses and expected to mislead and deceive the New Afrikan community.

Rising consciousness of the masses, political organization, and other things particularly evident in the 1960s and 1970s, made the white-appointed Black leadership method obsolete. It is still used at times, however, as is evident with Reagan's appointment of Pendleton to the U.S. Civil Rights Commission. Yet such appointments merely demonstrate the dwindling resources and time the Empire is able and prepared to put into deceiving New Afrikans. With the event of economic crisis, as experienced presently by American capitalism, resources for placating the colonized are, also, reduced. Naked force and acts which demonstrate contempt to the colonized's political intelligence are characteristic of such a period.

In recent times, however, the Empire's "liberal" wing and most moderates have been satisfied with the process of selecting handker-chief-headed Negro leadership through elections.

The elections, which are an apparatus of the Empire, can generally be relied upon to produce Negro leadership which is loyal to the white economic power structure that controls and finances, with the people's money, successful American political campaigns, and all American political jurisdictions (i.e., federal, state and local). Big business control over media, most professional politicians, and established campaign planners and "leaders" is generally enough to ensure that the elected are more loyal to big business than to their people.

The above analysis, although more or less correct in other situations, with other officials, fits Wilson Goode like a glove. Goode is a traitor. His commitment to the American government is far deeper than any favor he might have for persons bearing the same racial origin as he.

Wilson Goode actually presents nothing unique in the story of colonialism and oppression. We have seen his likes everywhere for years and still witness the same today. In Afrika there is Mobutu in the Congo, there are the Contras in Nicaragua, and there was Sadat and now the present Egyptian State leadership in the so-called Middle East (which is actually upper Afrika). This list could go on and on.

Essentially, every people and every struggle has its traitors. Goode is one. The material benefits of working for our enemy are more important to him than fighting for us.

In Azania (South Afrika) the masses now hunt down and destroy a Negro collaborator like Goode every week, and sometimes daily. Success in the New Afrikan revolution will require much of the same.

The only way to prevent what happened on May 13, 1985 in Philadelphia is by a successful New Afrikan national liberation struggle (i.e., the independence of New Afrika, the dismantling of the U.S. Empire). Successful New Afrikan struggle for an independent nation, politically, economically, and militarily, arms the New Afrikan population against such assaults, and at the same time disarms the assaulters. The only certain way to prevent atrocities sustained at the hands of your enemy at war is to defeat the enemy and to change or destroy the forces which cause that enemy to be your enemy.

With the independence of New Afrikan land in the Southeast and the establishment of a socialist New Afrikan state, the American government and imperialist economic powers will be defeated. With the growth of revolutions by all oppressed nations in America and by Americans, American imperialism will be destroyed. The Empire will be destroyed, and the white-American state will be transformed into a humane socialist nation/state or the American state will be absolutely eliminated.

With the occurrence of these social achievements, episodes like the MOVE incident of May 13, 1985 will be no more.

Florynce Kennedy

What do you believe is the principal cause or causes of what happened on May 13?

In the first place I think they are very complicated and embarrassing, especially to a Black person. I think that unfortunately because of the pathology of our society the kind of Black politician who will get to a position of responsibility might be a person who is so inclined to "bend over backwards" that he falls on his face and takes the Black and the white and the rest of the human race with him.

Philadelphia is an extraordinarily corrupt city. Most of our cities in America are corrupt. America is based on corruption. Every large city in America is probably part of an Indian treaty where we betrayed the people who actually owned the country. The entire country is predicated on fraudulent conduct and broken contracts. I think the Philadelphia story is a continuation of that pathology.

I think that the MOVE bombing was as much a result of fear of stylistic change. I think the MOVE people were only dangerous in that they were perceived to be dangerous because they were different. I'm sure the worst possible presentation of what they were about was put on, but as far as I heard and all I could understand is that there was some question of whether they were sanitary. I talked to a woman coming in on a Fire Island ferry who told me about her relatively wealthy husband who has a part of their house filled with dog feces. She called the Department of Health. She called all kinds of people, police and everyone else, and no one seems to be able to do anything about it. That was the type of accusation they made of the MOVE members: they had eccentric sanitary habits – and that could have been a lie.

The fear of Black ideological influence is so considerable and the paranoia of nonideological white people is such that they built the MOVE people into a monster. They were clearly eccentric, but what they were not, so far as I'm aware from what their enemies have said, anything like a danger.

As far as the Osage community was concerned, the Black people, as is the case with most oppressed people, they're very easily shamed. They're very easily made to feel guilty. They are very easily embarrassed by others of their numbers who do not attempt to conform. No matter how poor you are, you should wear your hair a certain way or do your best to try to wear it a certain way.

The MOVE people were eccentric. They were also political. But had they been political and ideological without being eccentric in their stylistics, they might all still be alive. They lost the support of the most natural constituency that they could have had by virtue of the fact that they were both eccentric and ideological – and I'm not clear as to what their ideology was. They were busy talking about their style of life and at least in the case of gay people or women who opt for choice or any of that, at least there's a following and a constituency within a constituency which either lines up beside them or along with them or at least tolerates them. But simply because the MOVE people had contemptuously rejected so many different, unimportant but crucial stylistic and lifestyle patterns, they were expendable. Except for those people who were concerned about them in terms of civil liberties, there was really almost nobody who was on their side.

The irony of it is that the Osage neighborhood was burned up along with the MOVE people. I don't have a better explanation than simply to say that this was a result of a pathological society. Killing is not at all important in our society. We'll kill anybody for any reason or no reason. We kill Indians. We kill anybody that makes us nervous. And the MOVE people clearly made Philadelphia nervous.

What significance, if any, do you attach to the fact that these events occurred under the administration of a Black mayor?

I think that the Black mayor and the neighbors may have been more outraged by the MOVE people because they were an embarrassment. I really believe that eccentric Black people, even serious, ideologically correct Black people like Farrakhan, upset Black people almost more than they do white people for different reasons and in different ways. I think that the difference between what Goode did and what is done by police throughout this country is simply the method. Killing Black people by city government is par for the course, but it is normally done by the police with guns. In this case it was done in a more American way with bombs. And it was more indiscriminate, more brutal, more totally berserk. It's obviously the work of a pathological society. But there's such a considerable amount of pathology in our whole society that no kind of pathological conduct should surprise us. I think the big mistake is to expect candidates from the Black community or even if we ever got any from the Native American community or Hispanic community, to be any better for having been oppressed. I think that is really the part that is so embarrassing.

I also think the kind of oppressed people who have not fought back against oppression tend to be seriously flawed. I'm not sure that they start out flawed but I think that the pressure of high office on a representative of an oppressed group, be it a woman, be it Black people, be it from the gay community and possibly from the socialist community, that unless there's a very strong support system, they will be as bad or worse than representatives from the oppressor community. Because once the oppressed begin to resist and reject oppression and withdraw consent to oppression, the oppressor gets a little careful, unless they are as Rizzo was, a total fascistic bully. So, I think in Wilson Goode you've got a flawed, weak person.

The mayor is probably rather stupid, but all the white people I know in Philadelphia – and there are not that many although I did lecture at the University of Pennsylvania during this spring since this happened – and I found that many white people who you would think should know better were very sympathetic toward Goode. In other words, they seemed to regard him as not all that bad. And Black people who are acceptable to not-good white people are quite often either weak, corrupt or accommodating or whatever. I just think America is so flawed and so pathological that Goode having been the person to mete out this horror is sort of par for the course. Because I don't know that the kind of Black person who floats to the top of the sewage of American politics in a corrupt city like Philadelphia would be any different, and maybe a whole lot worse, than the people who perceive them.

What do you think has to be done to prevent such an atrocity from happening again?

Well, the same thing that has to be done to keep people from being homeless all over the country. I think there is very little ideology even in the oppressed communities. I think that people are outraged. I think they complain a lot. I think they recount the horrors of what is being done by this administration or that union or this police group. But the fact is there is no ideology in this country of oppressed people against the establishment.

Any country that would allow the amounts of money to be spent on weaponry that we allow, that would sit by for a hundred million dollars to be sent to the Contras to destabilize the legitimate, sovereign government of Nicaragua when people are sleeping in Grand Central Station without homes; if we're going to permit the atrocity at Big Mountain where the Native Americans, the Indians as we call them, are being destabilized and moved and uprooted with their sacred graves being torn up; any country that allows these things—it would be pipe dreaming to talk about how to prevent a recurrence of this sort of thing. Little murders, little atrocities are happening every single hour.

I can speculate and say something that sounds intelligent about how to prevent it, but all I can say is, if we don't develop an ideology, if we don't act to respond to the major atrocities—for example, take the nuclear situation. Nuclear weapons make no sense at all. I think we ought to talk more about the fact that we probably never will use them and then consider the kind of money being wasted and the insanity of it all. I am not the least bit sure that we would ever use nuclear weapons. We've never had a war with Russia. With all the talk that we're doing, we're still trading more than raiding. We're raiding Nicaragua and we talk about Afghanistan. We have a thousand Afghanistans in this country, like the little war they call the Grenada rape.

So you see, I don't know how we can seriously talk about preventing any atrocity—municipal, state, county, federal, or international—as long as we are totally pathological as we seem to be. Although the bombing of the MOVE community was an atrocity, atrocities are so endemic to this country. The entire country is predicated on atrocities. To talk about preventing what was done to MOVE is to talk as if there is any rationality whatsoever in the bulk of the people or the agencies or the legislators or anyone else. The sanest of the legislators in this country are putting up with such shit that as far as I can see there's no basis for discussing anything rational such as preventing what was done to MOVE. How could you prevent it when everybody is crazy?

Carl Dix

What do you believe is the principal cause or causes of what happened on May 13?

First off, the cause wasn't ineptitude of the local officials or a lack of planning on their part. This murderous assault, including the bombing, was something that had been planned months in advance with documented involvement and support from the federal government (and probably a lot more involvement from the federal level that has never been documented).

The MOVE massacre was a calculated message of terror delivered by the U.S. rulers with the intention of having a chilling effect on those throughout society who have been moved by the developments of today either into active resistance or at least to the point of questioning whether they should take that step. Delivery of such a brutal message was necessitated by the situation faced by the U.S rulers. On the one hand, they are forced by the contradictions of their system and the current worldwide crisis to prepare for a global showdown with the rival Soviet-led bloc. Simultaneously, they are being shaken by revolutionary uprisings from Azania (South Africa) to Haiti to Peru. At the same time, they are enforcing conditions of increased poverty and degradation for large sections of people in the U.S., particularly large sections of Black people. They know that these conditions are creating great potential for explosions of mass resistance in the ghettos and barrios of the country.

The rulers have a vivid recollection of the 1960s where a similar mixture proved quite explosive. The ghettos were rocked by mass rebellions even as the U.S. faced national liberation struggles in Vietnam and many other parts of the world. The rulers are aware that the stakes for them are much higher today and that new outbreaks of protest and rebellion would be even more damaging to them than they were in the '60s. So, they are driven to lash out viciously, to say forcefully to the oppressed and others, "This is how far we'll go to deal with those who step out of line. This is the bottom line." (It also must be noted that this message of terror was swiftly underscored by the applause given to it by significant ruling class figures such as Attorney General Edwin Meese and L.A. Police Chief Darryl Gates.)

MOVE became the target of this brutal ruling class message because of their uncompromising spirit of resistance which had made them a frequent target for attacks by the authorities in Philly. This, plus their dedication to following the dictates of their own lifestyle and not getting caught up in "the system," made them a fitting example of the kind of "deviant" (and defiant) behavior that "resurgent America" will no longer tolerate. Thus unleashing the full force of the state on MOVE became a good way to deliver the intended message.

Upon hearing this kind of analysis, some have responded: "Where is the revolutionary activity that you claim they were out to suppress through this bombing?" Well, it's bubbling right beneath the surface, threatening to blow up in their faces. And it seems to me that all those who hate the oppression, brutality, and degradation that this system has historically forced Black people and others to endure have a responsibility to aid in exposing the MOVE massacre and building opposition to it.

What significance, if any, do you attach to the fact that these events occurred under the administration of a Black mayor?

Having a Black mayor in position to preside over the bombing and to take responsibility for it was a key part of the rulers' effort to force people to swallow this message of terror without protest and resistance, and it sheds some light on whose interests are really served by pursuing the strategy of placing Black faces in high places. (On this point of responsibility, I don't for a moment believe that a "hands-on manager" like Goode could have been unaware of what was planned, as he claims. Nor do I believe for a moment that such an assault could have been planned and carried out without getting the OK in advance from the highest levels of the ruling class.) Goode's role and the numerous justifications for the massacre that he and others spewed out were designed to spread confusion on whether or not the massacre should be seen as part of the escalating attacks on Black people. In addition, the rulers' anointed "spokesmen" for Black people were unleashed to call for investigations at the federal, state, and local levels and to appeal to people to withhold judgment until after these investigations (read: cover-ups) were completed. (In fact, after initial responses like "the most violent eviction in history" and "everybody opted for confrontation instead of negotiation," the silence emanating from Black elected officials and other "designated" Black spokesmen and leaders on this question has been deafening.)

All of this has not been without its effect. Many Black middle-class forces refused to condemn the bombing because they saw doing so as detrimental to their cherished strategy of advancing the situation of Black people through increasing the number of Black elected officials. Others latched on to Goode's story that he didn't know what was going down on Osage Avenue (or concocted new justifications for him) in order to avoid calling out the massacre and his role in it. And the relative lack of protest and opposition helped to create an atmosphere in which those who saw the massacre for what it was and wanted to fight it, especially those among the basic masses, felt isolated and suffocated.

This underscores a point I made in *Jesse Jackson, The Right Stuff for U.S. Imperialism.* That is that the increase in the number of Black elected officials, especially mayors in big cities, while a demand that Black people fought for in the 1960s and '70s, must also be seen as part of the rulers' counterinsurgency strategy to quell the uprisings in the ghettos in the '60s. In this way (and through other mechanisms) the rulers hoped to create a Black buffer strata capable of sitting on the heads of the masses in ways white officials no longer could. While this has had an effect in quelling resistance and spreading demoralization and confusion among some, as more and more people develop a clear understanding of the effects of this kind of class polarization among Black people, it will become possible to draw many more into a movement that can more forcefully and powerfully target the system that is responsible for all the atrocities that we face.

What do you think has to be done to prevent such an atrocity from happening again?

In a word, revolution! Nothing short of the armed overthrow of the U.S rulers, the smashing of their reactionary state apparatus and continuing to advance to eradicate every foul social relation left over from their dog-eat-dog set-up, is required to insure that atrocities like the MOVE massacre and the 1,001 other indignities the U.S. rulers force millions to endure here and worldwide are ended once and for all. I mean, are people going to continue to tell us that the surest way to advance our situation is to rely on getting more Blacks in elected positions when, after twenty years of applying that strategy and after more than 6,000 Blacks have gained elective office, the majority of Black people face conditions today that are no better than in the '60s, if not worse? (And, besides, in Philly they had elected a Black mayor, and he took responsibility for the massacre and said he'd do it again!)

Some reading this will dismiss all thoughts of making revolution as unrealistic and impossible. But the rulers of the U.S. think it is a real possibility and have historically taken very real measures to suppress those they fear might lead such a revolution and those sections of society they fear might rally behind such leadership. And they continue to do so today. (In fact, the MOVE massacre was one such measure.) And while in the U.S. today the numbers of people involved in active resistance are still relatively small, there are developments that point to the potential for this situation to change drastically and to do so quite rapidly. As Bob Avakian, Chairman of the Revolutionary Communist Party, U.S.A., put it in a recent interview in *Revolution* (Winter/Spring 1986, Number 54): "they [politicized elements in the U.S.] are responding to the growing and acute and explosive crisis that's shaping up internationally, in particular the threat of nuclear war; the threat of invasion directly by the U.S. in Central America, the carrying out of its present war moves through proxy forces already in Central America and its death squad and death-dealing policy against the masses of people there; its suppression of immigrants who are driven to this country in large part as a result of U.S. aggression against the people in those countries; the upsurge in South Africa and the clear role of the U.S. in backing up the state of South Africa against the masses of people there. All these things, and others, are calling people forth into struggle and impelling people into motion against the system and against the very real outrages it commits and the looming horrors that it's bringing onto the horizon. Very clearly that is what is going on, and it's important to recognize that it's the system and its very nature and its very operation and what the ruling classes in the world are compelled to do themselves that's calling people into motion against it. This system calls forth the forces that oppose it and ultimately calls forth the forces that will overthrow it."

C. Vernon Mason

Diane Thompson (DT): You have a lot of concern about the situation in Philadelphia. We were talking about that this morning and I was telling the audience about the petition "Draw the Line."...How are you involved with this petition, attorney Mason?

C. Vernon Mason (CVM): I signed the petition, Diane. A number of other people from New York: Reverend Ben Chavis, Professor John Henrik Clarke, Flo Kennedy, Cornel West, and as you mentioned Jitu, Justice Bruce Wright, Dr. Saundra Shepherd and a number of people, Manning Marable, who are here in the New York City area. I think that if we remember what happened in Philadelphia, and we also remember that the day afterwards, Mayor Goode got on the national media and said that he took full responsibility. I will always remember him saying that, almost in a fit of *pride*, or almost like dancing on the graves of the children and the people who had burned to death and had been shot. And ten thousand rounds of ammunition were shot into that house, and that bomb with a C-4 explosive, supplied by the FBI, and dropped on the residence itself. But almost in what could only be described as a fit of madness, Goode got on national TV and said that he would *"do it again"!* And he said it in a very, very arrogant, angry way, as though if there were other people he could have dropped some bombs on he would have done that also.

I think that we need to look at that for what it is. The police commissioner from Los Angeles was also on national TV that weekend along with John Conyers. Congressman Conyers condemned what happened. But this police commissioner said that only now could Wilson Goode be counted as one of his heroes. Now, I could imagine in the living rooms of people who have never wanted us to advance in this country and who found it

---

Excerpts from an interview with C. Vernon Mason conducted by Diane Thompson on WLIB, a Black-owned and oriented radio station in New York City. The broadcast aired November 6, 1985, at a time when the hearings of the Philadelphia Special Investigation Commission were about to conclude. The interview has been edited for publication.

comical and humorous that here we had a Black mayor who purportedly was in charge and who is taking responsibility for the burning of children to death and the killing of children. . . .

DT: It is obvious that a lot of other people liked Goode and the move that he made there with the MOVE house, because he represented a "good negro."

CVM: There's no question about that. I think it is something that we have to be cautious about applauding. That is, we are not just looking for people to change the players in the game. We are looking for people who will change the game itself and all that that represents. What has happened there is that for a number of organizations that have spoken out, city grants have been pulled back from those organizations because of this. A number of people in Philadelphia who are tied in with the administration cannot speak out about what is going on in Philadelphia. And I think that even the testimony that is going on right now [at the PSIC hearings] will indicate everybody is pointing the finger at each other. The fire commissioner is saying that he didn't get the order to put the fire out. The police commissioner is saying that he gave him the order. Goode now is saying that he was misled, that he didn't know what was going on. I think that what we really have to look at as Black people in this country is that this represents in the United States of America, 1985, while some of us are watching the program "North and South" on TV at night, this represents an even greater atrocity than what is going on in South Africa right now. Because we have not seen anything in South Africa in any of the coverage that would indicate that they are dropping bombs on Black neighborhoods in South Africa.

DT: Well, the situation in South Africa is blatant and it's honest. They let you know this is how we feel about you, this is what we're going to do. But this is so underhanded and so under the table. I was listening last night to them saying that the cranes that went in to clean up the ruins of the home had no business going in as soon as they did because the cranes actually dismembered some of the bodies. Then the question was asked, "was this intentional or not?" Now, if it wasn't intentional, it was downright stupid because they knew they had at least eleven bodies in there. And then to send in cranes to pick up pieces of wood without getting the bodies out – they knew what they were doing. Peo-

ple who operate cranes and people who order cranes to do that
and give them the green light know not to do that when there are
bodies under there unless they want to do that on purpose. . . .

CVM: . . . one of the things that I think has misled a number of
people is that it is not important what you think about MOVE. It's
not important what you think about the organization or the people. One of the things you hear from some of the people who are
on the other side in Philadelphia is, "it should have happened to
those people." And it's the dehumanization process: "Those people ate out of garbage cans and they were messing up our neighborhoods." One of the things Black folks got to remember is
whenever we fail to remember that even now in 1985, millions of
people feel the same way about us as a group. We can never really
be so assimilated that we take on that kind of belief system where
even – we've got all kinds of people in the Black community.
We've got people like MOVE, we've got ministers, we've got
scientists, we have people who are astronauts, we have everything and most of it positive in our communities. At the same
time, there are people, thousands and millions of people, who
don't like us and don't want us to advance as a group. So when we
start saying, "Well, it should have happened to them and these
people were not good and these people were terrorists and these
people were that," we buy into that same kind of belief system. I
just want to point that out because it's extremely important. A lot
of people feel that what happened to MOVE should have happened to MOVE. But if that can happen to MOVE what is the difference between, say, a Frank Rizzo, if he had been mayor bombing a Black neighborhood, and a Mayor Goode? If Mayor Frank
Rizzo had bombed a Black neighborhood then people would be
ready to riot. And I think we have to see that thing very, very
clearly. Because what that represents is that people, a lot of people, would do anything to be part of the system, such as Clarence
Pendleton who is part of the Reagan administration. There's no
question in my mind that he's forgotten a lot of lessons that we
should have learned as Black people in this country.

DT: You were talking about people forgetting and people talking
about Wilson Goode. Some people have said that the actions of
Wilson Goode, the attitude of Wilson Goode, has made Black
leaders look bad. Therefore, it is causing even more apathy
among Black voters. Black voters are discouraged now about
even voting for their own for elected office. Do you think that

Wilson Goode has done that to future Black candidates?

CVM: No. I think we need to look at that for what it is. I don't think that Black people should assume all the responsibility for actions of individuals, just as we don't all assume responsibility for people who commit crimes. That is certainly a problem we have to deal with, but I don't think we should all start feeling and thinking and acting like criminals because we have criminals in our community, just as I don't think we should assume the responsibility for what Wilson Goode did. I think we should be very, very clear and speak out and have standards of justice and standards of decency and standards of fair play that we apply to whoever is in that office. When Wilson Goode was elected we didn't need to think that the election of any person is nirvana or this is the end-all for us. We as people have to keep people, whoever we elect, accountable to the community. That's why we're trying to deal with this [Draw the Line] petition because we can't let Wilson Goode, because he's Black, think that he can drop bombs on the neighborhood and that he won't be criticized or taken to task for that. That way we would be shirking our responsibility. But I don't think people should get apathetic about that.

DT: Because if they do then they are allowing themselves to take on the same attitude as the rest of the population that clumps us all together and we're clumping ourselves together.

CVM: . . . One of the things that can de done in terms of what is being called for – Congressman Conyers spoke out about doing an investigation, a federal investigation into what happened when this thing first occurred. And I think that there should be a federal investigation to determine what was the involvement of the FBI, to determine what were the criminal acts committed, not by Ramona Africa, but by the people who were there, who were supposedly in charge, the people who gave the orders. The medical examiner [Dr. Hameli, a pathologist hired by the PSIC] was testifying yesterday and he said that the cause of death of a number of persons who died was homicide. Now somebody has to be held responsible for that. So one of the things that should be done is that those persons responsible should be prosecuted, be that Wilson Goode, be that Sambor who was the police commissioner, or the fire commissioner or whoever else was involved.

Stanley Vaughan

What do you believe is the principal cause or causes of what happened on May 13?

The principal cause of what happened on May 13, 1985 was simply an act of perpetual racism on behalf of the Philadelphia police and Philadelphia firefighters. Based on my experience in growing up in Philadelphia, but more so with my experience during the Civil Rights struggle in the 1960s, I have been victimized and have witnessed unnecessary acts of brutality and cowardly tactics administered by members of the Philadelphia Police Department against individuals and organizations who express clear opposition to the unequal system and the injustices impacting primarily on the Black population in Philadelphia.

Peaceful groups that no longer exist in Philadelphia lashed out against the system and later found themselves at war with the police.

Groups like the Student Non-Violent Coordinating Committee (SNCC), Congress of Racial Equality (CORE), the Revolutionary Action Movement (RAM), the Black Liberation Front (BLF), the Black Panthers and the Young Militants (YM), which I was a part of, all shared the same common objective and that was to rid the city of its discrimination and racial practices in housing and employment within the law enforcement agencies by fighting the system in a nonviolent manner. Those groups dedicated their lives towards changing a system which provoked Blacks into being victimized by racist policemen who played the roles of judge and jurors outside the courtroom and outside their jurisdiction in most cases. Needless to say that inside the courts the cry for justice was deliberately and visibly ignored, despite the multitude of evidence against the police, in the presence of many citizens who observed first-hand racism.

The tactics used to liquidate those peaceful groups in the 1960s were preposterous, barbaric, and inhuman, but not uncommon. The implementation of perjury, harassment, the planting of weapons and physical violence occurred in the Black communities, especially where so-called "militants," "activists," or "demonstrators" housed their organizations.

Those groups were used as prey and there was complete satisfaction on the part of the so-called "law enforcers" who condoned violence and destruction as long as Blacks were the subjects involved.

Most or all of those groups were subjected to raids by the Philadelphia police and like the MOVE organization, the intent of the police was to destroy all existing life. It is believed that a high percentage of Philadelphia's Finest are racist and without any doubt the citizens of Philadelphia have seen them demonstrate their ability and capability to destroy Black citizens by any means necessary.

The MOVE incident was not a unique or different type issue in Philadelphia! The method used to destroy MOVE was only different, this time it was more intense, more meaningful and more destructive. The firearms, tear gas, silencers, water cannons as usual were present, but this time an additive was used consisting of a military bomb and destruction by fire, in an effort to destroy all human life inside the MOVE house.

MOVE was a legitimate and friendly organization who just wanted to live their own lifestyles, unlike the KKK and other white supremacist groups who practice violence and racism.

MOVE cried out and appealed to the city adminstration, the politicians, and the courts for legal help! They had exhausted their entire legal means and efforts trying to get the politicians, the courts, and the so-called justice system to hear their plea to free their innocent brothers and sisters who were falsely and unjustifiably imprisoned in retaliation for the death of a policeman who is believed to be the victim of another policeman's bullet and who is currently enjoying his freedom walking the streets of Philadelphia today. Substantial evidence did not apply when it came to the MOVE conviction, just overall hate and racism involving judge, prosecutor, and a multitude of prosecuting witnesses, all policemen.

The principal cause of what happened on May 13, 1985 was definitely gross negligence, as the investigating committee concluded, but it was profound gross negligence on behalf of the Philadelphia policemen and firemen who pursued gunshots, a bombing and destruction of human life by fire while MOVE cried out to peacefully surrender.

It is my belief that the mayor lost control of the situation shortly after the bomb was dropped, and that is when the racist attitudes began to manifest themselves and take complete authority.

Previous mayors were always found to be out of town when a Black organization was scheduled to be raided by the police! This left the police commissioner completely in charge with the authority to do whatever he chose without interference. In the MOVE situation, the mayor did not vacate the city but it was like he was not around. He became invisible to the policemen and firemen in charge, specifically subsequent to the bombing, and soon after thousands of citizens in this country witnessed mutiny once again as they have seen in the past.

What significance, if any, do you attach to the fact that these events occurred under the administration of a Black mayor?

There are no significant reasons for the fact that the MOVE confrontation occurred under the adminstration of a Black mayor.

The situation would have occurred anyway but would not have been delayed for such a long period of time if a white mayor was in office.

Take the former mayor, Frank Rizzo, for instance! He would have taken immediate and direct action after the first complaint against MOVE. He would have used brutal force to destroy MOVE as he did in 1978, with pleasure, simply because they opposed the system. I must admit that probably the most and only significance attached to the fact that the event occurred under the administration of a Black mayor is the fact that MOVE, at first, characterized the mayor as being totally Black and understanding when it came to a Black issue. They assumed that this man was too a victim of injustices and racism. They assumed that his background as a sharecropper who was subjected to unfair treatment, as all Blacks are subjected to, would listen and help in some way to alleviate their sufferings. MOVE knew that they could not confront a white mayor who would denounce them simply because of their appearance alone. A Black mayor, a Black administration, and a Black community all deceived MOVE.

The magnitude of an entire city of Blacks ignored MOVE's plea for justice. Politicians placed their reputations ahead of dignity and concern for human life and justice for the brothers and sisters of MOVE. They refused to touch the situation or get involved, even though they were cognizant of the MOVE family being mistreated as early as 1978.

The confrontation would have occurred anyway, whether there existed a Black, white, red, or yellow mayor. The fact is that no one controls the Philadelphia police except the Philadelphia police! And where there is a situation involving Blacks such as MOVE, a "free-for-all" commences. Like an invitation to a party containing such words as, "Bring your own bottle," I can honestly believe from my ample experience during the 1960s that they were saying, prior to the May 13 confrontation, "Bring your own weapons," as long as they are the deadly ones.

The status of police misconduct and corruption in Philadelphia is overwhelming, but the status of racist activity perpetrated by the Philadelphia police against Black citizens is exceedingly more hostile than Mississippi, Alabama, and Georgia's racist activity combined today.

What do you think has to be done to prevent such an atrocity from happening again?

To prevent such an atrocity from happening again the City of Philadelphia will first have to clean house and rid itself of the evil racist forces that exist. They say that Billy Penn founded this city in 1682 and named it "Philadelphia," which comes from the Greek language, meaning "Brotherly Love." Well, I still say that the Indians were here first. Now, this is definitely a fictitious and deceptive act of perjury – to allow non-natives of Philadelpia to believe that this is really the "City of Brotherly Love."

Perhaps we could use the phrase, "The City of Brotherly Shove" like I've been hearing around town for many years. We could even use "Gestapo Cultural Land," or we could just call it any old thing that a slave might use while residing on some plantation.

I am not putting the blame on Billy Penn. I am sure his intention was to plan the town as a place of racial and religious freedom and equality for all. How can we call this city "the City of Brotherly Love" when hiring practices toward qualified Blacks are racially administered by most white employers? If the city's so-called officials believe in a democratic society, and they truly believe in Abraham Lincoln, George Washington, and even God and many other "long-haired," bearded historic figures whom they praise, then why won't they practice what they perpetually preach and what they have been teaching our children?

How can we call "Philly" what it is called when we can see as clearly as we can see a germ under a powerful microscope, discrimination in housing? A Black man, woman, or family cannot move into a community of their desire without some racist group of whites vandalizing their homes and making terrorist threats toward them. Is it "Brotherly Love" when the white father, mother, and kids all team up together to cast rocks at your windows, or firebomb your home, just because your skin color is a little darker? Yes, to prevent such an atrocity from happening again, like the MOVE tragedy, we would have to clean house and rid the city of those evil racist forces by trying to educate those white citizens in regard to the definition of love.

We must rid the police force of racists, bigots, and white supremacists, who shield their true identity behind the badge that bears the words: Integrity, Honor, and Service.

We must reinvestigate the entire police department and terminate those with racist attitudes and those with a chronic history of racist activities.

We must thoroughly investigate those members of the force who reside in areas such as Juniata Park, Elmwood, Tasker, Grays Ferry, the Northeast, and other sections of Philadelphia, where Black citizens are not welcomed and cannot express their freedom and rights to live wherever they want.

A policeman who resides in these areas will not deceive his neighbors by enforcing the law when a mob of white residents attacks an innocent Black family moving into his area! He will condone the activities of his fellow neighbors, therefore making him part of the problem and definitely not the solution.

We must investigate the current, as well as preexamine new applicants to the police force.

Those who do not comprehend the cultural and religious aspects of various races should not be part of any law enforcement agency.

There will always be recurrences of situations like the MOVE confrontation in Philadelphia, until the racist forces controlling city government are removed permanently.

Jitu Weusi

Part of the Continuing Holocaust

Tuesday morning we awakened to the news that an entire block of a West Philadelphia African-American community had been devastated with an unknown loss of life and property because the police were attempting to evict a single family from their home.

Recently an eviction in New York cost a 65-year-old grandmother her life and now the eviction of the MOVE family from a Philadelphia neighborhood wipes out an entire community of sixty homes with more than two hundred persons immediately made homeless.

History is Teacher

Over the years of our domicile in America, Africans have been the victims of countless senseless acts of brutality and destruction aimed at our community. These acts have been committed by private groups and individuals like the KKK and other white racist organizations, and these acts have been committed by agents of the state, like the police department and the U.S. Army.

About a year ago CBS television's *Sixty Minutes* focused on the town of Rosewood, Florida. Rosewood, which existed in the early 1900s, was a small Colored town in northern Florida that was totally destroyed by a white mob one night when news spread that a Black male had raped a white woman. The mob rode into town about midnight, fired some shots and set fire to all the homes and businesses in the town. The next morning Rosewood was a smouldering mass of ashes and ruins.

Other acts of devastation against African-American communities in Texas, Oklahoma, Georgia, and Illinois have taken place since the early 1900s.

First published in the *Daily Challenge*, a Black newspaper in Brooklyn, New York, on May 17, 1985. Reprinted here by permission of the author.

Philadelphia and MOVE

MOVE, or the Family Africa as they are commonly known in the African-American community of Philadelphia, is a communal-type, back-to-nature organization that established headquarters in the city in the early 1970s. Their members believe that Africans in America have become disastrously dependent upon modern technology and therefore are captive of it. MOVE members are taught to live their lives without any of the conveniences of modern technology. They live without bathrooms, running water, electricity, gas, telephone, and other items most of us classify as "necessities." MOVE families are vegetarians (they consume only products grown on farms) and live collectively in families that are composed of men, women, and children. MOVE members are nonviolent and don't engage in criminal activities. Their confrontation with Philadelphia authorities has occurred around their disregard for sanitation and child-rearing laws.

In 1975 and again in 1979 the Philadelphia police confronted members of the MOVE organization. Both confrontations resulted in destruction of property and loss of life to MOVE members.

Prepared with the history of past confrontations, it is inconceivable that the police did not know another similar confrontation would result in additional deaths and property damage.

Mayor Goode's Shame

Wilson Goode, an African-American, is the current mayor of Philadelphia. Goode rode to victory in 1983 on the heels of the Harold Washington uprising in Chicago and with the upsurge in Black vote power that produced the Jesse Jackson campaign.

Goode illustrated his disrespect for the African-American community in 1984 when he decided to support Walter Mondale over Jesse Jackson in the presidential primary election.

Being a long-time resident of Philadelphia, Mayor Goode was knowledgeable of the sensitive and explosive nature of any eviction of the MOVE organization. Why wasn't another method used to evict the group rather than a siege by the notorious Philadelphia police department?

When the siege began and it became impossible to dislodge the MOVE family without a massive dislocation of the entire community, why did Mayor Goode give the police permission to use bombs in a residential neighborhood?

More than any individual Wilson Goode must bear the weight of this loss of life and property suffered by the African-American community.

Backlash for Black Elected Officials

After the immediate impact of this tragedy has passed, the Philadelphia holocaust will pose long-standing questions to Black elected officials.

If white elected officials can arrest and apprehend infamous white killers and cultists without causing destruction and loss of life in Euro-American communities, why was this tragedy unavoidable? The Charles Manson family, the Hell's Angels, Nazi groups, and Klan organizations have been arrested, all without massive sieges and dislocation.

Why then did an African-American elected official, with a large staff and ample knowledge of a sensitive situation, make such a destructive and devastating blunder?

Black voters may decide that rather than voting for robots like Wilson Goode they would prefer to have known racists like former Philadelphia Mayor Frank Rizzo or New York Mayor Ed Koch remain in office. At least with them in office, their actions will be predictable and expected.

The Philadelphia tragedy will be historic if it serves as a barometer by which we can evaluate the type of African-American that we should elect to office.

In the past anyone with dark skin was acceptable. Now we must begin to weigh who these officials are that are elected to serve. If an African-American leader is elected to office and then proceeds to take actions that are harmful and destructive to the African-American community, it is our duty to demand the resignation or impeachment of that official immediately.

In the future before the African-American community votes for any African-American official to represent their interest, they must thoroughly investigate that person's background and associations and decide if they are truly concerned about our livelihood.

Alice Walker

"Nobody Was Supposed to Survive": The MOVE Massacre of '85

"Under questioning by commission members, Mr. Goode said he thought he managed the crisis well with the information he had at the time. But he said that he realized in retrospect that his subordinates had not given him enough data to make proper decisions, such as dropping a bomb on the MOVE house. *He was first asked for permission, which he granted, to use the device 17 minutes before it was dropped from a helicopter."* (My italics.) *New York Times,* Oct. 16, 1985.

"Mr. Goode also said that Mr. Sambor had violated his orders not to involve police officers in the assault who might hold what the Mayor called a 'grudge' from participating in a confrontation with the radical group at another MOVE house in 1978. *Several officers involved in that siege participated in the assault this year."* (My italics.) *New York Times,* Oct. 16, 1985.

"One of two people known to have survived an inferno that killed 11 people said that police gunfire drove fleeing members of the radical group MOVE back into their blazing house in the May 13 confrontation with police. . . ." *New York Times,* Oct. 31, 1985.

"(Detective) Stephenson's log also gives a gruesome glimpse of just what kind of deaths MOVE was forced to endure. Excerpts of entries concerning the search for bodies revealed, '15:35 – The body of a female was recovered 10 feet from rear door, 8 feet from west wall. On her foot, left, was a black Chinese slipper and was lying on her right side facing the rear wall. No other clothing . . . head and chest appeared to be crushed, can't recall hair – all photographed.

'16:05 – The body of a child was recovered under the female. Same area. No description. Only bones.

'17:50 – Left forearm with clenched fist recovered at door. . . .

'19:45 – Adult male from waist down recovered, no descriptions. Some skin . . .

'11:30 – The body of one Negro/male was lifted from the front area with his heart outside the chest area by crane . . . no arms, legs missing from thighs down. No head. . . ." *Revolutionary Worker*, Nov. 14, 1985.

"According to the report, [The Commission on the MOVE "confrontation"] *Goode paused only 30 seconds before approving the dropping of the explosives."* (My italics.) *Philadelphia Inquirer*, March 2, 1986.

"Negotiation with MOVE was never seriously considered. . . ." (Ibid.)

"A long gun battle ensued. The commission says the 10,000 rounds of ammunition fired [into the house] was 'excessive and unreasonable,' especially given the presence of children in the residence.

"In addition, the report notes that work crews found only two pistols, a shotgun and a .22 caliber rifle in the rubble of the MOVE compound." (Ibid.)

"Once the firing began, it could have been quickly put out if the Fire Department immediately had used high pressure Squrt water guns it had trained on the house. However, . . . Sambor and Fire commissioner William C. Richmond hastily made the "unconscionable" decision to let the fire burn, hoping to force the MOVE members to flee." (Ibid.)

"At least two adults and four children attempted to escape after the house caught fire, but police gunfire prevented them from fleeing." (Ibid.)

"Nobody was supposed to survive." Ramona Africa, *New York Times*, January 7, 1986.

How Does It Feel?

I was in Paris in mid-May of 1985 when I heard the news about MOVE. My travelling companion read aloud the item in the newspaper that described the assault on a house on Osage

Avenue in Philadelphia occupied by a group of "radical, black, back-to-nature" revolutionaries that local authorities had been "battling" for over a decade. As he read the article detailing the attack that led, eventually, to the actual bombing of the house (with military bombing material supplied to local police by the FBI) and the deaths of at least eleven people, many of them women, five of them children, our mutual feeling was of horror followed immediately by anger and grief. Grief: that feeling of unassuageable sadness and rage that makes the heart feel naked to the elements, clawed by talons of ice. For, even knowing nothing of MOVE (short for Movement, which a revolution assumes) and little of the "City of Brotherly Love," Philadelphia, we recognized the heartlessness of the crime, and realized that for the local authorities to go after eleven people, five of them children, with the kind of viciousness and force usually reserved for war, what they were trying to kill had to be more than the human beings involved, but a spirit, an idea.

But what spirit? What idea?

There was only one adult survivor of the massacre: a young black woman named Ramona Africa. She suffered serious burns over much of her body (and would claim, later in court, as she sustained her own defense: "I am guilty of nothing but [of] hiding in the basement trying to protect myself and...MOVE children"). The bombing of the MOVE house ignited a fire that roared through the entire black, middle-class neighborhood, totally destroying over sixty homes and leaving two hundred and fifty people homeless.

There we stood on a street corner in Paris, reading between the lines. It seems MOVE people never combed their hair but wore it in long "ropes" that people assumed was unclean. Since this is also how we wear our hair, we recognized this "weird" style. Dreadlocks. The style of the ancients: Ethiopians and Egyptians. Easily washed, quickly dried—a true wash and wear style for black people (and adventuresome whites) and painless, which is no doubt why MOVE people chose it for their children. And for themselves: "Why suffer for cosmetic reasons?" they must have asked.

It appeared the MOVE people were vegetarians and ate their food raw because they believe raw food healthier for the body and the soul. They believed in letting orange peels, banana peels, and other organic refuse "cycle" back into the earth. Composting? They did not believe in embalming dead people or burying them in caskets. They thought they should be allowed to "cycle" back to the earth too. They loved dogs (their leader, John Africa, was called "The Dog Man" because he cared for so many) and never killed animals of any kind, not even rats (which infuriated their neighbors) because they believed in the sanctity of all life.

Hummm.

Further: They refused to send their children to school, fearing drugs and an indoctrination into the sickness of American life. They taught them to enjoy "natural" games, in the belief that games based on such figures as Darth Vader caused "distortions" in the personalities of the young that inhibited healthy spontaneous expression. They exercised religiously, running miles every day with their dogs, rarely had sit-down dinners, ate out of big sacks of food whenever they were hungry, owned no furniture except a few pieces they found on the street, and refused to let their children wear diapers because of the belief that a free bottom is more healthy. They abhorred the use of plastic. They enjoyed, apparently, the use of verbal profanity which they claimed lost any degree of profanity when placed next to atomic or nuclear weapons of any sort, which they considered *really* profane. They hated the police, who they claimed harassed them relentlessly (a shoot-out with police in 1978 resulted in the death of one officer and the imprisonment of several MOVE people). They occasionally self-righteously and disruptively harangued their neighbors using bullhorns. They taught anyone who would listen that the American political and social system is corrupt to the core – and tried to be themselves, a different tribe, within it.

Back home in America I heard little of the MOVE massacre. Like members of MOVE I don't watch TV. The local papers were full of bombings, as usual, but bombings in Libya, Lebanon, El Salvador, and Angola-Mozambique. There seemed to be an amazingly silent response to the bombing of these black people, the majority of them women and children, presided over, after all, by a black mayor, the honorable Wilson Goode of the aforementioned City of Brotherly, etc. (Meanwhile there was incredible controversy over the filming of a movie in which no one is killed and a black man slaps a woman!*) Nor do I yet know what to make of this silence. Was the bombing of black people, with a black person ostensibly (in any case) responsible, too much for the collective black psyche to bear? Were people stunned by the

---

The Color Purple

realization that such an atrocity – formerly confined to Libya or Viet Nam – could happen to us? Did I simply miss the controversy? Were there town meetings and teach-ins and pickets round the clock in every city Wilson Goode and his police officers appeared? Or did the media (and Philadelphia officials, including the black mayor of which black Philadelphians were so proud) succeed in convincing the public that the victims were indeed the aggressors and deserved what they got? Ramona Africa, after all, was arrested for assault and sentenced to prison for "riot"- and it was *her* house that was bombed, her friends, colleagues and loved ones who were slaughtered.

Thumbing through the stacks of articles I've been sent on the MOVE massacre, I see that an earlier assault on their house occurred in 1978, when a white man, Frank Rizzo, was mayor. Under Rizzo, MOVE people were evicted, often imprisoned, their neighborhood destroyed, and many of them killed. And why?

Through both administrations the city officials and MOVE neighbors appeared to have one thing in common: a hatred of the way MOVE people chose to live. They didn't like the "stench" of people who refused, because they believe chemicals cause cancer, to use deodorant. Didn't like orange peels and watermelon rinds on the ground. Didn't like all those "naked" children running around with all that uncombed hair. They didn't appreciate the dogs and the rats. They thought the children should be in school and that the adults and children should eat cooked food; everybody should eat meat. They probably thought it low class that in order to make money MOVE people washed cars and shovelled snow. And appeared to enjoy it.

MOVE people were not middle class. Many of them were high school drop-outs. Many of them mothers without husbands. Or young men who refused any inducement to "fit in." Yet they had the nerve to critique the system. To reject it and to set up, in place of its rules, guidelines for living that reflected their own beliefs.

The people of MOVE are proof that poor people (not just upper and middle class whites and blacks who become hippies) are capable of intelligently perceiving and analyzing American life, politically and socially, and of devising and attempting to follow a different – and to them, better – way. But because they are poor and black this is not acceptable behavior to middle class whites and blacks who think all poor black people should be happy with jherri curls, mindless (and lying) tv shows, and Kentucky fried chicken.

This is not to condone the yelping of fifty to sixty dogs in the middle of the night. Dogs MOVE people rescued from the streets (and probable subsequent torture in "scientific" laboratories), fed, and permitted to sleep in their house. Nor the bullhorn aimed at airing their neighbors' backwardness and political transgressions, as apparently they had a bad habit. From what I read MOVE people were more philosophical than perfect; I probably would not have been able to live next door to them for a day.

The question is — did they deserve the harassment, abuse, and finally the vicious death other people's intolerance of their lifestyle brought upon them? *Every bomb ever made falls on all of us.* And the answer is no.

"The real reason for the government hit-squad is no secret: MOVE is an organization of radical utopians. Their political activity, their allusions to Africa, their dreadlocks, all speak rejection of the system. For this, they have been harassed, besieged, framed, beaten, shot, jailed and now bombed. The reported shout from the MOVE compound this last fateful Monday was: 'We ain't got a fucking thing to lose.' " *Revolutionary Worker* leaflet, May 16, 1985.

How does it feel
to watch your neighbors
burn to death
because you hated
the sound
of their dogs
barking
and were not yourself
crazy
about compost heaps?

How does it feel
to hear the children
scream in the flames
because you said
the clothes they wore
in winter
were never enough
to keep them warm?

How does it feel
to know the hair
you hated
spreads like a fan
around a severed head
beside the door?

How does it feel
to "take full responsibility"
as the mayor said
for an "absolute
disaster"
to your soul?

How does it feel to massacre
the part of yourself
that is really,
well-
considering the nappy hair and the watermelon rinds
and naked black booties
and all-
pretty much
an embarrassment?
What *will* the white people
think!

How does it feel, folks?
The bad image is gone:
you can talk now.
How does it feel?

When they come for us
what can we say?

Our beliefs are
our country
Our hair is
our flag
Our love of our children
is our freedom.

We too, fucking yes,
sing America.

B | The "Draw the Line" Campaign

In response to the May 13 massacre, Black and other activists on the East Coast drafted a "Draw the Line" statement and waged a persistent, year-long campaign to have it published in a major Philadelphia newspaper. The efforts of "Draw the Line" were important because after May 13 there was a concerted effort by the authorities to suppress and keep out of the public eye any criticism or condemnation of the bombing, and thus to give the impression that no one was seriously questioning it and in fact everyone was going along with it. And with various efforts also afoot either to support or excuse Mayor Goode's role, the "Draw the Line" statement and campaign worked to help change the perception that it is acceptable for a Black mayor to sanction the bombing of a group like MOVE.

From the outset, "Draw the Line" attempted to unite broad sections behind the statement and also rallied respected individuals – representing various political and social trends – whose many years in the struggles of Black and other minority nationalities gave them a right as well as responsibility to speak out against the MOVE bombing.

"Draw the Line" was controversial. Some welcomed its timeliness and uncompromising stand; others pondered and hesitated; and still others took a hands-off approach. But the weight of the unfolding evidence of a premeditated massacre swung significant numbers over to take a stand. Letters, a phone campaign, and media appearances to promote "Draw the Line" were undertaken. An impressive list of signatories was gathered nationwide – from Black intellectuals, activists, theologians, and artists, along with the signatures of progressive people of all nationalities.

While the considerable cost of publishing the "Draw the Line" statement as a paid advertisement represented a problem, the most serious obstacle came from the Philadelphia newspapers. The *Philadelphia Inquirer* would not run the statement. In December 1985, "Draw the Line" was tersely informed in a letter that the *Inquirer* had "decided not to accept this advertisement." The *Inquirer* rejected it on the basis of its content and would not elaborate any further. In an emergency letter, the Draw the Line Ad Fund pointed out: "While the people of Philadelphia are inundated every day with the official 'terms of debate' in their daily papers and in national TV shows...the powers-that-be are evidently determined to prevent them from hearing a different and opposing viewpoint."

The *Philadelphia Tribune*, a Black-owned newspaper supportive of Mayor Goode, also refused to accept the ad. "Draw the Line" organizers sought a personal meeting with the newspaper's publisher and forwarded to the *Tribune* a proposal from Dr. Carlton B. Goodlett, publisher of the *San Francisco Sun-Reporter*, a major Black newspaper in the San Francisco area. Goodlett offered to publish, for free, "Draw the Line" in the *Sun-Reporter* once the ad was published in the *Tribune*. But the *Tribune* still refused to accept the ad, saying that still so soon after the bombing, the atmosphere was "not right" for it. In response, Dr. Goodlett went ahead and published the statement in a weekend edition of the *Sun-Reporter*.

"Draw the Line" organizers continued to push forward and in February 1986 an important benefit for the campaign was held in Harlem. The following month, publication of the final report of Mayor Goode's Philadelphia Special Investigation Commission once again focused attention on the events of May 13, and "Draw the Line" immediately called a press conference in New York City. With the commission's report summarizing May 13 as a terrible but unintended mess, the message and stand of "Draw the Line" stood out all the more sharply. Two major Black-owned weeklies in New York, the *Amsterdam News* and the *City Sun*, ran front-page articles on the "Draw the Line" campaign; it was gaining important attention and more respect for its tenacity and continuing efforts to condemn the bombing.

Remaining firm in its resolve to break into the Philadelphia papers, in the spring of 1986 "Draw the Line" resubmitted the ad, with a slight wording change, for publication in the *Philadelphia Inquirer*. But they were again informed that the ad was unacceptable. And while another newspaper, the *Delaware County Daily Times*, ran an article on "Draw the Line," it too refused to accept the ad.

The ad was also resubmitted to the *Philadelphia Tribune*. Here there was a somewhat changed attitude. In part this seemed to reflect the deteriorating situation for Mayor Goode, who was finding himself more and more on the defensive as facts continued to spill out about May 13 and his role in those events. Reversing its previous censorship, the *Tribune* now agreed to publish "Draw the Line" as a paid ad. Finally, after a successful eleventh-hour fund-raising effort, the "Draw the Line" statement hit the Philadelphia newsstands when it was published in the May 23, 1986 edition of the *Tribune*, with over one hundred signatures on it.

A letter to supporters from "Draw the Line" declared that an important victory had at last been won, but also stressed that the publication of the statement "represents a beginning. Draw the Line has seen the light of day, but we cannot allow it to fall into the shadows." Below is the statement and the signatories. (Because of space limitations, it was not possible in the ad to list all the signatories.)

Endnotes

Introduction

For this and following chapters the source for quoted testimony from the Philadelphia Special Investigation Commission (PSIC) is the transcript of the hearings on file at the main branch of the Philadelphia Free Public Library, Government Publications room. The citations used here will follow that of the transcripts in the following order: name of witness, date of testimony, a.m. or p.m. session, and page number.

Another source available to the reader is the *Philadelphia Inquirer's* excerpts of testimony from the PSIC hearings published in two supplements entitled "The MOVE Transcripts," 28 October 1985 and 3 November 1985. The hearings were also televised by WHYY (Channel 12) and radio broadcast by WHYY (91FM) in Philadelphia.

During the first weeks of the hearings, the *Philadelphia Inquirer* and the *Philadelphia Daily News* did not publish due to a strike. Other publications which reported on the hearings during this period include the *New York Times*, the *Philadelphia Tribune*, the *Delaware County Daily Times*, *USA Today*, *The Times* (Trenton, New Jersey), and *Temple University News*.

Citations from the "Findings, Conclusions and Recommendations of the Philadelphia Special Investigation Commission," 6 March 1986, follow the text and page numbering from the bound edition released by the commission. This report was also published in a special edition of the *Philadelphia Daily News*, 7 March 1986.

Citations from testimony at Ramona Africa's trial, unless otherwise noted, are from the author's personal notes.

1. "A Neighborhood No More," *Philadelphia Inquirer*, 19 May 1985.
2. Ibid.
3. Ibid.
4. Letter to friends and supporters from MOVE women prisoners incarcerated at the State Correctional Institution, Muncy, PA, February 1986, p. 3.
5. Author's interview with MOVE spokesperson Gerald Ford Africa, May 1985.
6. See chapter 5 for more on this incident.
7. "'That Empty Spot' Was Her Family's Home," *Philadelphia Daily News*, 15 May 1985.
8. "A Neighborhood No More," *Philadelphia Inquirer*, 19 May 1985.
9. Ibid.
10. Ibid.

11. "Rendell Says City Was Told in June It Had Basis to Act," *Philadelphia Inquirer*, 18 May 1985.

12. "Six Bodies, 2 of Children, Taken from MOVE Rubble," *Philadelphia Inquirer*, 15 May 1985.

13. "Goode: The Right Decision, Despite the Consequences," *Philadelphia Inquirer*, 15 May 1985.

14. "How Others Would Handle Explosive Situation/Goode's Got Mayors' Support," *Philadelphia Daily News*, 16 May 1985.

15. CBS television broadcast of *Face the Nation*, "Siege in Philadelphia: MOVE and the Mayor," 19 May 1985. See also "MOVE Letter Threatened Fire," *Philadelphia Inquirer*, 20 May 1985.

16. "The Philadelphia Massacre: Reality and Future Shock," *Revolutionary Worker*, 20 May 1985. See also "City Reports No Automatic Guns," *Philadelphia Inquirer*, 18 May 1985.

17. "Goode, 2 Aides Differ on MOVE," *Philadelphia Inquirer*, 17 May 1985.

18. "Minority Cops Defend Sambor," *Philadelphia Daily News*, 22 May 1985.

19. CBS, *Face the Nation*, "Siege in Philadelphia." See also "MOVE Letter Threatened Fire," *Philadelphia Inquirer*, 20 May 1985.

20. CBS, *Face the Nation*, "Siege in Philadelphia." See also "Congress to Investigate?" *Philadelphia Daily News*, 20 May 1985.

21. "City Combs the Rubble for Answers," *Philadelphia Daily News*, 15 May 1985.

22. Author's interview with Clifford Bond, May 1985.

23. "MOVE House Is Bombed; Blaze Involves 60 Homes/Gunfight Continues After Blast," *Philadelphia Inquirer*, 14 May 1985.

24. Author's interview, 14 May 1985.

25. "The Findings, Conclusions and Recommendations of the Philadelphia Special Investigation Commission" (hereafter referred to as "PSIC Findings"), 6 March 1986, p. 45.

26. Ibid., p. 52. The PSIC wrote of MOVE: "They threatened violence to anyone who would attempt to enforce normal societal rules" (ibid., p. 19). For more on this, see chapter 7.

27. "Those Who Promote City Worry," *Philadelphia Inquirer*, 15 May 1985.

1 | The Plan

1. "After Worst Day of His Career, Goode Moves Agressively," *Philadelphia Inquirer*, 15 May 1985.

2. Ibid.

3. Ibid.

4. "Goode: the Right Decision, Despite the Consequences," *Philadelphia Inquirer*, 15 May 1985.

5. Ramona Africa, "Long Live John Africa! Long Live John Africa's Revolution!" (a public letter), 13 May 1986.

6. "Sources: Planners Doubted Intelligence Info," *Philadelphia Daily News*, 15 May 1985.

7. "MOVE Mom, Kids Routed During Raid," *Delaware County Daily Times*, 14 May 1985.

8. Police officer George Draper's testimony, PSIC hearings, 8 October 1985, p.m. session, pp. 15-16.

9. Police officers George Draper and John Cresci's testimony, PSIC hearings, 8 October 1985, p.m. session, pp. 5-12.

10. See District Seven Supervisor of the Department of Licenses and Inspection Jules Pergolini and Chief of District Operations Rudolf Paliaga's testimony regarding the police's requested and unrecorded drive-by inspections, PSIC hearings, 11 October 1985, a.m. session, p. 18.

11. Wilson Goode's testimony, PSIC hearings, 11 October 1985, p.m. session, pp. 103-4, and Leo Brooks' testimony, PSIC hearings, 16 October 1985, a.m. session, pp. 9, 10, 21-23.

12. Brooks' testimony, PSIC hearings, 16 October 1985, a.m. session, p. 24.

13. Sgt. Herbert Kirk's testimony, PSIC hearings, 11 October 1985, p.m. session, pp. 4-6. Kirk retired four months before the May 13, 1985 massacre.

14. Ibid., p. 7. Kirk's testimony represented the most extensive public elaboration of the elements of this plan. Details of the plan first emerged in August 1985 (see "Assault Planned in 1984," *Philadelphia Daily News*, 20 August 1985).

15. Kirk's testimony, PSIC hearings, 11 October 1985, p.m. session, pp. 12-14.

16. Ibid., pp. 13, 22.

17. "How the Bomb Decision Was Made," *Philadelphia Inquirer*, 17 May 1985.

18. Kirk's testimony, PSIC hearings, 11 October 1985, p.m. session, p. 21.

19. Ibid., p. 47, emphasis added.

20. Ibid., pp. 28-29.

21. Ibid., pp. 33-35.

22. Brooks' testimony, PSIC hearings, 16 October 1985, a.m. session, p. 32.

23. "Hands Off Osage," *Philadelphia Daily News*, 11 June 1985, emphasis added.

24. PSIC exhibit 37A (memorandum from the office of District Attorney Edward Rendell which was sent to Mayor Wilson Goode), dated 21 June 1984, p. 2.

25. "Police Face Off with Gunman at MOVE House," *Philadelphia Inquirer*, 4 May 1984.

26. District Supervisor of the Pennsylvania Board of Probation and Parole – Philadelphia office Yvonne Haskins' testimony, PSIC hearings, 10 October 1985, p.m. session, pp. 115-17. See also "Parole Jumper Didn't Warrant Raid on Osage House," *Philadelphia Daily News*, 17 May 1985.

27. "Police Out in Force at MOVE House," *Philadelphia Inquirer*, 9 August 1984.

28. Kirk's testimony, PSIC hearings, 11 October 1985, p.m. session, pp. 54-55.

29. Ramona Africa, "Memorandum in Support of Motion to Dismiss" (written for Civil Action Case No. 85-3), filed in the United States District Court for the Eastern District of Pennsylvania, p. 6.

30. Lucien Blackwell's testimony, PSIC hearings, 22 October 1985, p.m. session, p. 73.

31. "PSIC Findings," p. 27.

32. Ibid.

33. Goode's testimony, PSIC hearings, 15 October 1985, p.m. session, p. 43, emphasis added.

34. "Goode Says He's 'Fully Accountable' for Siege," *Philadelphia Inquirer*, 14 May 1985.

35. See, for example, Sambor's testimony, PSIC hearings, 17 October 1985, a.m. session, pp. 4-9, and 18 October 1985, a.m. session, pp. 27-30.

36. See Ramona Africa, "Facts Regarding May 13 Confrontation" (a public letter), October 1985, p. 7.

37. Sambor's testimony, PSIC hearings, 17 October 1985, a.m. session, pp. 71-72.

38. Brooks's testimony, PSIC hearings, 16 October 1985, a.m. session, p. 53.

39. Ibid.

40. Ibid., pp. 54, 61, 62.

41. Sgt. Albert Revel's testimony, PSIC hearings, 24 October 1985, a.m. session, pp. 84-85. See also "Officers: Water Was 'Diversion,' " *Philadelphia Inquirer*, 25 October 1985.

42. Sambor's testimony, PSIC hearings, 17 October 1985, p.m. session, pp. 55-56.

43. Ibid., pp. 53-54.

44. "Goode Cites Arrrest Warrants as Basis for Siege Decision," *Philadelphia Inquirer*, 14 May 1985.

45. See "Goode: the Right Decision, Despite the Consequences," *Philadelphia Inquirer*, 15 May 1985. See also "Affidavit of Probable Cause for Arrest/Complaint-Rider," Warrant #127802, signed by Civil Affairs Officer Theodore Vaughan, 11 May 1985, pp. 3-4.

46. "PSIC Findings," p. 35.

47. Ibid.

48. Irene Pernsley's testimony, PSIC hearings, 10 October 1985, p.m. session, pp. 194-95.

49. Ibid., p. 195.

50. "PSIC Findings," p. 35.

51. Ramona Africa, "Facts Regarding May 13 Confrontation," p. 18.

52. "PSIC Findings," p. 36. See also Draper's testimony, PSIC hearings, 5 November 1985, a.m. session, pp. 16-17, and "Africa Questions Officer about Motive of Probe," *Philadelphia Inquirer*, 30 January 1986.

53. "The Calm Amid the Threat," *Philadelphia Inquirer*, 13 May 1985.

54. "Talks/Settlement Hopes Foundered on Issue of Future Arrests," *Philadelphia Inquirer*, 14 May 1985.

55. Ibid.

56. Ibid.

57. "MOVE Gives Up Its Guns; Barricades Are Removed," *Philadelphia Inquirer*, 10 May 1978.

58. Author's interview with MOVE spokesperson Gerald Ford Africa, May 1985.

59. Irv Homer's testimony at the trial of Ramona Africa, 27 January 1986. See "Birdie Takes Stand," *Philadelphia Tribune*, 28 January 1986. Further, PPD Civil Affairs Officer George Draper admitted during the trial of Ramona Africa that he heard MOVE's early morning broadcast for the PPD to contact the three media personalities. When asked if he felt negotiations were a real possibility, Draper said yes but that "I didn't do anything about it." See "Cop: Didn't Talk When MOVE Asked," *Philadelphia Daily News*, 17 January 1986.

60. Author's interview with Chauncey Campbell, September 1986.

2 | The Assault

1. "Six Bodies, 2 of Children Taken from MOVE Rubble," *Philadelphia Inquirer*, 15 May 1985.

2. Goode's testimony, PSIC hearings, 15 October 1985, a.m. session, p. 66.

3. "Police Prepare to Evict MOVE/Members Threaten Officers," *Philadelphia Inquirer*, 13 May 1985.

4. "Neighbors Are Put Out," *Philadelphia Daily News*, 13 May 1985.

5. Novella Williams' testimony, PSIC hearings, 22 October 1985, p.m. session, p. 44.

6. Author's interview, summer 1985.

7. From film footage aired on Philadelphia TV station WCAU (Channel 10), *MOVE: What Really Happened?*, 13 August 1985.

8. Author's interview, summer 1985.

9. "What Phila. Police Brought to Bear Against MOVE," *Philadelphia Inquirer*, 11 August 1985.

10. Goode's testimony, PSIC hearings, 15 October 1985, a.m. session, pp. 49-50.

11. Ibid., pp. 52-53.

12. Brooks' testimony, PSIC hearings, 16 October 1985, a.m. session, p. 59.

13. Goode's testimony, PSIC hearings, 15 October 1985, a.m. session, p. 52.

14. "What Phila. Police Brought to Bear Against MOVE," *Philadelphia Inquirer*, 11 August 1985.

15. Ibid. The presence of an antitank gun was revealed at the PSIC hearings.

16. Sambor's testimony, PSIC hearings, 17 October 1985, p.m. session, pp. 46-47.

17. Revel's testimony, PSIC hearings, 24 October 1985, a.m. session, p. 47.

18. Ibid.

19. "Police Storm Osage Ave. House," *Philadelphia Daily News*, 13 May 1985.

20. Sambor's testimony, PSIC hearings, 17 October 1985, p.m. session, p. 116.

21. "How the Bomb Decision Was Made," *Philadelphia Inquirer*, 17 May 1985.

22. Sambor's testimony, PSIC hearings, 17 October 1985, p.m. session, p. 121.

23. Author's interview, 14 May 1985.

24. Sambor's testimony, PSIC hearings, 17 October 1985, p.m. session, pp. 121-22.

25. "PSIC Findings," p. 39.

26. Ibid.

27. "What the Phila. Police Brought to Bear Against MOVE," *Philadelphia Inquirer*, 11 August 1985.

28. Ibid.

29. "Talks/Settlement Hopes Foundered on Issue of Future Arrests," *Philadelphia Inquirer*, 14 May 1985.

30. Author's interview, summer 1985.

31. See "Day of Friction Between Media, Police," *Philadelphia Daily News*, 14 May 1985, which reports that Janet McMillan, Robert J. "Bo" Terry and Gregory Lanier of the *Philadelphia Inquirer* were "searched without cause, their notes and film rolls confiscated and held [by police] . . . police found [*Philadelphia Daily News*] reporter Edward Moran and photographer Michael Mercanti holed up in a house near the MOVE site. They were charged with burglary until police could verify they had the owner's permission to use the house. Photographers Denis O'Keefe and Rick Bowmer had their film confiscated. Authorities held Bowmer's equipment." See also "Assignment: Philly's Fiery Fiasco," *American Photographer*, August 1985, p. 82, which reports that the police took a roll of film from Gregory Lanier and exposed it.

32. "What Phila. Police Brought to Bear Against MOVE," *Philadelphia Inquirer*, 11 August 1985.

33. The original plan to enter 6219 Osage Avenue was changed, according to the PPD, because it was felt to be highly probable that MOVE members would locate themselves in 6219, which was a vacant property. Further, two police officers, disguised as workmen, had entered 6219 on May 11 and attempted unsuccessfully to insert spike mikes (eavesdropping equipment) in the common wall between 6219 and 6221. The officers' presence was detected by MOVE and thus the PPD felt that their plan to use 6219 had been compromised. See Sgt. Edward Connor's testimony, PSIC hearings, 25 October 1985, p.m. session, pp. 10-11.

34. James Phelan's testimony, PSIC hearings, 1 November 1985, p.m. session, pp. 14, 44.

35. Ibid., pp. 38-41.

36. The extensive damage done to MOVE's house and adjoining houses during the morning hours of May 13, 1985 was established during the questioning of witnesses at the PSIC hearings, including Gregore Sambor (17 October 1985, p.m. session, pp. 134-42) and the testimony of police officers John Reiber and Lawrence D'Ulisse (29 October 1985, a.m. session, pp. 37-40, 68-71).

37. Connor's testimony, PSIC hearings, 25 October 1985, p.m. session, pp. 68-70. Connor testified that he did not think the body he saw was dismembered. Previously, the *Philadelphia Inquirer* wrote: "In private conversations, Connor has said that what he saw was a headless torso,

according to one city official" ("Hours before MOVE Bomb, Blasts May
Have Killed 2," *Philadelphia Inquirer,* 4 September 1985).

38. Goode's testimony, PSIC hearings, 15 October 1985, a.m. session,
p. 94.

39. Brooks' testimony, PSIC hearings, 16 October 1985, pp. 25-26.

40. Connor's testimony, PSIC hearings, 25 October 1985, p.m. session,
pp. 18-25, 46-47.

41. Sambor's testimony, PSIC hearings, 18 October 1985, a.m. session,
p. 12.

42. Ibid.

43. "PSIC Findings," p. 40.

44. Ibid., p. 39.

3 | The Bomb

1. "MOVE House Is Bombed; Blaze Involves 60 Homes/Gunfight Continues After Blast," *Philadelphia Inquirer,* 14 May 1985.

2. "Mayor and Police Didn't Listen, the Owner of MOVE House Says,"
Philadelphia Inquirer, 14 May 1985.

3. Ibid.

4. Author's interview with a representative of the Citizen's Committee
for Humanity and Justice, 8 October 1985.

5. Ibid.

6. Press conference at City Hall, 13 May 1985. Film footage from the
press conference containing this statement was also played at the PSIC
hearings during Wilson Goode's testimony, 15 October 1985, a.m. session, p. 88.

7. According to information provided by PSIC investigator Thomas
Mower at the commission hearings, discussions between Gregore Sam-
bor and Lt. Frank Powell concerning the placement of explosives on
MOVE's roof took place as early as noon, May 13, 1985 (Thomas Mower's
testimony, reading notes from a private interview with Lt. Frank Powell,
PSIC hearings, 30 October 1985, p.m. session, p. 121).

8. See "PSIC Findings," pp. 12-13.

9. Paul Geppart's testimony, PSIC hearings, 24 October 1985, p.m. session, pp. 91-92.

10. Revel's testimony, PSIC hearings, 23 October 1985, a.m. session,
pp. 16-17.

11. Brooks' testimony, PSIC hearings, 16 October 1985, p.m. session,
p. 46.

12. Sambor's testimony, PSIC hearings, 18 October 1985, p.m. session, p. 140.

13. Sgt. Revel brought before the PSIC a two-page memorandum which he testified was present at a May 9, 1985 planning session for May 13. The memo states: "If for some reason entrance is not gained through the walls for the gas teams, bomb men will go onto roof and drop gas into 6221. Shaped charges, 4 locations on or at hatch entrances." (Revel's testimony, PSIC hearings, 24 October 1985, a.m. session, p. 84. See also "Officers: Water Was 'Diversion'", *Philadelphia Inquirer*, 25 October 1985.)

14. Goode's testimony, PSIC hearings, 15 October 1985, p.m. session, pp. 23-25.

15. Brooks' testimony, PSIC hearings, 16 October 1985, p.m. session, pp. 57, 58, 61. In his testimony, Wilson Goode indicated that he had paused for thirty seconds and then gave approval for dropping the bomb on MOVE.

16. "Technical Data Say C-4 Is Stronger Than Tovex TR-2," *Philadelphia Inquirer*, 8 August 1985, and "Explosive C-4: 'Designed for Destruction,'" *Philadelphia Daily News*, 8 August 1985.

17. "Explosive C-4: 'Designed for Destruction,'" *Philadelphia Daily News*, 8 August 1985.

18. "Official Statements On Bomb," *Philadelpha Inquirer*, 8 August 1985.

19. Detective William Stephenson's handwritten log, 13 May 1985, pp. 2-3, reads: "Sgt. Edward Connor, Lt. Frank Powell explained attack plan to staff who were present. To place explosive shape charges (C-4) on both sides of 6221 Osage in an attempt to activate tear gas."

20. "Explosive Discrepancy," *Philadelphia Daily News*, 31 July 1985.

21. "Excerpt from Sambor Memorandum and Interviews with Two Officers," *Philadelphia Inquirer*, 15 August 1985, Sambor's emphasis.

22. Ibid.

23. "Explosive Heavier Than Officer Said," *Philadelphia Inquirer*, 1 August 1985.

24. "City Admits Use of 2d Explosive," *Philadelphia Inquirer*, 8 August 1985.

25. Stephenson's report to the PPD (as distinguished from Stephenson's handwritten log), 13 May 1985, p. 7. Stephenson was wrong about the amount of C-4, but not about its existence in the bomb.

26. "Officers' Attorney: Sambor, Brooks Knew of C-4," *Philadelphia Inquirer*, 13 August 1985. Also, FOP attorney Robert Mozenter reported that if Lt. Frank Powell had been informed by police officer William Klein that C-4 had been included in the bomb, Lt. Powell would have approved of its use.

27. Ibid.

28. Ibid.

29. "Excerpt from Sambor Memorandum and Interviews with Two

Officers," *Philadelphia Inquirer*, 15 August 1985.

30. Goode's testimony, PSIC hearings, 11 October 1985, p.m. session, p. 108. See also "Goode: The Right Decision, Despite the Consequences," *Philadelphia Inquirer*, 15 May 1985.

31. Philadelphia Police Department Inspector John Tiers' testimony, PSIC hearings, 23 October 1985, a.m. session, p. 68. Gregore Sambor did admit in his testimony that shaped charges were tested in preparation for the MOVE siege and that "part of that testing was also in company with members of a Federal agency that had some expertise in both these areas, the tactical and the explosives" (Sambor's testimony, PSIC hearings, 17 October 1985, a.m. session, pp. 98-99.

32. See PSIC Counsel William Lytton III's questioning of Gregore Sambor regarding participants at May 9 planning meeting for May 13, PSIC hearings, 17 October 1985, a.m. session, pp. 101-2.

33. Sambor's testimony, PSIC hearings, 17 October 1985, p.m. session, p. 8.

34. Ibid., 18 October 1985, p.m. session, p. 53.

35. Connor's testimony, PSIC hearings, 25 October 1985, p.m. session, p. 107, emphasis added.

36. Philadelphia Police Department Chief Inspector John Craig's testimony, PSIC hearings, 23 October 1985, p.m. session, p. 94.

37. Sambor's testimony, PSIC hearings, 18 October 1985, a.m. session, p. 96. While testifying that he could not be certain, Sambor stated that federal agents on the scene could have been either from the FBI or the Bureau of Alcohol, Tobacco and Firearms, and that they would have been in the vicinity of Sixty-second Street and Addison, placing them within the police perimeter (Sambor's testimony, PSIC hearings, 17 October 1985, p.m. session, p. 148).

38. A letter from Special Agent in Charge Wayne G. Davis to William H. Brown III, chairman of the PSIC, dated 22 October 1985, reads: "On October 12 and 15, 1985, it was brought to the attention of management officials of the Philadelphia Office of the FBI that a quantity of approximately thirty 1¼ pound blocks of C-4 explosive was delivered to the Philadelphia Police Department by an agent of this office in January 1985." The letter was read at the PSIC hearings, 25 October 1985, p.m. session, pp. 111-12.

39. From PSIC's biographical sketches of personnel hired by the commission, entitled "Investigative Staff" and "Consulting Experts," undated.

40. Phelan's testimony, PSIC hearings, 1 November 1985, p.m. session, p. 62.

41. "Thumbnail Sketches of Commission Members," *Philadelphia Inquirer*, 23 May 1985.

42. "PSIC Findings," 6 March 1986, p. 42.

43. Ibid.

44. Ibid.

45. "Goode Comments on Controversy," *Philadelphia Daily News*, 16

May 1985.

46. "Sambor: Bomb Not Flammable," *Philadelphia Daily News*, 15 May 1985.

47. Frank Rossi, "A Demolitions Expert's View," *Philadelphia Inquirer*, 9 August 1985.

48. Charles King's testimony, PSIC hearings, 5 November 1985, a.m. session, pp. 72-74.

49. Ibid., pp. 83, 124. See also "PSIC Findings," 6 March 1986, p. 47.

50. "PSIC Findings," 6 March 1986, p. 47. Police officer William Klein claimed the bomb contained two sticks of Tovex and 1¼ pounds of C-4. The PSIC's explosives expert, James Phelan, testified that the bomb had to contain at least two sticks of Tovex *and* another 3¼ pounds of C-4. See Phelan's testimony, PSIC hearings, 1 November 1985, p.m. session, pp. 59-61.

51. PSIC photo exhibits 329 through 337 included PPD surveillance photos taken on May 12, 1985 and were displayed at the commission hearings, 23 October 1985, a.m. session, pp. 38-45. Further, Captain Edward McLaughlin testified at the hearings that MID Detectives Benner and Boyd shared with the planners of May 13 their knowledge that a gas can was hauled up to the roof by MOVE members on May 2. McLaughlin also testified that in the year preceding May 13, MID had on ten occasions taken photos, mostly aerial, of the MOVE property.

52. Photographs taken on May 13 showing gasoline cans on MOVE's roof appear in the *Philadelphia Inquirer*, 17 May 1985 and 26 May 1985.

53. "How the Fire Spread Past MOVE," *Philadelphia Inquirer*, 26 May 1985.

54. In addition to Goode's admitted belief that gasoline was probably stored at MOVE's house, there are the mayor's changing statements about the bomb and why he approved of its use. On the one hand, Goode stated in a televised address on May 14, 1985 that MOVE "had built a tunnel and was in possession of explosives with the potential to blow up the entire block" ("Goode: The Right Decision, Despite the Consequences," *Philadelphia Inquirer*, 15 May 1985). Indeed, the criminal charge of possession of incendiary devices was a key part of justifying the assault against MOVE. Yet, the very next day, May 15, Goode said that had he known any incendiary materials were in the MOVE house, he would not have approved the use of the bomb. Goode also claimed not to have read a police affidavit containing allegations that MOVE was believed to have been in possession of explosives ("Goode Says He Didn't Know of Explosives," *Philadelphia Inquirer*, 16 May 1985). No explosives or incendiary devices were ever found in the MOVE house.

55. Sambor's testimony, PSIC hearings, 18 October 1985, a.m. session, p. 75.

56. William Richmond's testimony, PSIC hearings, 30 October 1985, a.m. session, p. 67.

57. Goode's testimony, PSIC hearings, 15 October 1985, p.m. session,

p. 32.

58. Brooks' testimony, PSIC hearings, 16 October 1985, p.m. session, p. 68.

59. Richmond's testimony, PSIC hearings, 30 October 1985, a.m. session, pp. 79-80.

60. "MOVE House Is Bombed; Blaze Involves 60 Homes/Fire One of City's Worst Ever," *Philadelphia Inquirer*, 14 May 1985.

61. Engine 57 of the Philadelphia Fire Department set up a street level deluge gun at the corner of Sixty-second Street and Osage Avenue. Its streams of water were not directed at the MOVE house. Instead, the operator of the deluge gun was instructed to direct water at 6219 Osage Avenue (Deputy Fire Commissioner Frank Scipione's testimony, PSIC hearings, 30 October 1985, a.m. session, pp. 56-57).

62. Philadelphia Police Department film footage aired at the hearings of the PSIC, 29 October 1985. Interestingly, the PPD claimed it had a total of only thirteen minutes of film footage for all of May 13, 1985.

63. "60 Homes Lost in MOVE Blaze," *Philadelphia Daily News*, 14 May 1985.

64. Richmond's testimony, PSIC hearings, 30 October 1985, a.m. session, p. 92.

65. Scipione's testimony, PSIC hearings, 30 October 1985, a.m. session, pp. 83-84.

66. Sambor's testimony, PSIC hearings, 17 October 1985, a.m. session, p. 8.

67. Detective Stephenson's report to the PPD, 13 May 1985, p. 9.

68. Richmond's testimony, PSIC hearings, 30 October 1985, a.m. session, p. 102.

4 | The Alley

1. "The MOVE Transcripts," *Philadelphia Inquirer*, 3 November 1985. The identities of those believed to have perished in the MOVE house and their approximate ages come from Birdie Africa and Dr. Ali Hameli, the pathologist who headed the PSIC's medical team. Members of the MOVE organization have never identified who was in the house on May 13, 1985. Other pathologists have disagreed with Dr. Hameli's conclusions about the identities of the remains, including those of Tree (Katricia Dotson) and Vincent Leaphart. Thus it is possible that other or more people may have been killed.

2. "3 MOVErs Slain; 60 Homes Burn," *Philadelphia Daily News*, 14 May 1985.

3. Ibid. See also "The Tunnel Question Figured in the Strategy," *Philadelphia Daily News*, 15 May 1985.

4. "Gunfight or Not? Answers Keep Changing," *Philadelphia Daily News*, 17 May 1985. One month after this story appeared, Zachary Stalberg, editor of the *Philadelphia Daily News*, wrote a signed editorial in which he stood by his newspaper's account of what transpired in the back alley. The editorial states in part, "Our account of an early evening shootout was based on three police sources. The three were not in the alley but said they received their information from officers who were. All three were trusted sources of Joe O'Dowd, one of the most respected reporters in town and a man with 14 karat gold instincts" ("Letter from the Editor," *Philadelphia Daily News*, 17 June 1985).

5. "Goode, 2 Aides Differ on MOVE/Accounts of Events Conflict," *Philadelphia Inquirer*, 17 May 1985.

6. "Q: Shootout? A: Yes. Yes. No.," *Philadelphia Daily News*, 17 May 1985.

7. Stakeout officers William Trudel and Markus Bariana's testimony, PSIC hearings, 31 October 1985, p.m. session, pp. 157, 160-62, 172-75, and Sgt. Donald Griffiths' testimony, PSIC hearings, 31 October 1985, p.m. session, pp. 180-81.

8. Trudel's testimony, PSIC hearings, 31 October 1985, p.m. session, pp. 162-73. See also testimony of Lt. Dominick Marandola, who commanded all of the police firing teams on May 13. Lt. Marandola testified that he told Sgt. Donald Griffiths "to holler numerous times out the back door to instruct the MOVE members to surrender, they would not be hurt, they could escape the fire by coming in the rear kitchen door," and that "we stayed in the kitchen area until the kitchen caught fire" (31 October 1985, a.m. session, p. 57). Sgt. Griffiths was identified by witnesses at the hearings as being the officer who stated he shot a MOVE member in the back alley.

9. "3 Officers Tell How They Saved Birdie Africa," *Philadelphia Inquirer*, 9 June 1985. This account from stakeout officers is consistent with their testimony at the PSIC hearings. See Stakeout Officer James Berghaier's testimony, PSIC hearings, 1 November 1985, pp. 115-17.

10. "MOVE Death Toll Reaches 11/Goode to Pick Panel for Probe," *Philadelphia Inquirer*, 16 May 1985.

11. "Officer Says Five People Fled Fiery MOVE House," *Philadelphia Inquirer*, 30 June 1985.

12. Birdie Africa's testimony, PSIC hearings, videotaped 12 October 1985 at the law office of David S. Shrager and aired 31 October 1985 at the PSIC hearings. See also "The MOVE Transcripts," *Philadelphia Inquirer's*, 3 November 1985.

13. Birdie Africa's testimony, PSIC hearings, 31 October 1985, pp. 111-12 (page numbers follow preliminary transcript released by the PSIC to the press on 31 October 1985). Birdie testified that the only item he saw in Conrad Africa's hand was a wrench used to unbolt the garage

door.

14. "Had Others Agreed to Surrender?", *Philadelphia Daily News*, 22 May 1985.

15. Birdie Africa's testimony, PSIC hearings, 31 October 1985, p. 127.

16. "The More They Try to Whitewash the Dirtier They Get," *Revolutionary Worker*, 2 September 1985. Further, word went through a crowd at Sixty-second Street and Larchwood Avenue that two children had been killed. See "MOVE House Is Bombed; Blaze Involves 60 Homes/Gunfight Continues After Blast," *Philadelphia Inquirer*, 14 May 1985.

17. Stephenson's testimony, PSIC hearings, 31 October 1985, p.m. session, pp. 72-74.

18. Stephenson's handwritten log, 16 May 1985, p. 35.

19. "Log: Cop 'Downed' MOVE Member," *Philadelphia Daily News*, 20 August 1985.

20. Ibid.

21. Stephenson's handwritten log, 16 May 1985, p. 35.

22. Griffiths' testimony, PSIC hearings, 31 October 1985, pp. 189, 191. See also "Committee Hears Differing Accounts of Police Actions," *Philadelphia Inquirer*, 1 November 1985.

23. Philadelphia Fire Department Batallion Chief John Skarbek's testimony, PSIC hearings, 31 October 1985, p.m. session, p. 123.

24. This was reported by the TV news media in Philadelphia, 19 August 1985. Further, Detective Stephenson's handwritten log detailing the excavation and discovery of MOVE bodies on May 14, 1985 reads: "1720 [5:20 p.m.] Resumed excavation of rear area. 1750 [5:50 p.m.] Left forearm with clenched fist recovered at door..." Stephenson later reported to PSIC investigator Edward Scott, when he was interviewed in private by Scott, that someone had told him the fist was from Conrad Africa (14 May 1985, pp. 23-24).

25. Stephenson's handwritten log, 14 May 1985, p. 18. This information concerning the search for a souvenir was added to the left-hand margin of Stephenson's handwritten log by PSIC investigator Edward Scott when Scott interviewed Stephenson in private. The insertion is alongside Stephenson's notation about stakeout officer John Lacon reporting being grazed by a bullet fired by MOVE. The insertion reads in part: "Officer was at scene touching something. Informed he could not touch anything as it was evidence. 'I wanted a souvenir as he got shot...'"

26. "For Most Police, the Job Is to Wait and to Stay Alive," *Philadelphia Inquirer*, 14 May 1985.

27. Police Officer William Stewart's testimony, PSIC hearings, 31 October 1985, a.m. session, p. 123.

28. Ibid., p. 124.

29. Ibid., pp. 105-8.

30. Stewart's statements given to PSIC investigator Frank Eccles during a private interview. (See Frank Eccles' testimony, reading from notes

of interview with Stewart, 31 October 1985, p.m. session, pp. 10-11. See also "After Light Moments, More Dark Questions," *Philadelphia Inquirer*, 1 November 1985).

31. Stewart's statement to PSIC investigator Frank Eccles during a private interview. (See Frank Eccles' testimony, reading from notes of interview with Stewart, 31 October 1985, p.m. session, pp. 11-12).

32. "Gunfight or Not? Answers Keep Changing," *Philadelphia Daily News*, 17 May 1985.

33. Dr. Hameli testified that the bodies of the MOVE people were found within the basement area and that none were reported to have been found outside of the MOVE house, 5 November 1985, p. 64. Dr. Hameli's testimony was based upon information and photographs provided to him by city agencies, including the Philadelphia Police Department. Dr. Hameli was not present during any of the excavation of 6221 Osage Avenue.

34. "How the Fire Spread Past MOVE," *Philadelphia Inquirer*, 26 May 1985.

35. Richmond's testimony, PSIC hearings, 30 October 1985, a.m. session, p. 92.

36. Dr. Ali Hameli's testimony, PSIC hearings, 5 November 1985, p.m. session, pp. 97-105. Dr. Hameli also testified that an object lodged in the chest of Frank James Africa might also have been a firearm ammunition but at the time of his testimony Dr. Hameli did not have the results of laboratory tests. Previously another item found in the body of Frank James Africa by Dr. Hameli was thought to be an unspent bullet. It was then reported by the New York City Police Department to be "not a projectile from a firearm" but a steel part of a steam valve! The identification was based on the opinion of none other than a plumber consulted by the New York City Police Department (see "MOVE Test Shows Object Isn't a Bullet," *Philadelphia Inquirer*, 14 August 1985).

37. Hameli's testimony, PSIC hearings, 5 November 1985, p.m. session, pp. 97-107. See also PSIC document #371: "Report of the FBI Laboratory," 23 October 1985.

38. Stephenson's handwritten log, 17 May 1985, p. 36.

39. Hameli's testimony, PSIC hearings, 5 November 1985, p.m. session, pp. 42-44, 111. According to Dr. Hameli, the only other remains believed to be from Tree Africa consisted of a small jaw segment.

40. Ibid. (including the testimony of Dr. Ellis Kerley, a member of the PSIC's medical team, 5 November 1985, pp. 22-23).

41. Ibid., pp. 75-80. Four of the bodies had been released to family members by the time Dr. Hameli began his investigation. Dr. Hameli had two of the bodies exhumed. Because of the deterioration of the two bodies and the hardening of tissue, retrieving embedded items was, according to Dr. Hameli, a very difficult task and it was not possible to remove and test all of these items. Thus more bullet fragments may have been lodged in the bodies. Further, there were objects other than bullet

fragments in many of the bodies (e.g., brick fragments) which Dr. Hameli felt did not result from falling debris but by a much more powerful explosive force. Whether or not these propelled objects caused death is unknown.

42. "PSIC Findings," p. 52.

43. Exchange between Fire Commissioner William Richmond and PSIC member Henry S. Ruth, Jr., PSIC hearings, 6 November 1985, p.m. session, p. 186.

44. "PSIC Findings," p. 53.

45. "Officers Say Shots Hit Them on Osage," *Philadelphia Inquirer*, 3 July 1985.

46. Stakeout officer Walter Washington's testimony at the PSIC hearings, 1 November 1985, a.m. session, p. 22.

47. "For Some MOVE Members, the Battle Changed Little," *Philadelphia Inquirer*, 15 May 1985.

5 | Mr. Mayor: Frank Rizzo

1. "Pogroms in the Heartland," *Revolutionary Worker*, 5 August 1985.

2. Ibid.

3. "A Group that Chose to Live on the Very Brink," *Philadelphia Inquirer*, 9 August 1978.

4. Fred J. Hamilton, *Rizzo: From Cop to Mayor of Philadelphia* (New York: The Viking Press, 1973), p. 67.

5. Ibid., p. 69.

6. Ibid., p. 73.

7. Ibid., p. 74.

8. Ibid., p. 76.

9. Ibid., p. 76n.

10. Ibid., p. 80.

11. Joseph R. Daughen and Peter Binzer, *The Cop Who Would Be King*, (Boston: Little, Brown and Company, 1977), p. 118.

12. Ibid., p. 140.

13. Ibid., p. 174.

14. "MOVE Credo: Revolution 'Ain't Verbalized...,'" *Philadelphia Inquirer*, 9 May 1980.

15. "Armed Group Defies Police in Philadelphia," *New York Times*, 18 June 1977.

16. "MOVE Commune Mourns Death of Baby," *Philadelphia Inquirer*, 30 March 1976. Six MOVE members were arrested by the police during

this altercation, among them Conrad Hampton Africa, and hit with criminal charges including riot and reckless endangerment. See also "Commune Members Clash with Police; Six Arrested," *Philadelphia Inquirer*, 29 March 1976.

17. "MOVE Group Sues City," *Philadelphia Inquirer*, 12 May 1976, and "4 Black Judges Cited in MOVE's $26 Million Suit," *Philadelphia Tribune*, 15 May 1976.

18. Ramona Africa, "Long Live John Africa's Revolution" (letter to supporters and friends), released after May 13, 1985, undated, p. 13.

19. "MOVE Members Claim Baby's Death Is Result of Beating by Sheriffs," *Philadelphia Tribune*, 13 November 1976.

20. "Powelton Finds Its Tolerance Taxed," *Philadelphia Inquirer*, 17 July 1977.

21. "Police Grab 19 in MOVE Rally," *Philadelphia Inquirer*, 17 April 1978.

22. "MOVE Routed in Gun Battle with Police . . . an Officer Killed, the Group's House Leveled," *Philadelphia Inquirer*, 9 August 1978; "MOVE Rifle Shot Ramp, Police Say," *Philadelphia Inquirer*, 10 August 1978.

23. "MOVE Rifle Shot Ramp, Police Say," *Philadelphia Inquirer*, 10 August 1978.

24. "The Mayor: Grief Filled with Rage," *Philadelphia Inquirer*, 9 August 1978.

25. "Their Pain Becomes Anger for the Death of a Colleague," *Philadelphia Inquirer*, 9 August 1978.

26. "The Neighbors Saw It Coming Many, Many Times" and "Their Pain Becomes Anger for the Death of a Colleague," *Philadelphia Inquirer*, 9 August 1978.

27. "Their Pain Becomes Anger for the Death of a Colleague," *Philadelphia Inquirer*, 9 August 1978.

28. Hamilton, *From Cop to Mayor*, p. 81. The boycott did not succeed.

29. "600 Protest Police Blockade of MOVE," *The Evening Bulletin*, 5 April 1978.

30. "Council: MOVE Blockade Stays," *Philadelphia Inquirer*, 14 April 1978. Blackwell, whose district encompasses the Osage Avenue neighborhood, was still a city councilman when MOVE members were massacred in 1985. He upheld Mayor Goode and the city administration for their actions.

31. "Hundreds Protest Rizzo and Police," *Philadelphia Inquirer*, 18 August 1978.

32. Ibid.

33. Ibid.

34. "Bell Orders Probe of Phila. Police," *Philadelphia Inquirer*, 18 August 1978.

35. Hamilton, *From Cop to Mayor*, pp. 82-83.

36. "The Finale at MOVE: A Senseless Tragedy," *Philadelphia Inquirer*, 9 August 1978.

37. Throughout this book, the less exact but more commonly used term, "Black middle class," is employed instead of the more precise and scientific "Black petty bourgoisie," and refers in the main to Black small property owners and shopkeepers, the owners of small commercial enterprises, self-employed working people, the intelligentsia, bureaucrats, and supervisory and management personnel.

6 | Mr. Mayor: W. Wilson Goode

1. Of the original twelve defendants, Consuela Dotson and Sandra Davis had their cases severed and were tried separately. Both were acquitted of murder charges in the death of Ramp, but Dotson was convicted of criminal conspiracy and five counts of simple assault in connection with injuries suffered by other officers and firemen on August 8, 1978. All charges against another defendant, Davita Johnson, were dropped. MOVE has argued that Davis and Johnson "who were in MOVE headquarters on August 8, 1978, who had murder charges on them from the death of James Ramp, who had the same evidence against them that MOVE members did, are out on the street now simply because they are not MOVE members" (Ramona Africa, "Supplement A" to "Civil Action No. 85-3, Memorandum in Support of Motion to Dismiss," point 11, p. E.

2. "9 MOVE Members are Convicted of Killing Officer," *Philadelphia Inquirer*, 9 May 1980.

3. "MOVE 9 Waive Jury, Will Defend Themselves," *Philadelphia Inquirer*, 12 December 1979.

4. "9 MOVE Members are Convicted of Killing Officer," *Philadelphia Inquirer*, 9 May 1980.

5. "2 Officers Say They Saw MOVE Member Armed," *Philadelphia Inquirer*, 31 January 1980.

6. "MOVE Scores a Point on Police Film," *Philadelphia Inquirer*, 28 December 1979.

7. "2 MOVE Defendants Are Ejected," *Philadelphia Inquirer*, 4 January 1980.

8. "MOVE Rifle Shot Ramp, Police Say," *Philadelphia Inquirer*, 10 August 1978.

9. "Firefighters, Injured in MOVE Battle, Unsure Where Shots Came From," *Philadelphia Inquirer*, 24 January 1980; "MOVE Trial Hears Tale of Heroism," *Philadelphia Inquirer*, 25 January 1980.

10. "MOVE Says Police Inside House Fired," *Philadelphia Inquirer*, 10 January 1980.

11. This was the testimony of two of the nine imprisoned MOVE members who testified at the trial of Ramona Africa. Phil Africa testified on 30 January 1986 and Delbert Africa on 3 February 1986.

12. "Lawyers for MOVE Expect their Clients to be Convicted," *Philadelphia Inquirer*, 2 March 1980.

13. "9 in MOVE Get 30 Years for Killing," *Philadelphia Inquirer*, 5 August 1981.

14. "The MOVE Verdict is Explained," *Philadelphia Inquirer*, 7 February 1981, emphasis added.

15. Ibid.

16. "MOVE Leader Cleared," *Philadelphia Inquirer*, 23 July 1981.

17. "Goode Consolidates Power After Philadelphia Primary," *New York Times*, 19 May 1983.

18. "Election of Black Mayor in Philadelphia Reflects a Decade of Change in City," *New York Times*, 10 November 1983.

19. "New Mayors and New Outlooks for 2 Major Cities/First Black to Lead Philadelphia Emphasizes Voluntarism," *New York Times*, 3 January 1984. For the full text of Goode's inaugural address, see *Philadelphia Inquirer*, 3 January 1984.

20. "W. Wilson Goode Biography," prepared by the office of the mayor, undated, p. 1.

21. Ibid. Other sources on Goode's background are "A Manager for Mayor/W. Wilson Goode," *New York Times*, 10 November 1983, and "Goode Sworn In; Calls for Unity," *Philadelphia Inquirer*, 3 January 1984.

22. "At Last/Hopes of Many Fulfilled," *Philadelphia Inquirer*, 3 January 1984.

23. "Philadelphia Blacks: More Get to the Top, but Most Are Low on the Ladder," *New York Times*, 2 March 1986.

24. Ibid.

25. Ibid.

26. Ibid.

27. Ibid.

28. Ibid.

29. Ibid.

30. Ibid.

31. Ibid.

32. "On Black Mayors, Murder, and Whitewashes," *Revolutionary Worker*, 19 August 1985.

33. Ibid.

34. "Demonstrators 'MOVE' on City Hall," *Philadelphia Tribune*, 31 May 1985.

35. "National Committee to Probe the Incident," *Philadelphia Daily News*, 20 June 1985.

36. Sonia Sanchez, at a meeting of the National Commission of Inquiry held at Howard University, Washington, D.C.; also cited in "On Black Mayors," *Revolutionary Worker*, 19 August 1985.

37. Author's interview with Consumers Party representative Cardell Johnson, January 1987. She was found not guilty on all counts.

38. "Rev Forms 2nd Panel on MOVE," *Philadelphia Daily News*, 6 June 1985; "MOVEr: City Wanted 'to Kill Us'," *Philadelphia Daily News*, 17 June 1985.

39. "Interview with Carl Dix/Draw the Line," *Revolutionary Worker*, 10 March 1986. For more on the "Draw the Line" campaign, see Appendix B.

40. "Police Raid House but Find Only a Construction Site," *Philadelphia Inquirer*, 16 May 1985.

41. "Rowhouse Searched in False Alarm," *Philadelphia Inquirer*, 18 May 1985.

42. Ibid.

43. "Dreadlock: Their Wearers Being Hassled," *Philadelphia Tribune*, 21 May 1985.

44. "For Their Locks, Objects of Dread," *Philadelphia Daily News*, 22 May 1985.

45. Ibid.

46. "Goode: Clash with Cult 'Not Over Yet,'" *Philadelphia Daily News*, 18 May 1985.

47. "City Eyes 2 Other MOVE Houses," *Philadelphia Daily News*, 21 May 1985.

48. Statement released at a press conference, 17 August 1985, signed by "We, the Neighborhood People of Fifty Six Street." See also "MOVE Neighbors Fear Osage Repeat/Say Cops Not Needed," *Philadelphia Tribune*, 20 August 1985.

49. Comment of one of the Fifty-sixth Street residents at a press conference (attended by author), 17 August 1985.

50. Author's interview with Clifford Bond, May 1985.

51. "Neighbors Became Victims," *Philadelphia Daily News*, 14 May 1985.

52. "Block Leader Says He'd Act Same Way Again," *Philadelphia Inquirer*, 16 May 1985.

53. "Burned, Bribed, and Muzzled: A Neighborhood Story," *Revolutionary Worker*, 2 September 1985.

54. Ibid.

55. "City Combs the Rubble for Answers," *Philadelphia Daily News*, 15 May 1985.

56. "Suddenly, Neighbors' Lives Are Destroyed" and "After the Fire, Smoldering Emotions, *Philadelphia Inquirer*, 15 May 1985.

57. "Helping Hands Raised in Rebuilding Efforts," *Philadelphia Daily News*, 15 May 1985.

58. Ibid.

59. "Congressmen, HUD Chief See Stricken Area," *Philadelphia Inquirer*, 18 May 1985.

60. Ibid.

61. "Most MOVE Neighbors Have Gotten Only $2,500," *Philadelphia*

Inquirer, 15 June 1985.

62. "Law Assures Payment to Osage Fire Victims," *Philadelphia Inquirer*, 4 July 1985, and "Blackwell: Insurance Shouldn't Affect MOVE Damage Claims," *Philadelphia Daily News*, 19 April 1986. On July 3, 1985 Mayor Goode signed a law which stipulated that victims of the fire would be fully compensated without regard to any insurance payments. This did not apply to the owner of 6221 Osage, Louise James. The city has refused to grant James any compensation (even though James was not living at 6221 Osage on May 13, 1985). Instead the city put a lien on James' property and billed her for the cost of demolition work! James lost more than her house; her son and brother were killed on Osage Avenue (see "City Liening on MOVE House Owner," *Philadelphia Daily News*, 31 May 1985; "MOVE Suit Demands a Grand Jury Probe," *Philadelphia Tribune*, 11 June 1985).

63. "Groundbreaking/Osage Residents Look Ahead Confidently," *Philadelphia Inquirer*, 16 July 1985. A year later, many of the houses had still not been completed.

64. "Another Kind of Horror," *Philadelphia Daily News*, 15 May 1985.

65. Ibid.

66. Ibid.

67. "For Some MOVE Neighbors, the Ordeal Has Just Begun," *Philadelphia Inquirer*, 14 June 1985.

68. Ibid.

69. "Another Kind of Horror," *Philadelphia Daily News*, 15 May 1985.

70. "For Some MOVE Neighbors, the Ordeal Has Just Begun," *Philadelphia Inquirer*, 14 June 1985.

71. "Burned, Bribed, and Muzzled: A Neighborhood Story," *Revolutionary Worker*, 2 September 1985.

72. "Ramona Africa: Shots Blocked Exit," *Philadelphia Inquirer*, 3 July 1985.

73. "Jackson Calls for a Federal Jury Probe," *Philadelphia Inquirer*, 4 July 1985.

7 | The Hearings

1. "Commission Members" from "The MOVE Transcripts," *Philadelphia Inquirer*, 28 October 1985.

2. Ibid.

3. Ibid.

4. Ibid.

5. "PSIC Findings," p. 2.

6. PSIC chairman William Brown III's opening statement at the commission hearings, 8 October 1985, a.m. session, p. 5.

7. Ibid., pp. 5, 7.

8. "Philadelphia Panel Pledges Impartial Inquiry," *New York Times*, 9 October 1985.

9. "MOVE Commission Is Tested and So Is Philadelphia," *Philadelphia Inquirer*, 9 June 1985.

10. Letter from William Gray III to the PSIC, cited in "On Black Mayors, Murder, and Whitewashes," *Revolutionary Worker*, 19 August 1985.

11. "Someone Has to Answer for MOVE," *Philadelphia Inquirer*, 4 July 1985.

12. Ibid.

13. "Sambor Rumored on Way Out," *Philadelphia Tribune*, 2 July 1985.

14. Ibid.

15. "Mayor: Cops Ought to Testify," *Philadelphia Tribune*, 16 July 1985.

16. "MOVE Panel Wins Challenge," *Philadelphia Inquirer*, 17 July 1985.

17. On November 13, 1985 Police Commissioner Gregore Sambor announced his resignation, which went into effect on January 30, 1986.

18. Former Police Commissioner Joseph O'Neil's testimony, PSIC hearings, 8 October 1985, a.m. session, pp. 56-62, 70-71.

19. "Murderers Open Hearings in Philly," *Revolutionary Worker*, 14 October 1985. See also "Communists Scream: 'Smash Police Terror,'" *Delaware County Daily Times*, 9 October 1985. The transcript of the hearings records only that there was an "interruption from audience," 8 October 1985.

20. The *Delaware County Daily Times*, which filled the void left by a strike at Philadelphia's two major daily newspapers, gave front page coverage to the disruptions at the opening of the hearings (*Delaware County Daily Times*, 9 October 1985).

21. Draper's testimony, PSIC hearings, 8 October 1985, p.m. session, pp. 61-63.

22. Clifford Bond's testimony, PSIC hearings, 9 October 1985, p.m. session, p. 16.

23. Cassandra Carter's testimony, PSIC hearings, 9 October 1985, a.m. session, pp. 22-23.

24. See, for instance, "Throughout City Hall, a Hands-Off Approach/ The MOVE Transcripts," *Philadelphia Inquirer*, 28 October 1985.

25. Water Department Commissioner William Marrazzo testified that Gregore Sambor requested information about the size and condition of the sewers on the 6200 block of Osage Avenue. Marrazzo also offered his department's "TV equipment to inspect any sewers, if that would be of some service to the Police Department." Marrazzo testified that he believed the PPD requested information about the sewers because of the "general tunnel theory" (Marrazzo's testimony, PSIC hearings, 10 October

1985, p.m. session, pp. 133-35.

26. Clarence Mosely's testimony, PSIC hearings, 10 October 1985, p.m. session, p. 86.

27. Louise James' testimony, PSIC hearings, 9 October 1985, p.m. session, pp. 86-87.

28. LaVerne Sims' testimony, PSIC hearings, 9 October 1985, p.m. session, p. 90.

29. Louise James' response to question from PSIC member Bruce Kauffman, PSIC hearings, 9 October 1985, p.m. session, p. 105.

30. Sims' testimony, PSIC hearings, 9 October 1985, p.m. session, p. 127.

31. Goode's testimony, PSIC hearings, 15 October 1985, p.m. session, p. 28.

32. Chuck Stone, "Saving Goode, Shaming Philadelphia," *Philadelphia Daily News*, 23 October 1985.

33. "PSIC Findings," p. 38.

34. Ibid., p. 43.

35. Brooks' testimony, PSIC hearings, 16 October 1985, p.m. session, p. 128.

36. Ibid., p. 119-20.

37. Sambor's testimony, PSIC hearings, 17 October 1985, a.m. session, p. 8.

38. Ibid., p. 7.

39. See testimony of Wilson Goode, Leo Brooks, Gregore Sambor, and William Richmond at the final day of the PSIC hearings, 6 November 1985, a.m. session, pp. 3-117, and p.m. session, pp. 3-202.

40. "MOVE and the Mayor," *Philadelphia Daily News*, 4 March 1986.

41. "Report on MOVE Finds Goode 'Grossly Negligent' in Decisions," *Philadelphia Inquirer*, 2 March 1986.

42. "MOVE Panel's Verdict Focuses the City's Choices," *Philadelphia Inquirer*, 4 March 1986.

43. "For Osage Residents, 'the Truth,'" *Philadelphia Inquirer*, 3 March 1986.

44. Ibid.

45. Ibid.

46. Throughout the hearings various commission members asked members of the PPD if the MOVE children were considered to be hostages. For example, Gregore Sambor was asked if the PPD believed MOVE would use their children as hostages to prevent the police from peacefully entering the MOVE house (see Sambor's testimony, PSIC hearings, 17 October 1985, a.m. session, p. 84). In raising this issue, the PSIC would often point to PPD directives concerning hostage-taking or barricaded-persons situations which call for the deployment of police officers specially trained in talking the offender(s) into surrendering, which the PPD did not attempt in dealing with MOVE. The PSIC's preference for portraying the MOVE children as hostages (a) casts MOVE adults as

hostage takers of their own children and, (b) allows the PSIC to cover up the calculated and murderous nature of May 13 by faulting the PPD for failing to abide by its own directives. Significantly, Sambor didn't agree with the PSIC's view of the MOVE children as hostages; they were all – adults and children – considered to be MOVE and dealt with accordingly (see Sambor's testimony, PSIC hearings, 18 October 1985, p.m. session, pp. 63-65.

47. "PSIC Findings," p. 69.

8 | The Trial

1. "Ramona Africa Asks Why Only She Was Charged," *Philadelphia Inquirer*, 7 January 1986.

2. Prosecutor Joseph McGill made this point in both his opening and closing statements to the jury (14 January 1986 and 7 February 1986), as did Judge Michael Stiles in his charge to the jury, 7 February 1986. Judge Stiles's instruction that the dropping of the bomb was not a matter for the jury's consideration had a direct impact on the outcome of the trial; as one of the jurors said, "If we had to deal with that [the bombing], we'd still be there deciding" (see "The Verdict: 'Nobody Was Right,'" *Philadelphia Daily News*, 10 February 1986).

3. "Who Was John Africa?" (magazine section), *Philadelphia Inquirer*, 5 January 1986.

4. "Osage Resident Tells Africa Trial of 'MOVE Heat,'" *Philadelphia Inquirer*, 15 January 1986.

5. Prosecutor McGill's closing statement to the jury, 7 February 1986.

6. For example, in 1974 seven MOVE members were bound and gagged when they refused to be quiet during a court hearing. In 1976 the Pennsylvania Supreme Court voiced its disapproval and ruled instead that an unruly defendant has waived his right to be present at trial and should be removed while a defense attorney proceeds with the case. This was the court decision Judge Malmed relied upon in ejecting MOVE defendants tried for the murder of James Ramp (see "Bowing to Precedent: No Gags for MOVE," *Bulletin*, 20 January 1980).

7. "Osage Resident Tells Africa Trial of 'MOVE Heat,'" *Philadelphia Inquirer*, 15 January 1986.

8. See "Tapes of MOVE Threats Played at Africa Trial," *Philadelphia Inquirer*, 16 January 1986.

9. Letter appears in "The Text of MOVE's Letter," *Philadelphia Inquirer*, 20 May 1985.

10. See "2 Cops Describe MOVE Shootings," *Philadelphia Daily News*, 21 January 1986.

11. PPD photographs (exhibits C28 through C30) were introduced at Ramona Africa's trial by Prosecutor McGill, 17 January 1986.

12. Testimony of PPD ballistics expert, Police Officer Jachinowitz, at the trial of Ramona Africa, 22 January 1986.

13. Police Officer Anthony McBride testified about where he said weapons were found in MOVE's house (see "Weaponry Described in Africa Trial," *Philadelphia Inquirer*, 22 January 1986).

14. Imprisoned MOVE member Phil Africa's testimony at the trial of Ramona Africa, 30 January 1986.

15. Imprisoned MOVE member Delbert Africa's testimony at the trial of Ramona Africa, 3 February 1986.

16. Ibid.

17. Imprisoned MOVE member Phil Africa's testimony at the trial of Ramona Africa, 30 January 1986.

18. Ramona Africa's response to Judge Stiles during her direct examination of Sue Africa, 4 February 1986.

19. Imprisoned MOVE member Sue Africa's testimony at the trial of Ramona Africa, 4 February 1986.

20. "MOVE Mother Lectures Court," *Philadelphia Daily News*, 5 February 1986.

21. Goode's testimony at the trial of Ramona Africa, 24 January 1986. For press coverage, see "Goode Testifies in MOVE Case," *Philadelphia Inquirer*, 25 January 1986; "Ramona Africa Questions Mayor Goode About Honesty," *The Daily Pennsylvanian*, 27 January 1986.

22. Sambor's testimony at the trial of Ramona Africa, 28 January 1986. For press coverage, see "Sambor is Challenged by Africa," *Philadelphia Inquirer*, 29 January 1986.

23. Ramona Africa, letter released to supporters, friends of MOVE, and the media, undated, p.12.

24. Sambor's testimony at the trial of Ramona Africa, 24 January 1986.

25. "Bye, Bye Birdie," *Philadelphia Daily News*, 29 May 1986.

26. "Dad Guides Birdie Africa to a New Life," *Philadelphia Daily News*, 30 May 1986.

27. "Bye, Bye Birdie," *Philadelphia Daily News*, 29 May 1986.

28. Ibid.

29. Ibid.

30. Prosecutor McGill's cross-examination of Birdie Africa in a closed courtroom at the trial of Ramona Africa, 27 January 1986. Press and spectators watched his testimony via video cameras in an adjacent courtroom.

31. "Youth Says Africa Was Not Armed," *Philadelphia Inquirer*, 28 January 1986.

32. Ibid.

33. Ramona Africa's summation to the jury, 7 February 1986.

34. "The Ramona Africa Verdict," *Philadelphia Inquirer*, 11 February

1986.

35. "Radical Acquitted on 10 Charges, Convicted on 2, in Philadelphia Bombing and Fire," *New York Times*, 10 February 1986.

36. "Guilty on 2 Counts, Ramona Faces Jail," *Philadelphia Daily News*, 10 February 1986.

37. "The Verdict: 'Nobody Was Right,'" *Philadelphia Daily News*, 10 February 1986.

38. McGill's comment on the sentencing of Ramona Africa, aired on evening news, Channel 10 (WCAU) in Philadelphia, 14 April 1986.

39. Letter from Rev. Paul M. Washington to Judge Michael Stiles, 11 April 1986. The full text reads: "Dear Judge Stiles: May 13th, 1985 was a day unlike any other that any of us have seen. Of the thirteen people in 5221 [sic] Osage Avenue that day, eleven died, two escaped. I question at this time, in the light of what Ramona Africa has endured both in her house as well as in jail since that date, if there is still reason to sentence her to a continued period of incarceration? I ask that you sentence her to time served, she has suffered enough."

40. Statement of Black youth at a Free Ramona Africa rally, 14 April 1986, tape recording of rally obtained by author.

41. Statement of a Black woman activist in Philadelphia at a Free Ramona Africa rally, 14 April 1986, tape recording of rally obtained by author.

42. Excerpt from Ramona Africa's statement at her sentencing, 14 April 1986. See also "Ramona Eligible for Parole in 5 Months," *Philadelphia Daily News*, 15 April 1986.

43. Excerpt from Ramona Africa's statement at her sentencing, 14 April 1986.

44. Novella Williams' comment on the sentencing of Ramona Africa, aired on evening news, Channel 10 (WCAU) in Philadelphia, 14 April 1986.

45. "Court OKs 24-Hour MOVE Vigil," *Philadelphia Daily News*, 13 May 1986.

46. "MOVE: A Day of Symbols," *Philadelphia Daily News*, 14 May 1986.

47. "Memorial," *Philadelphia Inquirer*, 14 May 1986.

48. "The Statement Issued by Mayor Goode," *Philadelphia Inquirer*, 13 May 1986.

49. Author's interview, May 1986.

50. Author's interview, May 1986.

9 | The Larger Context

1. CBS, *Face the Nation*, "Siege in Philadelphia." See also "Congress to Investigate?", *Philadelphia Daily News*, 20 May 1985.
2. "How Others Would Handle Explosive Situation/Tactics Expert Defends Tovex," *Philadelphia Daily News*, 16 May 1985.
3. "Experts on Police Procedure Criticize Bombing of House," *Philadelphia Inquirer*, 15 May 1985.
4. Ibid.
5. Editorial from *Chicago Sun-Times*, cited in "In the Wake of Philly Massacre, the Murder and the Lies," *Revolutionary Worker*, 27 May 1985.
6. Richard Poe, "Preemptive Strike/A New Kind of Policing," *East Village Eye*, June 1986.
7. Donald Goldberg and Indy Badhwar, "Blueprint for Tyranny," *Penthouse*, August 1985.
8. Ibid.
9. Ibid.
10. Ibid.
11. Poe, "Preemptive Strike," *East Village Eye*, June 1986.
12. Goldberg and Badhwar, "Blueprint for Tyranny," *Penthouse*, August 1985.
13. Ibid.
14. Ibid.
15. Ibid.
16. Ibid.
17. Ibid.
18. Ibid.
19. Ibid.
20. Poe, "Preemptive Strike," *East Village Eye*, June 1986.
21. Ibid.
22. "Experts on Police Procedure Criticize Bombing of House," *Philadelphia Inquirer*, 15 May 1985.
23. Poe, "Preemptive Strike" *East Village Eye*, June 1986.
24. "PSIC Findings," pp. 57, 58, 61, 62, 63, 64.
25. "Crisis Management/Emergency Preparedness Program," from "Fact Sheets for Press Briefing," from the office of W. Wilson Goode, 10 March 1986.
26. See "Protestors on Black Family: 'We Want Them Out,'" *Philadelphia Daily News*; and "400 Protest at Home of Blacks in S.W. Phila," 21 November 1985, "Protest Held at 2d Home," 22 November 1985, "Blaze Chars Home Bought by Blacks," 13 December 1985, all in the *Philadelphia*

Inquirer. The Black family decided to move out of the neighborhood. While their house was unoccupied but still filled with the family's belongings, it was torched.

27. "Crisis Management/Emergency Preparedness Program," specifically "Friday 22 November 1985" and "Operations Plan/Mayor's Declaration of November 22 1985, Effective: Duration of Declaration," from "Fact Sheets for Press Briefing," from the office of W. Wilson Goode, 10 March 1986.

28. "Correspondence from Philly/Amerikkka Needs Black Mayors and Officials and Racism Too," *Revolutionary Worker,* 9 December 1985.

29. "34 Charged for Defying S.W. Phila. Protest Ban," *Philadelphia Inquirer,* 1 December 1985.

30. Poe, "Preemptive Strike," *East Village Eye,* June 1986.

31. "Police Department's Oversight and Organization," from "Fact Sheets for Press Briefing," from the office of W. Wilson Goode, 10 March 1986.

32. "Police Department Training," from "Fact Sheets for Press Briefing," from the office of W. Wilson Goode, 10 March 1986.